Canadi
Public Speaking

Melanie Novis

PEARSON

Prentice
Hall

Toronto

National Library of Canada Cataloguing in Publication

Novis, Melanie
    Canadian public speaking / Melanie Novis.

ISBN 0-13-035830-4 1.
    Public speaking. I. Title.

PN4121.N69   2004 808.5'1   C2003-902745-7

Copyright 2004 Pearson Education Canada, a division of Pearson Canada Inc., Toronto, Ontario

All Rights Reserved. This publication is protected by copyright, and permission should be obtained from the publisher prior to any prohibited reproduction, storage in a retrieval system, or transmission in any form or by any means, electronic, mechanical, photocopying, recording, or likewise. For information regarding permission, write to the Permissions Department.

ISBN 0-13-035830-4

Vice-President, Editorial Director: Michael J. Young
Acquisitions Editor: Marianne Minnaker
Marketing Manager: Ryan St. Peters
Associate Editor: Jennifer Murray
Production Editor: Charlotte Morrison-Reed
Copy Editor: Karen Hunter
Production Coordinator: Heather Bean
Page Layout: Heidi Palfrey
Art Director: Julia Hall
Interior and Cover Design: Amy Harnden
Cover Image: PhotoDisc

14 15 16 CP 13 12 11

Printed and bound in Canada.

Contents

Chapter Nine   Clear Speech and Articulation   181

Chapter 10   Delivery Methods   200

Chapter Fifteen   Listening   275

Chapter Sixteen   Sample Speeches   288

Foreword

I first met Melanie Novis in the exhilarating atmosphere of the university, where I spotted an outstanding student, one of those inspired by the teaching of Professor Rosalie van der Gucht. It was she who had invited me to do a lecture tour extending throughout South Africa. I was there to talk on the English Speaking Board philosophy that encourages the individuality of Every Single Being.

I think the best way I can underline the importance of the title of this book is by quoting a key statement of ESB philosophy, "there are as many brands of spoken English as there are regions where English is spoken – but everyone needs an oral passport, the kind of English which can be understood anywhere in the world English is spoken, and which causes neither ambiguity nor embarrassment."

I have met Melanie Novis in her progress through a brilliant professional career. Her presence evokes an atmosphere of trust in what she is teaching. Her methods are built on a sound understanding of the interrelationship of voice, speech and language.

My personal note to all public speakers, whether their audience be five or five hundred, is: "Remember, it is not what is said nor what is heard – but what has been *received*, which is truly communicated."

Christabel Burniston,
President of the English Speaking
Board International, England

Preface

Einstein once said, *"Everything should be made as simple as possible, but not simpler."* He was talking about physics. Let us talk about public speaking and let us make it simple. Public speaking is a skill and because it is a skill, it can be learned.

Canadian Public Speaking will be the roadmap you need to assist you in acquiring a vital life skill, the ability to stand up in front of a group and express yourself effectively.

The objectives of this book are:

- to show you that public speaking is a skill that can be learned and mastered;

- to help you diminish your fear of public speaking;

- to give you the skills, techniques, and know-how to speak publicly;

- to enable you to deliver your message and present who you are with clarity, competence, and confidence; and

- to equip you with a vital asset that will give you a competitive advantage in the working world that awaits you.

Success in life is not wholly dependent upon good academic grades. If you are unable to present yourself and your ideas confidently, success may be elusive.

This book is designed to help you master the skill of speaking in public in a way that is straightforward and easy. By embracing the hands-on, direct, practical approach used in this book, you will walk away with concrete methods and techniques which you can apply when presenting information to your professors, instructors, fellow students, prospective employees, and general audiences.

Canadian Public Speaking offers the reader a total approach to effective speaking. It is divided into the three major components of public speaking: the verbal (what you say), the non-verbal (what you show/what we see), and the vocal (how you sound). This text examines and offers methods on how to prepare and structure both an informative and a persuasive speech. A short, easily adaptable method for impromptu speaking is also included. We will also examine how to deliver the speech.

The theme of authenticity and congruency runs throughout the book and, as such, the student will be made aware of the impact of the non-verbal on the audience. Body language, eye contact, proxemics and the use of audio-visual aids is also discussed. Often students pay little attention to the vocal component of their speech, however, this component is very important. The advantages of a well-modulated, commanding voice are also addressed. Practical exercises for improving articulation, projection and vocal variety will help the student improve the vocal aspect.

In order to properly equip yourself for your future employment, two chapters are devoted to interviewing and listening skills. Interviews with well-known Canadian figures are interspersed throughout the book and the student will be able to glean tips and information from those accomplished speakers.

The final chapter of the book contains examples of famous speeches and student speeches that illustrate the methodology and techniques used to structure an effective speech.

As the student moves progressively, or even selects a pertinent section of the book, he or she will be provided with practical tools, skills, methods, and ideas that will help him or her to become a proficient, confident speaker capable of speaking in every situation.

My message to each student is simple: Be yourself, be authentic, be congruent, and be prepared. After all, that's not too difficult, is it?

Acknowledgments

My interest and love of the spoken language began at the age of ten when I began attending private speech lessons on a weekly basis. Today my career as a teacher of speech and oral communication has spanned thirty years and I have had the privilege of working in schools, universities and corporations internationally.

My thanks and acknowledgements go to a succession of speech teachers who inspired and motivated me. They are Hinda Cohen, Josie Matthews, Professor Rosalie van der Gucht, Christabel Burniston, David Beeching, and Shelagh Snell.

Many thanks to the following individuals for their interviews, speeches, and general insights: Edward Greenspan, Evan Solomon, Silken Laumann, Dr. Robert Buckman, Diane Francis, Jeffrey Hemmelgarn, Professor Hank Davis, Richard Bradshaw, Buzz Hargrove, Josey Vogels, Jim Van Horne, Fred Addis of The Leacock Museum, Dr. Carl Spadoni, Xiang Zhang, Wendy Ng, Catherine Driscoll, Albert Kohl, Dr. Mary Barrie, Dr. Bruce Meyer, and all my students.

I would also like to thank my reviewers Jill Tomasson Goodwin, University of Waterloo; Signe Gurholt, New Brunswick Community College; Susan Lieberman, Grant MacEwan College; and Panteli Tritchew, Kwantlen University College for their thoughtful suggestions.

For their unswerving support and help in bringing this book to fruition, I would like to express my gratitude to my husband, Jim, my children Lindi and Adam Lazarus, Bernice Lester, David Miller and my editors, Jennifer Murray and Adrienne Shiffman. Their guidance, patience and steadfastness have been invaluable. I have learned a lot from you and I thank you.

To students of public speaking who will be reading this book, it is my pleasure to share with you my lifetime's work. I trust that Canadian Public Speaking will help you become a confident, effective speaker.

Public Speaking

Mend your speech a little,
Lest you may mar your fortunes

—Shakespeare, *King Lear*

LEARNING OBJECTIVES

- To understand the skill of public speaking

- To learn to diminish the fear of public speaking

- To build confidence

- To recognize the obstacles to effective communication

- To understand the importance of the persona of the public speaker

- To learn how to make effective eye contact

- To manage your visual impression

- To learn four different types of gestures

- To cultivate variety in body language

- To develop congruent and appropriate nonverbal skills

"What? Me give a speech? No, thank you, I'll avoid that at all costs!" is a very common lament.

There comes a time during every student's university or college education when it is impossible to avoid speaking in front of a group. We are always communicating and presenting: in one-on-one situations, before our fellow students, our peers, our professors, at meetings, during tutorials, when defending a thesis, making an announcement, or even when asking for a student loan.

What will you do when 20 percent of your final mark is allocated to a speech? Avoidance is no longer an option. No longer can you luxuriate in the safe enclave of silence. Instead, you must go in the direction of the fear and conquer it.

To learn and to master the skills of effective public speaking is not the daunting task you might imagine it to be. Help is at hand. This book will teach you how to be prepared for the moment when you need to express your ideas with ease and eloquence.

How do you go about turning a private liability into a public asset? You have already begun by reading this textbook.

However, reading a book to learn the skill of public speaking is akin to learning tennis from a book. You need to actually go out there and practise the skill. This book can offer you theoretical instruction, yet to accomplish and master the skill of public speaking you need to experiment, practise, and apply what you read in order to develop competence when speaking in public.

Each one of us can tell a story; give an opinion; or present an argument to a friend, an acquaintance, or a family member. In a private comfortable setting, speaking comes naturally. Yet what happens when conditions change and we are no longer engaged in a one-on-one interaction? As the number of individuals in the audience increases, so does the fear factor. All of a sudden it is hard to express our ideas in clear, captivating language, to relate directly to the listener, and to command their attention. If we focus on being prepared, composing a well-structured message, analyzing our audience, taming those butterflies, articulating with clarity, and blending in a mixture of good supporting material, we will capture the intellect and heart of the listener. After all, public speaking is just an enlarged conversation with an audience.

A VALUABLE SKILL UNDERSTOOD

Consider the two words comprising the phrase, "public speaking." It encompasses "public," which suggests more than one person and "speaking," which is to verbally articulate your message.

The basic rule of speaking in public is: have something to say and then say it effectively. Design the message so as to capture the attention of the audience, keep them interested in and riveted upon your speech, and pave the way for them to retain or be influenced by your message.

As a student your aim is to get a solid education, but to attain success in the workplace you will need to master the additional skill of public speaking. In this text we will look at contemporary speaking, but the words of Aristotle, who wrote one of the earliest studies of public speaking 2300 years ago, still resonate today. He stated, "It is not sufficient to know what one ought to say, but one must also know how to say it." This book will teach you how to say it.

In class you will be called upon to present the results of your academic studies, to explain a concept, to demonstrate an experiment, to instruct, to convey the results of your research, to argue a particular point of view, or to make a proposal. As you move into the "real" world you may have to present yourself at a job interview, persuade someone to hire you, run for political office, motivate a group of individuals, market a product, deliver a business presentation, give a report, or request funding for a project. Perhaps you will even have to make the toast to your grandmother at her eightieth birthday party or give a speech at a friend's wedding. There is no escaping speaking in public. Success will result from competent speechmaking.

We begin the process of learning the skill of public speaking with a self-evaluation. Start by filling in the Personal Evaluation form below.

FORM 1.1 | **Personal Evaluation**

1. How do you rate yourself as a public speaker?

   Excellent   Very Good   Good   Fair   Needs Improvement

2. Do you experience nervousness prior to giving a speech?

   Always   Sometimes   Never

3. Are you able to diminish your nervousness by preparing and practising?

   Yes   No

4. How would you rate your knowledge of how to structure a speech?

   Very Good   Good   Poor

5. Can you deliver a talk with confidence?

   Yes   No

6. Do you use vocal variety when you speak?

   Yes   No

7. Do you make good use of body language and gestures?

   Yes   No

8. Do you make genuine, effective eye contact with members of the audience?

   Yes   Sometimes   No

9. Are you able to locate, design, and incorporate visual aids to enhance the effectiveness of your speech or presentation?

   Yes   No

10. Does the question and answer period intimidate you?

    Yes   No

11. List the qualities you believe a good speaker should possess.

12. Which of these qualities do you now have?

13. List your public speaking strengths.

FORM 1.1	Personal Evaluation (continued)

14. What areas of public speaking would you like to improve upon?

15. What kind of initial impression do you leave with others?

16. What impression would you like to convey to an audience?

Keep this evaluation as your benchmark and refer to it from time to time. You will see how your answers/responses change as you continue to learn and to master public speaking.

Every time we speak we are conveying an impression to the listener. Be genuine, authentic, and just be yourself, but also consider the skills and techniques you will learn from this book. Watch speakers whom you admire and note the methods and techniques they employ. If they work for you, adopt them. In the words of Ralph Waldo Emerson (1841, p. 21) from his book, *Self Reliance*:

> *Insist on yourself; never imitate. Your own gift can present every moment with the cumulative force of a whole life's cultivation; but of the adopted talent of another you have only an extemporaneous half-possession. That which each can do best, but none but his Maker can teach him.*

EXERCISE

Here is a simple exercise to catapult your entry into the arena of public speaking.

1. Students divide into pairs.
2. Partner A interviews Partner B.
3. Partner B gives Partner A the following information:
   Name
   Background
   Academic Studies
   Work
   Family
   Interests
   Unique quality
   Describes someone who she regards as a really good public speaker

4. Now Partner B interviews Partner A. Partner A offers information relating to the topics listed above.

5. Partners A and B go to the front of the classroom.

6. Partner A introduces B to the listening group based on the knowledge gathered during the interview process.

7. Partner B introduces A to the listening group.

8. When you return to your seat, write down two things that you did well during the introduction.

9. Write down two things you would do differently next time.

10. Request positive, constructive feedback from the listening group. Positive, constructive feedback is not: "You spoke far too quickly, I couldn't understand a word you said." It means giving feedback that offers a solution presented in positive language such as, "Your message was clear and interesting. If you spoke at a slower pace and used more pauses, it would be easier to follow."

Use this simplified evaluation as a guide when offering positive, constructive feedback:

FORM 1.2	Evaluation of a Speech

Speaker's Name: _____

Topic: _____

Please write comments on:

1. Vocal

_____

_____

2. Eye Contact

_____

_____

3. General Delivery

_____

_____

4. Gestures and Language

_____

_____

FORM 1.2	Evaluation of a Speech (continued)

5. Choice of Topic and Audience Interest

_____

_____

6. Opening

_____

_____

7. Development of Topic and Interest Arousal

_____

_____

8. Conclusion & Impact

_____

_____

9. Achievement of Purpose

_____

_____

10. Visual Aids

_____

_____

11. Speaker's Attitude

_____

_____

12. I suggest the following improvements

_____

_____

_____

_____

Elements of Public Speaking

Public speaking is a transaction which involves three elements: the speaker, the message, and the audience or listener. These elements are crucial and interdependent as shown in Figure 1.1 below.

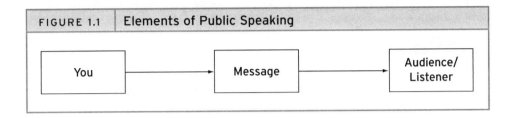

| FIGURE 1.1 | Elements of Public Speaking |

You → Message → Audience/Listener

As the speaker you will plan, organize, and structure a message that takes into account the audience for whom the message is intended. You will select a particular channel through which to convey your message. The channels used in public speaking are the visual channel, which incorporates your appearance, gestures, body movements, eye contact and visual aids; and the auditory channel which is comprised of the sound of your voice and the words you select. We will examine all of these aspects during the course of this book.

Another important element to which you need to give some thought is congruency. Congruency is the harmony between what you say and how you say it, at the time you say it. In other words, when you say, "I am happy to be here with you today," your voice, your facial expression, and your posture should reflect those words. Saying those words in a dull, monotonous voice while displaying a deadpan face and droopy posture is at odds with your message and your intention.

What you say and how you say it makes an impact on your audience. A study by Albert Mehrabian (Mehrabian, 1972)—a professor of psychology at UCLA known for his work in the field of nonverbal communication—offers a communicative breakdown for feeling and liking. According to Mehrabian, the impact of your message is assessed in the following three areas:

1. Verbal. What you say.
2. Vocal. How you sound.
3. Nonverbal. How you use body language and gestures, your appearance, your visual aids, and your environment.

   The results of the study revealed that of the impression we impart

   7 percent is verbal

   38 percent is vocal

   55 percent is nonverbal

   Even though your verbal message—which is the content—accounts for only 7 percent of the impression you make, you must pay great attention to this component. As a student, close attention will be paid to your content so you should aim for the best 7 percent that you can achieve. Prepare the content diligently and judiciously. The verbal aspect of an impression will be discussed in Chapters 3, 4, 5, and 6, the nonverbal aspect will be covered in Chapter 7, and the vocal component is examined in Chapters 8 and 9 of this book. You, the speaker, incorporate all three components: the vocal component emanates from you, you are in charge of selecting and organizing the verbal content, and you are your best visual aid.

Using this breakdown, incorporate these three elements as you do the following exercises:

EXERCISE

1. Prepare a one-minute speech on "My Pet Peeve." Describe this pet peeve using vivid descriptions and tell the audience why it is a pet peeve of yours and finally, tell them how you would like to resolve it.

2. Here is a list of 12 virtues. Choose one virtue and speak about it for one minute.

   Sincerity

   Humility

   Silence

   Chastity

   Order

   Frugality

   Justice

   Resolution

   Moderation

   Tranquility

   Cleanliness

   Industry

3. Describe the person who has been the most influential in your life.

4. Choose a partner. Describe a frustrating situation as clearly as possible. Once you have finished your description, your partner will repeat back your message. Ask yourself, "Am I sending the message properly?" "Has it been received as intended?" Switch partners and repeat the exercise. Discuss ways in which you could have improved your description. Ask yourself, "Was I credible? Was I concrete and specific in my choice of words? Did I convey my frustration and my reason in a convincing manner?"

These exercises could very well replicate an everyday personal interchange, so they should be relatively easy to do.

We all have the ability to communicate an idea or opinion. Now let's examine one factor which holds many speakers back, the fear of public speaking.

THE FEAR OF PUBLIC SPEAKING

I've suffered a great many catastrophes in my life. Most of them never happened.

—Mark Twain

"I am so nervous about the speech I have to give tomorrow. How will I cope? What if I make a fool of myself? I may forget my message and then what will I do?"

Nervousness before a presentation is a normal phenomenon. More people fear public speaking than death. In fact, the comedian Jerry Seinfeld made a comment on this fact and said, "So, in other words, more people would rather be in the coffin than delivering the eulogy."

The fear of public speaking can be addressed and conquered. Even professional speakers experience stage fright before standing up in front of an audience, but then they think about harnessing that nervous energy and using it positively, aiming to make those butterflies fly into formation.

The feeling of nervousness is very similar to the feeling of excitement, so let excitement propel you to deliver a speech that is dynamic.

There is an old saying that suggests that worry is a lot like a rocking chair. There's lots of action but it gets you nowhere. There is no point in giving in to the paralyzing fear, which hinders the attainment of your public speaking goals. Let us go in the direction of the fear and conquer it.

Famous individuals have faced and dealt with fear, so you are not alone. Taking a course in public speaking and reading this text will assist you on your path to confident speaking.

Let's look at some of the fears we encounter before speaking. Do any of these apply to you?

- I am frightened of speaking in front of a large group
- I am afraid of making a silly mistake or embarrassing myself
- I speak quickly in order to get through the speech
- I am fearful that I will forget my speech
- I cannot make eye contact with the audience
- I need notes to help guide me through my speech
- I feel very tense throughout the speech
- My voice sounds wooden and dull
- I am afraid of making gestures
- I am anxious while preparing my speech
- I want to escape
- I dread the question and answer period
- I feel as if I don't have anything of value to say
- I feel I will be judged harshly
- I avoid speaking in public
- My heart beats faster
- My face flushes
- My stomach is in knots
- My palms sweat

- I forget to breathe
- I sway from side to side
- I feel lightheaded
- My hands tremble
- My mouth is dry
- I fidget continuously
- My voice cracks
- My jaw is tense

If you look back at all the comments you have checked you will notice that much of your fear originates from your thought patterns and that fears manifest themselves physically, for example, in the sweating of the palms of the hands.

There are things you can do to help yourself and mitigate your fears. You can prepare, practise, use positive thinking, relax, and breathe properly.

Techniques to Build Confidence

Be prepared   Know your material and organize it efficiently. Know your audience and appeal to their needs and motivations. Prepare your notes in detail. You can reduce them to key points and place them on cue cards, deliver them from a manuscript, or use overheads or PowerPoint as your guide. Chapters 3 and 4 will give you details on how to prepare a speech.

Practise   Practise the speech aloud at least six to ten times before delivering it. Practice in the venue in which you will be presenting, if possible. Practice using the microphone and your visual aids. Practice delivering answers to the questions that you anticipate you will be asked. Remember to do the best you can, perfection will be elusive for a novice speaker. Refer to Chapter 13 on Practising the Speech for help.

Positive Thinking   Most of our fears do not come true. What are the chances of the audience getting up and leaving in the middle of your speech? How likely is it that they will fall asleep while you are speaking? What is the likelihood of you crumbling to the floor overcome by an attack of nerves? All those fears are highly unlikely to manifest themselves.

Consider this: Have you ever attended a speech and thought, "I hope the speaker fails!"? Probably not. Your audience wants you to succeed. They want to listen closely to your message. Shift your focus in thinking. Instead of thinking, "What will the audience think of me?" say to yourself, "I have a message to give you." This way your focus is outwards. You are thinking about giving something away. You cannot control your audience but you can control yourself and your thought patterns.

As you approach the front of the classroom, lecture hall, or podium, keep repeating these words over and over like a mantra:

I am prepared.

I am confident.

I want to give you a message.

Imagine that you own the speaking space and that this is comfortable territory for you. Approach the podium purposefully and use erect posture. When you reach the podium, place your notes down, take your time, look up at the audience, and make good eye contact with them. Then begin speaking.

Always learn your opening lines by heart so that you can make a direct connection with the listeners. Do the same for the conclusion. Practise saying these two "bookends" of your speech aloud, over and over, until you can speak in a natural and easy fashion.

When you make your initial eye contact, find the friendly faces in the audience, as they will provide you with additional confidence.

Here is an additional action you can take. Check the list of qualities below that you possess or aim for as a speaker.

Qualities

appealing	friendly	powerful
believable	funny	prepared
bright	gracious	quick-witted
capable	imaginative	rational
captivating	impressive	relaxed
commanding	informative	reliable
compelling	innovative	self-confident
composed	insightful	self-controlled
confident	inspirational	sincere
convincing	instructive	skilled
credible	knowledgeable	smart
dedicated	likeable	spontaneous
dynamic	logical	trustworthy
eager	motivated	unpretentious
effective	natural	warm
energetic	orderly	well-adjusted
enjoyable	original	well-informed
entertaining	outgoing	wise
enthusiastic	persuasive	witty
expressive	poised	zestful
forceful	positive	

Choose ten of the most appropriate qualities and place the phrase "I am" in front. Then say them aloud.

For example:

I am poised

I am positive

I am confident

I am impressive

I am relaxed

I am logical

I am knowledgeable

I am commanding

I am friendly

I am energetic

Before giving your speech, engage in this positive self-talk. You can stand in front of a mirror and speak the phrases you have selected. You can record them on a tape-recorder and listen to them or you can simply go over the phrases silently. The purpose of these self-affirming statements is to relegate all negative thinking to the background and ultimately eliminate the kind of thoughts that present themselves as obstacles to your success in public speaking.

Mental Imaging   Condition your mind for a positive performance. You know that your speech is coming up next week. You experience some degree of nervousness and feel a little bit of dread. The first step is to prepare thoroughly and then practice diligently. To build your confidence, picture yourself delivering a successful speech and picture the audience responding positively to your words. The speaking environment is warm and friendly and everyone wants you to succeed. Picture yourself feeling, "I am glad I am here and I have a message to give to you."

Do this **visualization exercise** every night for one week prior to your speech:

EXERCISE

1. Choose a quiet time of the day when there will be no distractions.
2. Find a comfortable chair to sit in.
3. Close your eyes and picture the room in which you will be speaking.
4. Picture yourself walking up to the front of the room energetically and purposefully. You radiate confidence.
5. See yourself looking out at the audience while making good eye contact and smiling. The audience smiles back.
6. The audience is friendly, supportive, and receptive.
7. Picture yourself speaking confidently, in a well-organized fashion, while the listeners hold on to your every word.
8. You are giving your audience something of value. Your information is interesting. Your visual aids are impressive.
9. You feel comfortable and committed to your audience.
10. Your speech ends and the audience applauds enthusiastically. You feel triumphant.

Visualization works very well for public speakers. Athletes have used visualization for decades. Kay Porter and Judy Foster, authors of *The Mental Athlete: Inner Training for Peak Performance* (1986) state, "If you 'visualize' yourself as a mediocre athlete, if you go into a workout or competition 'seeing' yourself performing on an average level or slower or less perfectly than those around you, this is the way you will perform in reality." On the other hand, if you picture yourself excelling and crossing the finish line in first place, this type of visualization can propel you to victory.

Mental imaging will help you develop a positive approach. By picturing the event over and over again, you can transform negative thinking and this will lead to producing the positive result you desire.

Breathing and Relaxation   When your thoughts thunder, "I am nervous!" you may tell yourself, "Oh stop it, don't be nervous!" Does this comment work to tame your emotions? Generally speaking, it will not. On the other hand, for some of you, it might. If it does not help to talk yourself out of your anxiety, try doing the following breathing and relaxation exercises. Breathing exercises help to bypass the mind and calm you down physiologically.

Breathing and Relaxation Techniques

1. Lie down and let your spine sink into the floor. Mentally list each part of your body. Beginning at your feet, tense and relax each part, eventually working upwards towards your face. Screw up your eyes, clench your jaw, and tense your whole face until it resembles a shriveled prune. Relax.

2. Now turn your attention towards your breathing. Close your eyes. Without any judgement, observe how your breath enters and leaves your body. Is the inhalation or exhalation longer?

3. Imagine your lungs are like two deflated balloons and, as you inhale deeply, your lungs and ribs expand. Breathe in slowly to the count of three and let your ribs move forward. Repeat this step three times. Now as you breathe in, let your ribs move forwards and sideways. Repeat three times. Next, let your ribs move forwards, sideways, and backwards on each breath. Feel the full expansion of your lungs for three more full breaths.

4. Breathe in to the count of three, expanding your lungs completely. Hold your breath until the count of three, exhale for three, and retain for three. (When you retain your breath, nothing happens at all.) This is one complete cycle of rhythmical breathing. Continue breathing in this manner for five minutes.

5. Now observe your breathing again. It should be deeper and fuller.

6. Slowly open your eyes and gently stretch your limbs.

7. Return to a seated position and notice how much calmer you feel.

To access this calm centre, it is important to practise rhythmical breathing every day for at least 30 days. It has been said that it takes 30 days to form a new habit and your aim is to train the lungs and ribs to work efficiently so they can serve to help you relax.

When you are sitting in the classroom waiting for your turn to deliver your speech, you can use this breathing technique. This time, sit erect in your seat, relax the palms of your hands in your lap, and lift your ribs. Unobtrusively, begin the rhythmical breathing and this will calm you down without anyone noticing what you are doing. When the time comes for you to speak you will feel calmer, much more centred, and in control.

This text will offer you an assortment of techniques for building your confidence while speaking. Choose the method or tool that works best for you according to the situation for which you are preparing. Do not be afraid of trying things out or getting them wrong. Get honest feedback from a friend, classmate or instructor. Then apply those suggestions that have merit. George Bernard Shaw, the famous English playwright, risked speaking in public, which was a nerve-wracking experience for him. He became a good public speaker and here is what he said about it, "I became a good speaker as other men became good skaters; by making a fool of myself until I got used to it."

Confidence Builders

1. Prepare

2. Practise aloud

3. Know the audience

4. Memorize the opening and conclusion of the speech

5. Visit the speaking venue

6. Use positive self-affirming statements

7. Do breathing exercises

8. Channel the nervous energy

9. Focus on your message

10. Visualize success

Here is another confidence builder which you can use during everyday spoken interactions or when you are called upon to speak on the spur of the moment in front of a group. This simple structure for impromptu speaking will provide you with a roadmap to reach your desired destination. It is called the PREW method.

The PREW method

P = Point of View

R = Reason

E = Example

W = Wrap Up

1. Offer your point of view on the selected topic.
2. Give your reason for your point of view.
3. Offer an example to support your viewpoint.
4. Give a wrap-up or conclusion to your talk.

Notice how the example adds colour and impact to your speech.

EXERCISE

1. Students should divide into pairs. Partner A gives partner B a topic upon which to speak. Partner B responds by speaking upon the topic while following the PREW method.
2. Switch roles.
3. Practise using the PREW method on a daily basis.

OBSTACLES TO EFFECTIVE COMMUNICATION

When preparing for your speech, give consideration to some potential obstacles that may sabotage your speech or hinder the effectiveness of your message. Pay attention to the following:

Physical and Mental Considerations   Can the audience see, hear, and understand you? Arrange the layout of the room so that no one has an obstructed view and make sure that you use sufficient volume when speaking so that the audience receives your message with ease. Analyze your audience (see Chapter 2) so that you can frame your message in a way in which the audience will understand you.

General Attentiveness   Is the audience alert? Have they been sitting for a prolonged period? If so, instruct them to stand and stretch for a few moments. If they have been sitting in darkness viewing many PowerPoint presentations prior to your speech, turn on the lights for a while so that you can engage the listeners once more.

Time   At what time of the day or evening are you delivering your speech? Is it at the end of the day on a Friday, when the audience's focus is more on the weekend than on listening to a speech? Are you speaking just before the lunch break when the listeners have food on their minds? If you have a choice, try and speak in the early morning when the audience is generally more alert.

Another issue around time and timing is adherence to the starting time and sticking to the allocated timeframe. Show your audience that you respect them by delivering your speech on time and do not exceed the specified time limit allocated for your speech.

Language   Do you need to adjust your language usage? Is the audience composed of individuals whose second language is English? Are you using technical terms with which the audience is unfamiliar? Make the necessary changes to accommodate your listeners' needs and their level of understanding.

Distractions   Is there construction occurring across the road from the room in which you are speaking? Have you asked the audience to turn off their cell phones? Is it very cold or too hot in the speaking venue? Do you pause when an individual enters the room and makes a noise while doing so? Try not to speak over an interruption. Simply stop for a few seconds and then resume speaking. If it is within your control, select a venue where the external distractions are at a minimum.

Environment   Create a comfortable environment by ensuring that the audience does not feel cramped. The environment should be conducive to the receipt and processing of your message. This includes monitoring the air-conditioning, the door, the lighting, the number and placement of seats, and the audio-visual aids.

Prejudice and Attitudes   A speaker needs to be trusted. Be sensitive and avoid offending anyone's religious, political, sexual, or social beliefs.

The Medium   The medium of communication can be via a speech, an e-mail, a letter, a video, a PowerPoint presentation, a postcard, or a meeting. Choose the medium or mediums that best achieve your objective.

Good communication takes into account three factors:

1. The task – What is to be done?
2. The place – Where is it being done?
3. The people – Who is involved in doing it?

Your task in public speaking is to give an effective speech. The place is the venue at which you will be speaking. The people are the audience to whom you will be speaking. Skill in dealing with these three factors can help or impede the effective presentation of your information.

YOU, THE MESSENGER

Men trust their ears less than their eyes

—Herodotus, The Histories, 5th c, B.C.

Imagine the following scenario:

During one hot, sweltering week in summer, Wendy performed her civic duty when she was selected as a juror on a drug case. The defendant, Judd Harper, elicited enormous sympathy but his defending counsel, Carol Dodge, did not serve him well. From the jury box, Wendy observed Carol's long red talons, rather than fingernails, with every gesture she made. Her thick, untamed, wavy, black hair cascaded over her shoulders and she constantly rearranged the errant strands that fell into her eyes. Carol fidgeted unnecessarily with the white collar poking out from under her lawyer's robes. When she delivered her opening address, Carol spoke with clarity and conviction, yet she consistently distracted her audience with her perpetual fiddling and fidgeting.

The court was this lawyer's stage. She was a player who did not do justice to her role. Her entrance was not imposing and her exit left her client with a guilty verdict.

How do we form an impression of an individual? Our first impression is a visual one, based on what we see. A second impression is formed when the individual speaks. Frequently, we form a first impression, and when we hear the speaker's thoughts articulated, we alter our initial observation.

Now, the lawyer in the previous story exhibited a visual impression and displayed mannerisms that, together, distracted and detracted from her message. She became the focal point in the courtroom, and her spoken words assumed secondary importance. The negative impact of her nonverbal communication overrode her verbal message.

According to Professor Mehrabian (1972), 55 percent of the impact of our message is nonverbal. During the initial phase of seeing someone we notice appearance, gender, age, race, posture, body language, and how effectively they make eye contact with us. As a speaker, you will note that your audience is doing exactly the same thing. We can use our appearance, posture, body language, and eye contact to appropriately deliver an impression that is congruent with our message. Congruency results from the synergistic combination of the visual, vocal, and nonverbal aspects of our message. Each element reinforces the others.

It takes the average audience 30 seconds to form a first impression of a speaker. That first impression is formed from the moment you enter the speaking arena, which could be the front of a classroom, a meeting room, a stage, an auditorium, or an outdoor venue. Always approach the podium with a sense of purpose and walk with a brisk pace, demonstrating a sense of eagerness while conveying the feeling that you want to be there. Once you reach the podium or the appointed area from which you will be delivering your speech, place your feet slightly apart and feel them firmly rooted on the floor. Keep your posture erect, with your sternum (the bone on your upper chest) raised. Feel comfortable, yet poised. A smile will put the audience at ease and demonstrate warmth. When you smile, do so in a genuine manner.

Eye Contact

Now you need to establish eye contact with your audience. Some people find it very hard to make genuine eye contact. To help you establish a nonverbal connection with your audience, find a friendly face in the audience and begin by making eye contact with this person. You will then feel more at ease. Scan the audience. When you make strong eye contact you can even draw in the unresponsive listener. In a small group setting, you will actually be able to make a direct eye-connection with each individual. In a larger audience of 100 to 1000 people, you can use the Z-sweep technique shown below.

To begin, direct your gaze at the back left-hand corner of the room. Look across the far end of the room as your eyes sweep to the back right-hand corner. Now let your eyes move diagonally from the back right-hand corner to the front left-hand corner of the room. Then sweep across the front section of the audience from the left-hand side to the right side.

When you use the Z-sweep, it will appear as if you have offered a nonverbal greeting with your eyes. You have shown a desire to communicate and connect with your audience.

Initially, when you employ this technique it may feel awkward or choreographed. But with repeated practice, it will become second nature to you, and your listeners will feel that you have connected with them nonverbally.

FIGURE 1.2	Z-Sweep

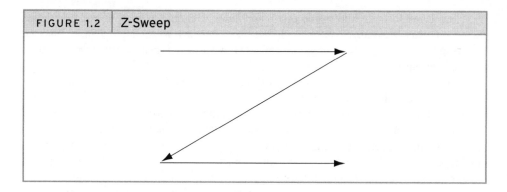

Frequently a speaker will "look" at an audience but not "see" them. Ensure that you do not "stare" at the listeners, but rather "soften" your eyes when making eye contact. Hold eye contact with one individual for the duration of one thought. Then switch to someone in another part of the room. Make eye contact with him or her and deliver a second thought. Never break eye contact in the middle of a thought—you will appear insincere and somewhat shifty. Complete your full thought before engaging with the next person. If your eyes keep flitting from person to person in rapid succession, you will convey a sense of unease. Make genuine eye contact with someone, hold it for five to nine seconds, which is the average duration of a thought, and then move on to the next person.

It has been suggested that if you are afraid of looking someone in the eye, then you should look at his or her forehead or chin. Unfortunately, this does not work. Let me show you why. Try the following exercise.

EXERCISE

1. Choose a partner. Partner A talks to Partner B and while doing so, Partner A looks at Partner B's chin. Now switch roles. Partner B talks to Partner A while looking at Partner A's forehead.

2. Ask for feedback. Did Partner B feel that Partner A genuinely connected with him or her? Did Partner A feel that Partner B made authentic eye contact with him or her?

In all likelihood, the answer will be "No." This points out how important it is to connect eye-to-eye. It is not intimidating to look at someone if you realize you can break eye contact after one thought and then move on to someone else. As a speaker, you will convey power and sincerity if you use your eye contact with skill.

Your eyes are an important medium to use when expressing yourself. Depending on how you use them, you will transmit different impressions. When your eyebrows are raised they may show surprise, nervousness, ridicule, scorn, or questioning. If you knit your eyebrows you may appear perplexed, indecisive, or worried.

Stand in front of the mirror and try knitting and raising your eyebrows. Notice the impressions those movements convey.

Oculesics is the word used for eye behaviour. Eye behaviour varies from culture to culture, so when relating with an individual on a one-to-one basis, avoid making rash judgements about that person as being hostile, sneaky, or insincere until you know about how eye contact is viewed according to his or her cultural background. North American culture encourages frequent eye contact, in fact, we should make eye contact for about 70 percent of the time in order to build a solid rapport. Your eyes are vehicles for conveying sincerity and interest in both your listeners and your subject matter. We can recall the words of Ralph Waldo Emerson, which reinforce the importance of the role that eyes play in communication: "When the eyes say one thing and the tongue another, a practiced man relies on the language of the first." In other words, we trust what we see before trusting what we hear.

When you enter the speaking arena, you make a nonverbal connection with your audience by making eye contact with them. When you close your presentation, stand firmly, and continue making genuine eye contact for a few moments. This will let the audience absorb your closing words and give a sense of finality to your talk. When you make pleasant, but not prolonged, eye contact with your listeners, you will engage them and help create a bond between you and your audience.

The Visual Impression

The next time you watch a speaker approaching a platform, notice how much you have learned about him or her before he or she begins to speak. Consider how the speaker transmits an image based on appearance, posture, movement, use of space, eye contact, gestures, and body language.

How would you like your audience to see you? As a confident, competent, and composed speaker? As a student who speaks with ease? Your body language conveys your level of confidence. Body movement and actions are a silent language; you can convey a message by making effective use of appropriate body language.

Practise walking up to the front of the classroom, and move with a sense of lightness and purpose. Walk at a brisk pace and you will convey enthusiasm and spontaneity. When you reach the spot from which you will speak, turn to face the audience, relax your arms to your sides, make eye contact, and greet the listeners. Say confidently, "Good morning. My name is _____ (state your name)." Through your voice, body language, and approach, you have communicated your importance and your purpose.

Over many years of teaching, I have seen and heard numerous speech horror stories. One young, energetic, medical student delivered an entire presentation with toilet paper hanging out of his pants. Another female student displayed a toothy grin—full of spinach—while delivering an acceptance speech. A second female student walked confidently up to the platform totally unaware that the back section of her skirt was tucked into her pantyhose.

These students, who had spent days preparing for their presentations, actually sabotaged themselves by not paying sufficient attention to their nonverbal communication. Below you will find some techniques meant to prevent such embarrassing situations from happening.

Prior to delivering your presentation, visit the restroom. Face the mirror and look at yourself from head to toe. Smile. Then turn around and check the view from the rear. Incorporate this preparation ritual as an integral step in your preparation routine to prevent incidents such as these from happening to you.

It is important to pay attention to your appearance. You should look appropriate for the occasion, the audience, and the topic. Refer to Chapter 14 on "Interviewing" for more detailed information on appearance.

Posture   We communicate nonverbally through our posture. Growing up, did your parents ever remind you to "stand up straight?" Good posture is not simply achieved by throwing the shoulders back. This posture can appear rigid and unnatural. Try this exercise: Imagine an invisible thread attached to you upper breastbone. Now walk about and picture this thread lifting you skywards. Now check your posture in a mirror. You will find that you have achieved erect posture. Try another exercise: Square, then relax your shoulders. Imagine yourself wearing an invisible crown and walk across the room. Practice walking this way for three to five minutes. To enforce good posture, practice this simple walk on a daily basis for 30 days. In this way, good posture will become a habit.

When you are speaking from behind a podium, place your hands on either side of the podium, and keep your posture erect. You may choose to lean in towards the audience to emphasize an important point, but you do not want to convey the impression that the podium is a physical support or crutch that you depend on to maintain an upright posture. Strive to maintain good posture whether in front of or behind a podium.

Movement and Space   We have discussed how to approach the lectern and the speaking area. If you choose to move while speaking in front of an audience, do so in a poised and comfortable way. When you move do so purposefully. Move to the left side of the platform and deliver a portion of your talk. At an appropriate and significant moment, often when you want to transition from one idea to another, walk to the right side or middle of the stage. Avoid giving the impression of pacing—don't make your movement from point A to point B too predictable and regular. Also avoid the "one-step," which occurs when you take one step and then stop. This conveys tentativeness. Always take at least two steps in a particular direction. It looks more natural. If you want to create a sense of intimacy, move towards your audience. When you diminish the distance between you and your listeners, communication is enhanced.

Proxemics is the study of space and distance between people in social and interpersonal situations. Anthropologist Edward T. Hall coined this term during the 1950s. Proxemics is influenced by culture. In North America, we are generally comfortable communicating with each other at arm's length, whereas in other countries and cultures, they are comfortable communicating with less distance between each other. The British tend to prefer more personal space than the French do. Be sure to take cultural differences into account when communicating, since the use of space conveys meaning.

Generally, there are four spatial zones. For public speaking, 4 metres or more is appropriate. When talking to strangers or acquaintances, a distance of 1.3 metres to 4 metres is appropriate. With friends, the distance diminishes. Most are comfortable with a distance of 45 centimetres to 1.3 metres. The intimate zone is 15 to 45 centimetres.

We must keep in mind that many listeners may experience physical discomfort when a speaker invades their personal boundaries by delivering a presentation at too close a distance. Allow the listener to preserve his or her "bubble" of private terrain. So, if we return to the original point of reducing the distance between the speaker and the audience, do so while being conscious of proxemics.

Gestures

Suit the action to the word, the word to the action, with this special observance, that you o'er-stop not the modesty of nature.

—Shakespeare, *Hamlet*

A gesture is the movement of any part of the body.

Why are gestures so significant for a speaker? Why is it that when we interact with our peers, gestures occur so naturally; yet, when we stand in front of an audience, we ask ourselves, "What should I do with my arms? How can I possibly use my hands and arms and feel comfortable doing so?" American writer Henry Thoreau said, "Average speakers inform and explain. Good speakers demonstrate. Exceptional speakers inspire." When you aspire to become a good speaker, you must embrace gestures to demonstrate, to emphasize, to emote, to describe, to locate, and to express yourself. The audience will grasp your message and retain more information when you offer them a visual reinforcement. Aim to develop a rich repertoire of gestures that will appear to be natural and spontaneous.

Think of your speech as an expanded conversation with an audience. Gestures need to be larger, too, when you are in presentation mode. In Greek theatre, when actors performed at the centre of an amphitheatre, their actions were **declamatory**. Declamation is over-exaggerated movement and action, used so an audience can see and understand the actors. A speaker is not an actor, but there is an element of performance in every spoken presentation. An actor assumes the role of a particular character, while a speaker remains authentic and genuine. The gestures a speaker uses will impact his or her message and add visual variety.

There are four basic types of gestures: the describing gesture, the emphatic gesture, the locating gesture, and the attitudinal gesture.

The describing gesture This gesture demonstrates dimension, number, shape, and size. When you use this type of gesture you are matching your words with your actions. For example, if you were saying, "She walked up a spiral staircase," you might accompany the words with a gesture that shows the index finger pointing upwards while making a rising circling motion. If you were describing a road zigzagging, your gesture would reflect that movement. When stating, "I will be covering the following three areas in my presentation," you could hold up three fingers to synchronize with your three points. These gestures add emphasis and impact while reinforcing your message.

The emphatic gesture This gesture throws emphasis on the point you are making. The statement, "We categorically deny these accusations," could be accompanied by a downward slashing motion of one hand while saying the word "deny." In the early 1960s, during the height of the Cuban Missile Crisis, Premier Khrushchev of Russia took off one of his shoes at the United Nations General Assembly and slammed it on the rostrum. This gesture was subsequently reported in all major newspapers across the world. Khrushchev used the gesture to add emphasis and impact to his message.

The locating gesture This gesture helps to illustrate direction or place. For example, when you want to identify a questioner during the question and answer period, you would point in the direction of that person to identify him or her. Assuming that you were speaking on the topic of "Canada's Climate," and said, "As we move from west to east, we notice distinct changes in climate"; you might use your arm to gesture when you say the words, "west to east"—first in a westward direction and then across in an eastward direction. By performing this gesture you help to illustrate the verbal message.

The attitudinal gesture Attitudinal gestures convey much about the speaker. They reveal the level of confidence, the level of passion for or disinterest in the subject, or they show whether the speaker is nervous or bored. If you were nervous and consistently touched your face, adjusted your glasses, flicked back your hair, played with coins in your pocket, or fiddled with a pen or pointer, your actions would reinforce your nervousness to the audience.

Former Prime Minister Pierre Trudeau displayed irreverence when he used an attitudinal gesture and pirouetted behind the Queen of England's back as he was seeing the Queen off on her flight to London. After bidding her farewell, he pirouetted down the runway. He pirouetted publicly again, a decade later, after proclaiming the constitution. His action this time might be interpreted as joy.

Attitudinal gestures are often unconscious. You can become aware of your unconscious attitudinal gestures by videotaping one of your presentations. After viewing the tape, you can then make conscious adjustments. For instance, once you know that you have been swaying consistently throughout your talk, you can make the decision to plant your feet firmly on the floor, and channel the nervous energy from your feet into your arms by gesturing. Make positive, concrete gestures that are congruent with your message.

In the classic Shakespearean play, *Hamlet*, Hamlet gives instructions to a group of actors in a play and his words still hold true today: "Speak the speech I pray you, as I pronounced it to you, trippingly on the tongue." Hamlet first instructs the actors to speak clearly and precisely. He later tells the actors, "Nor do not saw the air too much with hand, thus, but use all gently, for in the very torrent, tempest and (as I may say) whirlwind of your passion, you must acquire and beget a temperance that may give it smoothness" (III, ii, 1). In other words, he encourages them to temper their gestures, make them appear smooth, and avoid exaggerated, large movements. As Hamlet suggests, gestures should not be artificial, overdone, repetitive and overly bold; rather they ought to be incorporated, embraced and appropriately used.

Dos and Don'ts for Gestures

1. Smile in a genuine way as this warms up the audience towards you.
2. Use gestures to match the word. When you say, "Profits dropped steeply," use a downward slashing motion when you speak the word "steeply."
3. Do not over-gesticulate or use a repetitive pattern.
4. Avoid playing with coins in your pockets, your eyeglasses, your hair, a pointer, or a pen.
5. Diversify your gestures. The audience needs visual variety.
6. If you drop something, such as an overhead transparency or your notes, pick them up gracefully.
7. When using an outstretched hand as a gesture, keep the fingers together, not spread apart.
8. Keep gestures above waist-level so that they are visible to the whole audience.
9. Avoid jerky gestures, swaying, licking your lips and touching your face; these promote perceptions of nervousness.

10. Avoid the "Velcro effect." This occurs when the speaker keeps his or her upper arm glued to his or her sides while gesturing only from the elbow in a forwards or sideways motion. Allow the elbows to move out and away from the body.

11. Do not point at a member of the audience with your forefinger. If you want to indicate towards someone, turn your palm upwards and gesture in his or her direction. A pointing gesture may be perceived as being accusatory.

12. Make bold gestures when you deliver a presentation. If you are speaking from behind a podium, the gestures need to be higher so that the podium does not mask them.

13. Use your head and face as mediums of expression. Smile or nod at the appropriate moment. Reflect your feelings through your facial expressions.

14. Avoid closed body language, such as having both hands in your pockets, both arms behind your back, or crossed arms.

15. Make any adjustments to your clothing prior to the presentation.

16. Keep your gestures smooth, natural, and concrete.

EXERCISES

1. Do the following exercise with a partner: Turn on the television and select a show that has a television host speaking to an audience. Record the show for repeated use. Turn off the sound and try to interpret what the presenter is saying by watching his or her nonverbal behavior. Compare your impressions with your partner. Now play back the tape to check the accuracy of your nonverbal readings.

2. Generally speaking, what is the distance that we, in Canada, like to maintain between us for each of the following zones:

   the intimate zone

   the social zone

   the public zone

3. Which of the following gestures would convey a positive impression:

jingling change	smile
nod	drumming fingers on the lectern
making eye contact	crossed arms
moving calmly	frowning
staring	leaning forward
pausing	fiddling with a pointer
shuffling paper	jerky eye contact
both hands on hips	rubbing an eye
clearing your throat	leaning against a table
pointing with your palm facing upwards	

4. Here are some exercises to free your limbs and help you develop comfort while gesturing.

    (i) Let your arms drop limply at your sides.

    (ii) With the movement originating from your shoulder, shake your left forearm, wrist, and hand towards the front of the classroom. Keep your arm loose and relaxed and at shoulder level. Now extend your left arm to your left side. Keep your extended arm parallel with the floor and shake your arm sideways at shoulder height. Next, reach the arm skywards and shake the arm. Repeat these three shaking movements with your right arm.

    (iii) Roll your shoulders backward in a circular motion, ten times. Then roll the shoulders forwards in a circular motion, ten times.

    (iv) Circle your head in a clockwise direction, five times. Repeat this in a counter-clockwise direction, five times.

    (v) Stand comfortably on both feet then shake your left leg vigorously. Repeat this action with your right leg.

    (vi) Stand on the tip of your toes and stretch your arms upward toward the ceiling. Drop your heels back down to the floor. First, let the wrists flop, then flop the forearms, and then let the upper arms flop down to your sides. Now drop your head to your chest and bend forward from your waist until your arms are hanging freely from your shoulders. Your head hangs down and is completely relaxed. Swing your arms from left to right with a pendulum motion and let your body accompany that movement. Return to the centre and slowly uncurl from your waist until you resume your normal stance. Repeat this exercise and, this time, feel as if you are a floppy doll as you curl downward and start the swinging action.

    (vii) Maintain an upright position. Lift your chest and keep your chin parallel to the floor as you walk around the room.

    (viii) Massage your face and then pull different faces: smile, pout, drop your jaw, and show surprise.

5. Stand in front of the mirror and perform the following expressions and actions:

raised eyebrow	frown
smile	free, unstilted movement
pursed lips	nod
crossed arms	rapid breathing
hunched shoulders	sigh
aggressive, intense eye contact	clenched fists
tilted head	serene eye contact
arms loosely placed at the side	hands gripping the lectern
passive facial expression	slouch
feet firmly planted slightly apart	stiff posture

body angled away from the audience	legs crossed
stroking chin	biting nails
raise your arm and say "Stop!"	say, "You, you and all of you!"

How do you interpret each action or gesture?

Now gesture showing the following:

"I have a migraine."

"Definitely not."

"I am over here."

"She is tall and skinny."

"Profits plunged."

"You are all welcome."

"It is smooth."

"Be quiet."

"Go away!"

"There are two main issues."

6. Prepare a two- to four-minute speech that requires movement, action, and gestures. Deliver this to the class who will, in turn, give you positive and constructive feedback on your gestures. First, the class will tell you what you did well and then, they will offer suggestions for improvement.

7. Write 300 words on what you have learned about your own system of nonverbal communication.

When contemplating gestures, make them congruent with your message, and make sure that they match the context in which they are delivered. Avoid offending different cultures. A good gesture will be natural, graceful, vital, appropriate, and well timed. When your gestures reinforce your message, your listener will retain your information and recall it long after the presentation has been delivered.

As Christabel Burniston, M.B.E., President of the International English Speaking Board, (International) has said, "Let gesture be used easily and rhythmically, not as a conscious added embellishment but as an integrated part of harmonious transmission."

SUMMARY

This chapter explains the skill of public speaking and addresses the fear that most people experience when faced with giving a speech. Techniques to diminish the fear and build confidence are offered. In addition, the speaker learns to identify the barriers or obstacles to effective communication. The important role the visual impression plays in public speaking is examined. The visual impression is conveyed through appearance, movement, proxemics, space, and the effective use of eye contact. Appearance and dress should be appropriately dictated by the occasion. Clothing should be the backdrop to the message. To make a genuine connection with the audience, the speaker should make good eye contact with members of the listening group. The eyes should not dart from person to person, but rather connect with one listener for the duration of one thought. The speaker can then move on and renew eye contact with another individual. Erect posture conveys a sense of confidence, as does the ability to make good use of the speaking space. When moving towards the speaking area or podium, do so with a brisk pace. During the presentation move purposefully, yet avoid pacing up and down.

Keep in mind the four types of gestures that can be used to add impact to your talk: the describing gesture, the emphatic gesture, the locating gesture, and the attitudinal gesture. Refer to the list of dos and don'ts for gestures, which offers concrete tips to help you polish your nonverbal delivery.

SUGGESTED READING

Dimitrius, Ellen, and Mark Mazzarella. *Reading People*. New York: The Ballantyne Publishing Group, 1999.

Hall, Edward T. *The Hidden Dimension*. Garden City, New York: Doubleday, 1966.

Morris, Desmond. *Body Talk*. New York: Crown Publishing Group, Inc., 1994.

Nierenberg, G.I., and H. Calero. *How to Read a Person Like a Book*. New York: Hawthorn, 1971.

Rogers, Natalie. *The New Talk Power*. Virginia: Capital Books, 2000.

Burniston, Christabel. *Spoken English in Advanced Education*. Southport: The English Speaking Board, 1974.

REFERENCES

Aristotle, Nicomachean Ethics, written 350 BCE, translated by W.D. Ross.

Mehrabian, Albert. "A semantic space for nonverbal behaviour." *Journal of Consulting and Clinical Psychology* 35 (1970): 248–257.

Mehrabian, Albert. *Silent Messages*. Belmont, CA: Wadsworth, 1971.

Mehrabian, Albert. "Nonverbal Betrayal of Feeling." *Journal of Experimental Research in Personality* 5 (1971): 64–73.

Mehrabian, Albert. *Nonverbal Communication*. Chicago: Aldine-Atheron, 1972. 182.

Porter, Kay, and Judy Foster. *The Mental Athlete: Inner Training for Peak Performance*. New York: Ballantyne Books, 1986. pp. 64–71.

 WEBLINKS

ourworld.compuserv.com/homepages/har/les1.htm
This site offers relaxation exercises to manage anxiety.

www.mtsu.edu/~jpurcell/Taichi/taichi.htm
This site offers meditation and relaxation tips.

Interview Edward Greenspan

Edward Greenspan, Q.C., L.L.D., is a leading Canadian criminal lawyer, author, and extremely engaging speaker.

Q Which public speaker made an indelible impression on you?

A Clarence Darrow is regarded as the greatest criminal lawyer that ever lived. I have read all of his public speeches and his jury addresses and they had a pretty profound effect on me, in terms of his use of language, his choice always to use the simplest words and expressions rather than the words that the audience would not know. Yet, I sit back in admiration of his vast knowledge of words that he employs in his essays. I admire his honesty in trying to get beneath the surface of what he is talking about, to reach the hearts and the minds of the listeners.

Q What are the attributes and qualities of a good speaker?

A A good speaker has to win the audience over very quickly in a speech; they have to like the speaker…There has to be some humour. Humour is a good device to enhance the mood of the crowd toward you. So I'm attracted to people who begin with good humour. I also admire people who can begin fairly quickly and let me know in a very short period of time that they have an exceptional grasp of the subject. In other words, "Wow me," wow me with your knowledge. That always works. I am distracted by people who read their notes—not that you shouldn't refer to notes—but rather it is the sheer reading of notes that I find distracting. I don't like speeches that are not tightly written. I don't like meandering at all; it is very distracting. Very early on in the speech, I know whether the speaker has spent time structuring the speech.

Q What elements does a speech require?

A Speakers have to recognize their limitations and their strengths. If you're not funny, don't be funny; you can't go to a book, pick out a joke and deliver it when you know that everybody in your close circle says, "You're not funny." It is a mistake to try to be something you're not. But I do like the "warm up" in terms of the speaker warming the audience, and the audience warming to the speaker. Of course, if it is a very serious moment, you go right to it. You can't just be entertaining; you also have to be informative. During the death penalty debate that went on in Canada in 1986, I travelled across the country and debated against the death penalty, at a time when about 78 percent of Canadians were in favour of the death penalty. There was a free vote that Prime Minister Mulroney permitted so that every member could vote according to his or her conscience. This was, and still is, a pretty emotional topic. So I had to try to win people over to thinking that I was worth listening to in the first ten minutes. This is what you have to do in structuring your speech. Then you deal with your central points as oratorically and persuasively as you can… You have to take a point of view throughout your speech and end powerfully on this point.

Q How do you prepare your speech?

A Well, first of all it goes through a number of drafts—all of my thoughts are written. Humour is the hardest to write. I have to rework it a lot. I usually have a number of people look at it and some people listen to it....When it is finally done, I time it for the first time. If I have got 20 minutes or 25, I will never be caught going too long and I will never be caught going too short; whatever time they have allotted me, that is what they will get.

Q   **From the student's point of view, would you say that public speaking is a crucial skill in a professional and business world?**

A   Absolutely. There are two words in there, one is public and one is speaking. To be able to speak and convey an idea is essential. Public means two or more people. It does not have to be 500, it does not have to be 300, and it does not have to be 100. But, if I am sitting in a room and an accountant walks into the room, and has to explain to me an aspect of a financial statement, then I want a good explanation and a good explanation has to be delivered effectively. If the accountant is fumbling and stumbling, I stop paying attention; or if the accountant is not conveying the information to me in a language that I can understand, then he or she is failing as a public speaker.

Q   **I see a lot of people fearful of pausing. Can you comment on this observation?**

A   In a written speech, I put in brackets, "Pause." You always calculate how the speech sounds in order to make your position sound better. I don't like people who speak straight ahead; I prefer when they engage their entire audience. Look to the left, to the right, to the centre—then a second time, to the right, the left, then the centre.

Q   **There was a study done at UCLA as to why some speakers are more successful than others. They broke it**

down into the verbal, which is what you say, the vocal, how you say it, and the nonverbal. And the results were very surprising. The content accounted for 7 percent, the vocal 38 percent, and the nonverbal 55 percent.

A   Yes, the nonverbal is really important. But at the same time, a monotonous voice shows a lack of passion for the subject. When you are speaking on a subject, the one thing you don't want to convey to your audience is your disinterest in the subject. If you don't care about what you are talking about, why should they care? You must care. Perhaps I feel strongly about this point because I am a lawyer, an advocate. I go to court every day and I advocate a position on behalf of a client; I do believe in the adversarial process. When you are making a speech you are trying to win people over.

Q   **How do you ensure that a diverse audience understands you?**

A   You have to speak to the middle—to the centre. Every time you speak you are speaking to a diverse audience. It is not always a homogeneous group. They may be from similar socio-economic groups but they have diverse notions and diverse ideas. You have to pitch your idea in such a way that you don't lose your enemies too fast. Trying to pitch it to the middle is very difficult, but you have to do it.

Q   **The question and answer period—how do you deal with it as the speaker?**

A   I always summarize the question so that the audience understands what I am being asked, what I am going to answer. This also gives me control over how I want to answer it, because I may skew it a bit in my favour...You always want to refer back to what you said—always. You can give even greater importance to what you said in the context of the underlying question.

Q   Name one essential quality that a good speaker needs.

A   The one quality I consider essential for speakers is honesty. If I were asked a question that I thought I did not understand or couldn't grasp, I would say, "You know one of my nightmares is giving a public speech in front of 300 people where somebody would ask a question that I did not have the answer to, and I am now living my nightmare."

Why be embarrassed about being asked a question that you don't know the answer to? We're not all geniuses. It does not show vulnerability, but rather flexibility and honesty.

Q   What advice would you offer to novice speakers?

A   Know your subject. Always write out your thoughts. Always share the original speech with at least one or two other people. Listen to everybody who criticizes you. Reject some of what they say, but remember that they are the audience. Go over it no less than three times before you deliver it.

chapter two

Audience Analysis

For of the three elements in speechmaking—speaker, subject, and person addressed—it is the last one, the hearer, that determines the speech's end and object.

—Aristotle

LEARNING OBJECTIVES

- To learn the importance of analyzing your audience in order to tailor and target your message

- To evaluate your audience based on their demographics including knowledge of their age, gender, occupation, ethnicity, and education

- To know how to adapt your message by understanding the values and needs of your audience

- To familiarize yourself with the speaking environment

There is a Chinese proverb that states, "Square words won't fit into a round ear." As a speaker, it is important to take note of this advice. You can prepare a well-researched, well-constructed, and well-prepared talk but if you don't take into account who your audience, or the recipient of your message is, then your "square" words will not be received as you intended them. Here are a few guidelines. Remember it is not what is said that is important; rather, it is what has been received by the listener that is key. Frequently the speaker intends to convey a particular idea but the listener hears something different. Once you have prepared your presentation, listen to your words with your audience's ears.

When preparing your presentation, do a thorough audience analysis since this will shape the content, tone, and language of your message. An effective speaker will shape a "round" message to fit a "round" ear. As a presenter, public speaker, leader, or speech-maker, you have additional homework to do—find out who is in your audience.

KNOWING YOUR AUDIENCE

You need to gather information on the following:

1. prior knowledge of the audience
2. level of education and interest
3. gender
4. age
5. occupation
6. cultural, ethnic, or racial background
7. religion
8. group membership
9. attitude
10. values
11. needs
12. speaking environment

We will begin with an analysis of the demographics of the audience. Demographics incorporate the elements shown above.

Prior Knowledge of the Audience

Once you have decided upon your topic, you need to ask yourself, "What knowledge does the audience have on this subject? Are some members of the audience more informed than others?" The depth of their knowledge will influence and dictate the depth and breadth of the content of your presentation. For example, if you are giving a presentation on "Computers in the Home" to a group of stay-at-home parents who have come to learn how to access the Internet, and how to list birth dates, carpool schedules, and recipes on their computer, you must offer clear directions and instructions. To give a detailed technical talk about the inner workings of the computer shows you have not done your homework around audience analysis and you have misread your audience's needs.

How do you obtain this background information on the attendees? Well, begin with the person who first invited you to talk on the subject. Also, you can research on the Internet, visit the library, and use personal and professional connections as resources. Ask definitive questions like, How much experience does the audience have with computers?, How technically adept are they?, What do they want to know?, What do they need to know?, Have they done research on computers?, Are there any experts in the audience who will be more knowledgeable on the topic? Clearly, if you were directing your talk to an audience concerned with the more technical aspects of computers, the title and focus of your presentation would be different.

The Level of Education and Interest

What level of schooling does the audience have? Are they high-school graduates? Are they university graduates? Are they a group of retirees, some with a university education, others without? When you have discovered the educational level of the listening group, you will select the appropriate vocabulary, language, style, anecdotes, humour, and structure for your talk. You should carefully consider your speech purpose, your key message, your anecdotes, and examples. Tailor each to your audience's level of education and interest.

Let's assume you are giving a talk to a group of potential tourists to the Niagara region. The talk is entitled "Ontario's Niagara Region: A World-Class Holiday Destination at Our Doorstep." If your audience is comprised of a group of individuals whose only interest is to visit the casinos and gamble, you would deliver a very different key message compared to the one you would deliver to a group of history buffs.

Here is an extract of a talk that was delivered by Margaret Grisdale on this subject. Her audience was a group of tourists who love history. Margaret first attracts the attention of the audience by using a quotation. She continues to describe the many attributes of the unique, changing recreational area of Niagara. She then offers a historical context, and discusses architectural preservation. She caters to the educational level and interests of her audience.

Ontario's Niagara Region: A World-Class Holiday Destination at our Doorstep

Who first invented work; and bound the free and holiday rejoicing spirit down? Charles Lamb's question, posed in the early 1800s in his essay on *Work*, is as pertinent today as it was then. As dreary November settles in, we all think about escaping the routine of work—even if only for a few days. Let me tell you about a unique and charming place to which you can escape that is readily accessible from Toronto, where Canadian currency is accepted and which, undoubtedly, will offer an activity to appeal to you.

When selecting a holiday destination, it is often necessary to choose culture, sophisticated accommodation, and fine dining over scenic natural beauty and access to the outdoors. **Niagara-on-the-Lake** and the surrounding region combine all of these attractions. Here, you can engage in boating, biking, shopping, golfing, dining, stroll in a garden, retreat to a spa, or hunt for antiques. I have enjoyed a number of visits to the town—both long and short—and, in telling you about it, will focus on the theatre, the Niagara River Recreational Trail, and the wineries.

Site of the neutral Indian village of Onghiara, Niagara-on-the-Lake was settled at the end of the American Revolution by British Loyalists. Originally known as Newark, the town served as the first capital of the colony of Upper Canada until Governor Simcoe moved it to York. The historic houses and public buildings that you see here today, however, do not date from this period. With the exception of the powder magazine at Fort George, the town was destroyed by fire during the war of 1812. The town was soon rebuilt, following the war, and became an active commercial centre with a thriving shipping and ship building industry. By the end of the 19th century, the scenic beauty of the area made it a leading tourist attraction.

The Great Depression and World War II, however, ended the first wave of tourism: the historic houses and grand hotels lay in neglect, and the trains and boats stopped running. By the late 1950s a few forward-looking individuals began to restore the town's fine old buildings and, with the founding of the Shaw Festival in the 1960s, restoration began in earnest. One of the best things about this architectural preservation is that these lovingly restored buildings are in daily use. The inn or bed and breakfast that you select will very likely be one of them, and your host will take great pride in displaying its unique features. The ceilings in one of my favourite B&Bs, for example, are supported by charred beams, believed to have been salvaged from the great fire and used when the house was built in about 1816.

Gender

In this day and age, we need to be gender-sensitive. Before preparing your presentation, ask yourself, Is the audience composed of men or women?, Is the audience all-female?, Is it a completely male audience?, Is the audience heterosexual?, Is the audience homosexual? Consciously avoid sexist language, jokes, and anecdotes, and be sensitive to emotional "trigger" words. Many speakers, mistakenly, still engage in gender stereotyping. Be careful when you make the assumption that all women like fashion and all men like sports. Women like sports too, and some men are extremely fashion-conscious. You take the risk of offending or alienating your audience if you make inaccurate generalizations.

The words that you select should be chosen with care. Today, many words have become neutered. For example, an actress is now called an actor; we have househusbands, fire fighters, and police officers. Air hostesses are now referred to as flight attendants; we no longer have a man-eating disease, we have flesh-eating disease. We don't have a chairman who leads a meeting, we have a chair or chairperson. We don't address members of our class by saying "fellow classmates," we say "classmates." Most women are offended by the terms "gal," "doll," "chick," or "babe."

Always be sensitive towards gender and sexual orientation, and aim to craft your presentation by using language that is gender-sensitive, appropriate, and politically correct.

Age

The age of your listening group is a factor to be taken into consideration during the planning and shaping of your message. You should be able to find out the approximate age or age range of your audience. Are your listeners young, middle-aged, or elderly? Ask this important question. A speech on retirement planning would be viewed as totally inappropriate for a group of pre-adolescents. A talk on "How to manage money and save on an allowance" would be more relevant to them.

When Jennifer Walker, a financial adviser, gave her presentation on "Retirement Planning and Your RRSP," she successfully gauged the age and interest level of the audience. She was speaking to a group of people in the 25 to 45 years of age range. She opened the presentation in this way:

> Will you be able to support your lifestyle when you retire? How many baby boomers do you know who will have to continue working well into their sixties, even seventies? Having been in the financial planning industry for over nine years, I would like to share with you the most powerful retirement planning vehicle available to every person in this room, the Registered Retirement Savings Plan (RRSP). Let's spend the next few minutes together exploring the three main points in retirement planning: What, How, and Where?
>
> What is an RRSP? It is a personal retirement plan that is registered with the government to assist and encourage Canadians to save for their own retirement. RRSPs are not specific investments, but a vehicle used to hold a variety of investments and shelter them from tax. Contributions to an RRSP are tax-deductible, and the funds inside an RRSP grow tax-free.

Individuals in this age group would obviously be interested in planning for their financial security. Your talk would be accurately focused if you used this approach.

Occupation

There is a wonderful story about a preacher who relished telling stories. Once, a member of the audience asked him how he managed to have a story for every occasion. This was his reply:

> Let me tell you a story about a traveller who stopped at a country inn. While waiting for his meal to be prepared, he decided to take a walk around the property. When he went to the back of the garden, he saw a tall oak tree. On the tree was a target with three arrows in the bullseye. Beside the tree stood the innkeeper's son, Sam, holding a bow. The preacher was rather curious and asked Sam, "How do you manage to hit your target with such accuracy?" to which Sam replied, "It's really quite simple. First, I shoot the arrows and then I'd draw the target around it."

That method would certainly fail if we applied it to audience analysis. First define your target, then shoot your arrows.

Know the occupation or occupations of the attendees. If you are talking to a group of Olympic contenders, sports broadcasters, and members of the sports television industry, you could make a strong connection with them by including sports anecdotes and quotations.

Your presentation might open in the following way:

> Baron De Courbertin, founder of the modern Olympics, said, "The important thing in the Olympic Games is not to win, but to take part; the important thing in life is not the triumph, but the struggle; the essential thing is not to have conquered, but to have fought well.
>
> Today, as Olympic hopefuls, sports broadcasters, and television executives, we endure a constant struggle to reach the top, and then the challenge is to stay on top. We have fought the good fight and we ought to be proud of that.

Here the quotation used to open the presentation is pertinent to the occupations and interests of members of your audience.

Cultural, Ethnic, or Racial Background

There's an old saying that people like to do business with people who are like them.. This also applies to an audience listening to a presentation. An audience will naturally be inclined to listen more attentively to a message that is consistent with their interests, ethnicity, background, and values.

Canada is a country that is proud of its cultural, ethnic, and religious diversity. We embrace and celebrate our differences and are often held up to the world as a fine example of a country that has succeeded in creating a tolerant, multicultural society.

After having done your homework to find out the ethnic background and composition of your audience, make certain that your presentation demonstrates respect for those differences.

If your audience is culturally diverse, do extra research so that you target the needs of the audience with your speech topic; match your language, your visuals, and your body language to audience expectations.

A student was a giving a presentation on Chinese New Year to an ethnically mixed group and began with following words:

> What is the most important day of the year for you? Is it your birthday? Is it your wedding anniversary? And may I ask you, what day is the most important one for your entire family?
>
> If you are from a Western country, you would probably reply, "Christmas" or "Thanksgiving." If you are Muslim you might say "Ramadan," a Jew might respond with "Yom Kippur," and an Indian might say "Deepavali," which is a festival of lights.
>
> My answer would be "Today." And why you may ask? Well, today is the Chinese New Year, a time of celebration, a time for family reunion, and a time to give thanks.

This student took into account the fact that members of her audience embraced different religions and different traditions and she acknowledged this in the opening of her talk by posing specific questions. She easily drew her listeners into her talk, willing to listen to her message. She set the stage for a receptive audience.

Religion

Religion is very personal to every individual. As a speaker you should demonstrate respect and deference for the listeners' religious choices and beliefs. Canada's policy of multiculturalism emerged as a result of its prevalent tolerance of all religious and ethnic groups.

When preparing for a presentation to a religious audience, ask the following:

1. What is the religious make-up of the group?
2. Will the audience be open to my point of view?
3. Will my topic offend anyone?
4. How can I structure my talk in a way that the audience will respond without prejudice?
5. Have I done thorough research on the ethnic, religious, and cultural background of the groups?

6. What attitudes do they have towards my subject matter?

7. What needs do they have that should be met by my presentation?

8. Am I familiar with the theology, vocabulary, and sensitivities of my listening group?

The Reverend Dr. Andrew Stirling delivered his sermon on September 16, 2001 at the Timothy Eaton Memorial Church, five days after the horrendous terrorist attack on the World Trade Center in New York. Although he drew on the Christian tradition, he aimed to embrace all believers by choosing what might be considered non-offensive words. He concluded his sermon in the following way.

> I didn't know what to read. I thought: "What on earth, Lord, can I say? I am so filled with anger. I want revenge. I want those who have taken those innocent lives to suffer." I think we all felt that way, did we not? But in the light of day, and in the light of God, I want those who are the perpetrators to be called to justice.

Always keep in mind the fact that, for many individuals, religion is their life-guide and you would not want to offend or rile anyone. Your credibility as a speaker is established during your presentation, so it is important for you to demonstrate a respect for individual differences.

Group Membership

If you are speaking on campus, some members of the audience may belong to fraternities or sororities. Some may be members of the ski club, the debating society, or the computer club. If you are speaking to an audience of business executives, some may belong to the Certified General Accountants of Canada, while others may be members of the Financial Executives Institute. Do your research on the organizations and group affiliations and incorporate anecdotes, facts, and statistics that will be relevant to your listeners. For example, the audience of Financial Executives Institute will be impressed if you mention in your presentation that their Institute is a pre-eminent professional association representing 14 000 individuals from over 8000 corporations. It will be evident that you have done your research on their organization.

When addressing a group in Montreal, it would be wise to know if the audience is bilingual. If you were speaking to students from Université de Montreal, French would be the language of choice, whereas students from McGill University would expect a presentation delivered in English. You need to know that McGill University is an international university whose main language of instruction is English.

You can do further research and find out what the mission statement or vision is of the group you are addressing. Weave your knowledge of their organization into your presentation and you will definitely earn the respect of your audience. You are also conveying to your listeners that you have been diligent in researching and uncovering background information on the group that you are addressing.

There was a rather arrogant young speaker who once gave an address to a group of elderly folks. He made the following errors in his delivery—he spoke at a breakneck speed and shouted his message. He had not done his audience analysis. Mistakenly, he assumed that older people were hard of hearing; he also neglected to adjust the pace of his delivery so that he could be understood. With an older audience, place yourself in a position so that you are clearly visible to them. At the outset, state clearly in simple language the topic of your presentation. Slow down your pace of speech and take frequent pauses. Keep your sentences short and paint vivid pictures. Find out their needs and values since there will probably be a generation gap between the young speaker and her elderly audience.

The next three remaining elements lie outside the category of demographics, but are equally important in terms of audience analysis.

Attitude

An attitude conveys your disposition towards what you like or don't like, of what you approve or disapprove. This attitude may show your state of mind or feelings towards an idea, an individual, a particular group, or an event. For example, Falun Gong may be an accepted form of belief or religion in Canada, but in China it is banned. So clearly, a talk on this topic as a visiting lecturer to a conference in Beijing would be unsuitable. Discover whether your audience would be in favour of, or against, your proposed topic. You may need to reconsider your topic and speech purpose and tailor your message to meet the audience's needs and expectations.

If you were to address a group of individuals who believe in alternative medicine, they may have a closed mind to a talk entitled "The Flu Shot, Not the Flu." The talk may encourage the audience to avoid influenza by taking advantage of the free vaccinations offered by the Department of Health. Armed with the knowledge you gleaned by doing your audience analysis, you could begin your talk by acknowledging their belief in alternative medicine and then state that you are here to reveal an option, one that would guarantee an escape from the miserable illness of influenza.

The attitudes that members of the audience assume are frequently predicated on their beliefs and values. A belief is something in which you have faith or trust. Often, a belief cannot be supported with proof and it can be based on incorrect information. If you are speaking about "Eliminating Capital Punishment for War Crimes," knowledge of your listeners' belief system will help you to understand their point of view. You can then proceed to alter their opinion by providing examples, evidence, and stories on the impact of the cruel, inhuman elimination of a human life.

Values

Values are enduring principles that guide our behaviour throughout our lives. Values support our beliefs and attitudes. It is harder to change values than to change beliefs because they are so deeply ingrained in us. The value of courage emerged strongly when firefighters braved the fires of the World Trade Center after the September 11, 2001 terrorist attack.

Here are some examples of key values in Western society:

accomplishment	cleanliness	friendship
altruism	courage	greed
ambition	equality	happiness
beauty	forgiveness	harmony

helpfulness	justice	responsibility
honesty	loyalty	security
imagination	nurturing	self-respect
inclusion	orderliness	wisdom
independence	pleasure	work ethic
integrity		

Examine the attributes, beliefs, and values of your audience with extraordinary diligence, so your presentation reaches receptive ears. You can call attendees and ask them what their expectations are.

If you were developing a speech to be delivered to new immigrants on "Canadian Values and Culture," you might want to turn to the research done by Environics Research Group in July 1997 and printed in their report, *Focus Canada*. When the researchers posed the following question, "What things do you value most about being Canadian?" the value that topped the list was freedom/choices. This was followed by beauty/geography, climate/resources, health care/medical system, and finally quality of life. New immigrants are frequently drawn to Canada as a destination to call home because Canada represents freedom and freedom of choice to many. You could weave these values into your talk so that they resonate with the very values that your audience holds.

When speaking to members of your class, find out their interests, the academic courses that they are studying, the sports in which they participate, the extra-curricular activities in which they are involved, their future career plans. All this analysis will equip you with the information to frame and target your talk with more precision.

Needs

To be an effective speaker you cannot plan a presentation directed to, "To whom it may concern." Do not offer a generic presentation. We analyze our audience based on all the criteria we have discussed so far and now we need to understand human needs. Your audience will be motivated to listen to you when you address and satisfy their needs.

An audience of abused children will more likely be open to listening to a lecture by a sports hero who himself has emerged from an abusive environment to become successful. Here they can identify with his early beginnings where, like their own, his basic need for safety was undermined. The sports hero can structure his talk in a way to offer methods and a mindset that can provide these children with hope.

So we return to the theme of this chapter: know your audience, know their needs, and, consequently, tailor your message to your listeners.

THE SPEAKING ENVIRONMENT

To create a sense of comfort for yourself, find out as much as you can about the environment in which you will be presenting. If you are able, pay a visit to the venue. See if the layout is a U-shape, a V-shape, a boardroom-style setting, or an auditorium. Will you be speaking on a raised platform or will you be presenting on the same level as your audience? Will there be a podium? What is the height of the podium? (If you are short, make certain that there is a platform that can be placed behind the podium so that you can be elevated.) When the Queen of England visited Canada a few years ago, a photograph of her appeared on the front page of a national newspaper. The headline read, "The Hat of State," and it accompanied a photograph of her Majesty hidden behind a podium that was clearly too high for her stature. All that was visible above the podium was a picture of her hat!

If you have any control over your speaking environment, you may send a requisition form to those in charge of the classroom, meeting, conference, or presentation arrangements, as in Form 2.1 below.

What other environmental features will affect your presentation? The acoustics certainly will. Will you need a microphone? What type of microphone will best suit your purpose—a standing microphone or a lavalier microphone? Where are the light switches? You need to have quick access to your lighting for a PowerPoint presentation. You could solicit the aid of a classmate to lower or raise the lighting according to your presentation plan. In this case, you will need to practise with your classmate or colleague so that your timing is

FORM 2.1	**Requisition Sheet**

EQUIPMENT and FACILITIES

A large meeting room with chairs arranged

- in a "U" formation
- in an auditorium-style arrangement
- around circular tables

Audio/Visual Requirements

- ❏ VCR - VHS format
- ❏ Video camera - VHS format
- ❏ Monitor
- ❏ VHS tapes
- ❏ Flipchart
- ❏ Overhead projector
- ❏ Screen
- ❏ Slide projector
- ❏ Lavalier or stand-up microphone
- ❏ Podium
- ❏ Computer
- ❏ L.C.D. projector
- ❏ A remote mouse
- ❏ Microsoft PowerPoint '97
- ❏ PowerPoint Version 7
- ❏ Technician

perfectly synchronized. It is also a good idea to begin a presentation in full view of the audience, with the lights on, and during the question and answer period the lights should come on again. In this way, you make a better audience connection.

It will not serve you well if you do all your audience analysis and then, when you are presenting, you discover that the listeners cannot see or hear you. Make sure that the sight lines work in your favour. You do not want anyone to have an obscured view of you and your presentation materials.

A personal visit to the venue will help prepare you for the occasion. Go and sit in the back row of the venue. Sit in the seats situated at the sides of the room. If you were sitting in these seats, would you have an unobstructed view of the speaker and his visuals? You may need to rearrange the seating if it does not meet your requirements. Walk the journey from your seat or from the wings of the stage to the podium. In this way, you will familiarize yourself with your speaking environment and you will build your self-confidence.

Will you be a part of a speaking roster? What is your position on the agenda? Will you be speaking just before lunch, when the listeners' minds are focusing more on lunch than on a presentation? Will you be speaking just after lunch, at that time of day when people feel rather sluggish? Ask to present in the morning, if possible, as this is the time period when people are fresh and alert. If this is not possible and you do have to speak at an undesirable time, make the most of it and make certain that you are even more energetic and enthusiastic than usual.

The temperature in the room will affect the listeners. A room that is too hot or too cold will create a sense of discomfort. Know where the temperature dial is located and get it adjusted accordingly. Do this prior to the presentation.

You will also want to eliminate as many distractions as possible. Check that your speaking venue is not affected by construction noises and that there are no endless interruptions.

Size of the Audience

How many people will attend your presentation? If the group is a small one, you may prefer to create a U-shape setting, so that you can move about freely and diminish the distance between you, the speaker, and your audience. This is an arrangement that is often preferred by individuals who are conducting meetings, brainstorming sessions, or seminars.

If the group is small, yet formal, you may use a boardroom-style set-up with the listeners sitting around the table and you will then present from the head of the table. If you choose, you may sit down and present, but it is preferable to stand since this makes you the focal point of attention. You are occupying more space and also conveying a stronger presence when speaking from an upright position.

If the size of the audience is large, it is preferable to have an auditorium-style layout of the chairs. Knowing that you are addressing a large audience, it is important to remember to make eye contact with all areas of the hall, room, or theatre. Incorporate the left side of the room, the right side of the room, the central section, and the back of the room when making eye contact.

The size of the group will also dictate whether you need to use a microphone or not. When in doubt, ask a friend to visit the facility with you and stand at the back of the room. Say a few words aloud and your friend can offer you feedback as to the level of volume you need to use for this speaking environment. If your voice is capable of strong projection, you may not need a microphone. If there is the slightest chance that someone at the back might not hear you, use a microphone. The listeners do not want to work to receive your message so make it easy for them to hear you by employing appropriate volume. Your message will then be received effortlessly since you have taken an audience-centred approach.

Challenging Types of Audiences

The Inattentive Audience   Sometimes an audience appears bored and disinterested in your talk. They seem to be focused elsewhere or to be shifting about in their seats. Their attention span could also be limited. When you encounter this type of audience, introduce stories, anecdotes, and humour when appropriate. Let them know that the information you have to offer will be of benefit and interest to them. An inattentive audience can become engaged if you use audience involvement. Ask them for their experiences or opinions on the topic. Pose questions to which they can respond.

Pay attention to the nonverbal aspect of your presentation by using powerful visuals and cartoons to capture the audience's attention. Incorporate bold gestures, and make good use of your presentation space by moving about purposefully.

Use good vocal variety. Be expressive and, by picking up the pace of your delivery, the audience will become more alert. This does not mean, however, that you should race through your presentation. A dynamic voice will compel the audience to listen to you.

Keep the structure of your talk simple and easy to follow. Do not exceed the allotted time frame. In fact, finish five minutes early and the audience will be appreciative.

The Hostile Audience   When faced with a hostile audience, avoid emotional entanglement with them. Move away from emotions and stick with the facts. Support your points with solid evidence and, if necessary, offer additional data to corroborate your message. Have these facts on a PowerPoint slide or overhead. If those visual aids are not at your disposal, write down the facts and evidence on a chalkboard.

This might also be a good time to remind the audience of your credentials and your background. You can also offer an expert opinion relating to your subject matter.

A hostile audience might not be responsive to humour, so be cautious in this regard. When in doubt, you might be safer to avoid humour.

Use logical patterns to structure your presentation, such as the topical pattern, the spatial pattern, or the chronological pattern. It is hard to be hostile when confronted with a logical presentation in terms of both order and argument.

Speak in a voice that is calm, measured, and controlled. Do not let hostility cause you angst that, in turn, may negatively affect your vocal delivery.

Conduct the question and answer period by employing the methods suggested in Chapter 11. If you want greater control over this segment of your presentation, at the outset of your presentation suggest to members of the audience that they write questions on cards that you have distributed to them prior to the talk. Collect the cards, and select the questions that are of greatest concern to your listeners. Then respond to them in a calm, controlled, and confident manner.

FORM 2.2	Audience Analysis Worksheet

Topic: _____

Speech Purpose: _____

Speech Topic: _____

Audience: _____

Occasion: _____

Why is the audience attending this presentation? _____

_____

What knowledge does the audience possess on this topic? _____

_____

How did they get their information? _____

_____

What is their attitude towards this topic? _____

_____

Will they find the information interesting? _____

_____

What do I need to know about this particular audience? _____

_____

What is their educational status? _____

_____

What is their economic status? _____

_____

What are their occupations? _____

_____

What is the age group of the audience? _____

What do I know of their culture, ethnicity, and religion? _____

_____

How many people will attend the presentation? _____

Is the audience composed of male, female, or mixed gender? _____

Where is the presentation being held? _____

What is the layout of the room? _____

Where are the podium, microphone, chalkboard, and visual aids positioned?

_____

What time is the presentation? _____

How long will I speak for? _____

Will there be a question and answer period? _____

EXERCISES

1. Divide into pairs. Design a questionnaire to discover the demographics of your class. Circulate this questionnaire to your classmates and ask them to complete the information you require.

2. Get into small groups and plan a list of five topics for a presentation that would interest the members of your class.

3. You are going to deliver a presentation introducing a new computer system to a large organization. Your audience will be made up of top-level executives, the chief executive officer, the chief financial officer, the chief operating officer, mid-level executives, and secretaries. Prepare a list of questions you will pose to gauge the level of knowledge, attitude, aptitude, needs, and interest of the audience.

4. Prepare a questionnaire to distribute amongst your classmates. You will be presenting on a controversial topic, and you plan to uncover their feelings, beliefs, values, and attitudes. Choose one of the following topics:

   Euthanasia

   Working mothers

   Terrorism

   Student loans

   Corruption and the Olympics

   Abortion

   The right to protest

   Care of the elderly

   Marriage should be more difficult and obtaining a divorce should be made easier

   Cloning

   Homelessness

   Taxes

5. Select a speech from the Internet site **douglass.speech.nwu.edu** or **www.history channel.com/speeches.index.html**. Analyze the audience the speaker is addressing by finding examples that are revealing of the demographics of the group, the occasion, and the situation.

6. Your audience is a group of new immigrants to Canada. You represent the government and will present a comprehensive presentation on the various provinces and their demographics. Visit the Web site: **canada.worldweb.com/visitorinformation/ demographics/ 8114.html**, and gather demographic information on the provinces. Divide the class into 12 pairs. Each pair will then provide the demographic information on the province that they have chosen to present to the class.

SUMMARY

In this chapter we have examined the importance of audience analysis. Successful speakers carefully examine the demographics of their audience. They will find out as much as they can about the prior knowledge, gender, age, occupation, cultural, ethnic or racial background, religion, and group membership as it pertains to their audience. Next, prepared speakers will do an attitudinal analysis and discover as much as they can about the attitudes, values, and needs of the audience. Remember to be diligent when doing your environmental and situational analysis. Before you speak, visit the venue in which you will be presenting. Check the audio-visual equipment to make certain everything is correctly placed and in good working order. Check the podium height and the room arrangement.

Listeners are egocentric so always give the audience a "What's-in-it-for-me?" statement. For example, during the introductory segment of a presentation on "Becoming an Effective Presenter," include this type of statement: "By the end of my presentation you will have learned three vital skills which will assist you to become a confident, competent speaker." Shape your message, tailor your delivery appropriately, and structure your speech by using the method to which your audience would be most receptive. Remember, listen to your talk with your audience's ears, and deliver your message with authenticity, alignment and purpose.

SUGGESTED READING

Environics Research. *Focus Canada*. July, 1997.

Jeary, Tony. *Inspire Any Audience*. Texas: TPG Inc., 1997.

Maslow, Abraham H. *Toward a Psychology of Being*. New York: D. Van Nostrand Company, 1968.

Maslow, Abraham H. *Motivation and Personality*. New York: Harper & Row, 1970.

Noonan, Peggy. *Simply Speaking: How to Communicate Your Ideas with Style Substance and Clarity*. New York: Harper Collins Publishers, 1998.

 ## WEBLINKS

www.historychannel.com/speeches.index.html
A&E Television Networks, Home Page. 2002.

douglass.speech.nwu.edu
1995-2002 Douglass.

| Interview | **Evan Solomon** |

Evan Solomon is the host of CBC *Newsworld's* provocative show on print culture, "Hot Type," and co-host of CBC News: Sunday. He is the co-founder and the former editor-in-chief of *Shift Magazine* and his first novel is titled, *Crossing the Distance*. *Maclean's Magazine* named him one of the "100 Canadians to Watch."

Q   Which public speakers have left an indelible impression upon you?

A   If you're interested in rhetoric the classics are important. Growing up in my house you could hear recordings of Churchill and Martin Luther King. They are both great speakers. With respect to the present day, I'm a big fan of Bill Clinton's. He's a mesmerizing speaker. I would also say Richard Ford, the writer, and Coleman Barks. Monologists and storytellers, I find to be excellent speakers. Trudeau was a great speaker.

Q   Describe the attributes of a good speaker.

A   A good speaker makes a connection to the audience. They are passionate about their subject. Someone who's passionate about his subject and curious will make a connection to his audience. Intellectual passion and real emotion are important. I also like a speaker who does not read a speech. A speaker who reads from a PowerPoint presentation because somebody has told them that people only remember what they see three times does not use the efficiency of the gathering. If all you do is read the presentation to them, you may as well send them the presentation by email. What makes a speaker engaging is when you have something to say and have a curious, intelligent, interesting and passionate story. Take it to the next level. You don't have to just convey information. You are connecting, you are telling a story. Technology can deliver information but it cannot deliver inspiration. You listen to a speech for inspiration. You want to trigger ideas. You want to deepen an interest in the things that you are interested in, as well as deepen the connection with things you are passionate about. People are not only looking for information, they are looking for a different way of seeing. Whether the topic is delivered at an energy, engineering, or medical conference or whether it is a political speech, you need charisma to do that.

It's all about telling a story and conveying a message. Great speakers are people like Socrates and he never made speeches. He conducted a dialogue with the audience. Churchill wrote wonderful speeches. He delivered them with precision of language and he believed in every word. When Churchill said, "I have nothing to offer but blood, toil, tears, and sweat," you believed him. You knew he wasn't just going through the motions. A speaker has to have an authenticity to him or her. Politicians have such a difficult time. They are prepped, they are spun, dehydrated, and blow-dried, and terrified that they might offend someone. They deliver very bland, homogenized speeches and are told, "Don't get off message." Our Prime Minister has sold himself on his inability to give speeches. He's a little guy from Shewinigan who thinks a big speech makes him sound somehow arrogant.

Q   **What are the vital elements of a good speech or presentation?**

A   A presentation has a different goal. It is to convey a series of facts and information. Clarity in presentation is vital. If your goal is to inspire or generate ideas, then passion would be more important than clarity. Passion in the speaker I put up top because of the narrative arc to the story. Most people begin a speech by summarizing it first and then they'll tell you, "I'm going to be talking about x, y, and z." This is good for a presentation, but it can undermine a speech. At the beginning of a speech one can open with a story that creates a narrative tension, or open with unresolved ideas that will be resolved by the end of the speech. At the end there must be a payoff. So there is that element of instability that a speech needs at the beginning. You create a kind of pleasurable tension for the audience. The nature of a speech or a story is the presentation of a series of unresolved ideas/instability that leads towards a climactic resolution. That is followed by a denouement, which is what the audience can take away. I think a speech without those elements—which you see all the time—can be terrible. For example, some speakers start with their thesis. They circle around it for three–five minutes and then come back to it. They do this again and again through the speech in a series of what can sometimes be interesting circles but in the end they haven't gone anywhere.

There is something else I have to say that is important for a good speech, and that is the ability to adjust it to the audience's concerns, their mood, the tension, and topicality. An accomplished speaker is able to go off script and connect to the moment. It can be terrifying to try this on the spot. Again, there's that pleasurable discomfort of learning. When you experience the pleasurable discomfort, you are ready to learn or ready to be inspired, you are looking for a little bit of discomfort. A good speaker is bold enough to have an intimacy with an audience. This is scarce and this is what makes a speaker valuable. I'm a believer in a speaker who moves around on the podium but then, many speakers don't and they can be just as effective. What bothers me is when a speaker will hide behind a podium during a PowerPoint presentation. Do not rely on the crutch of illustrations.

Also, a speaker ought to be able to move from very, very serious things to very, very funny things. Humor and the human encounter are good ingredients for a speech. They invite people in and it ends with the payoff of that connection you've established. Finally and fundamentally, you have to convey good information and deliver the information you have promised.

Q   **How do you prepare for a speech and what is your method of preparation?**

A   I write it out in note form. I research the topic and I research the group. I talk to people who are usually hosting the event. I ask the question, "What is the greatest anxiety of the audience?" "Why is the audience coming here?" Bill Clinton could go into any room in any town and know more about the town than the people who lived there. He knew more about the issues of the time, of the town, the local area, or the company. He made an effort to connect with his audience through research. Once people know that you've made an effort to understand them, they will make an effort to understand you. How do you do that? The key is preparation. I don't speak from notes but I use them as a guide.

Q **Is the ability to give an effective speech or presentation a crucial skill in the business and professional world?**

A I would say it is a skill that is undervalued. It is a crucial skill that will enable you to hold a meeting and to deliver the speech that begins a meeting. Even on other occasions it is important. I find it depressing when I listen to wedding speeches that are horrible. These are not necessarily bad speakers, they're just not effective. They don't put in the time and the preparation to acquit themselves proficiently. The inability to express an emotion or a thought—that's terrible. The ability to speak well is becoming an invaluable skill. Scarcity increases value and abundance decreases value and good communication that cuts through the noise is a scarce and, therefore, valuable skill. If you embrace the skill of speaking effectively, you become more valuable. What we can bring to an issue will be how we are judged.

Q **Are there any speaking habits that annoy you?**

A It depresses me when someone is simply reading a text or when somebody delivers a PowerPoint presentation. You can barely see the speaker who is surrounded by darkness while reading from the PowerPoint. This is redundancy and displays the inability to understand the efficiencies of technology. People have spent time and money to gather together. Don't bore them with something that they could have received in an email. Use the live audience to your advantage. The other thing is phoniness, somebody who is clearly shilling something without passion. They're not using the medium of a live event properly. If the speaker doesn't care, why should I?

Q **What detracts from a good speech?**

A The flat Canadian accent is so neutral. It doesn't lend itself to oration. Coleman Barks, who is a sensualist poet and a beautiful speaker from the South, can carry language that can soar and drop, that has hills and dales. That ability to be very expressive—the French language has it. We have to make a great effort to squeeze out the little drops of emotion here in Canada but it can be done. Some people can do it wonderfully. Peter Gzowski spoke with passion. Voice must have modulation and expression and convey the height and depths of the range of the language.

Q **Ralph Waldo Emerson said, "It is a luxury to be understood." How do you ensure that a diverse audience understands your message?**

A Of course you cannot be assured that everyone will understand you. We always misunderstand each other. With regards to Bill Clinton, if there were 100 people in the room and he thought 99 got his message, he would direct his speech to the one person he thought he still needed to bring on side. You know you've connected if you see smiles in the crowd, if people are laughing. You need empathy and the ability to understand the position of the other. Are they freaking out or are they falling asleep? A person who cannot read the faces of the audience is a bad speaker. A speaker needs a great degree of empathy. This is the priority. He or she is someone who understands the core concerns of the audience he or she is speaking to.

Q **How important is it to use aphorisms, quotations, and anecdotes in a speech?**

A It's wonderful. Nietschze wrote a book of aphorisms that's not to be trifled at. But I think a speech that relies too heavily on stringing together "quotes dotcom" is boring. An aphorism, a quote, or an anecdote is great when they decorate the structure of the speech. These are the things that allow you to become comfortable in the house that you've built. But there has to be a structure underneath it and I think it's important not to rely too heavily on it. The aphorism, the quote, the anecdote can distill a thought, it can open a speech, it can close it. It helps the audience see the speaker. Often you will find in a speech that people respond most to that. It humanizes the experience. Aphorisms can buffer a point. And they bring in an historical perspective, in fact. More and more, I find that my speeches have become historical explorations. We all have rearview mirror prophecy.

Q **What prepared you for your role as a public speaker?**

A I always start with thinking that the best form of learning is dialogue. Most of the best ideas have been generated through dialogue. My education was to learn how to express, defend, and debate ideas. There is a great quote by Emerson that every kid should read. It was from his essay, "Self-Reliance," written in 1841. He says, "A foolish consistency is the hobgoblin of little minds, adored by little statesmen and philosophers and divines. With consis-

tency a great soul has simply nothing to do. He may as well concern himself with his shadow on the wall. Speak what you think now in hard words, and tomorrow speak what tomorrow thinks in hard words again, though it contradicts everything you said today" (*Essays: First Series*, 1841). What he's saying is that when you speak strongly about something and you're proven wrong, then you need to adjust.

Q **What advice would you offer to novice speakers?**

A For a novice speaker the idea is simply to get up there and have fun. Express yourself. Try out different voices, by which I mean, it's all right to imitate the best speakers styles, to try them on until you find your own unique voice. Explore the language. The language is a very interesting country. Also, don't be afraid of humiliation. Humiliation is not such a terrible place to be, in fact, it can be instructive. And don't be afraid to be afraid. You learn by failing. That's how science works. Science is about failure. And finally, know that when you are speaking, you are trying to accomplish something different than when you are writing. Speaking is about a connection, not just about information. It's about an emotional connection at a live event. It's about telling people a story. If you do that, then you're in good shape.

chapter three

Preparing a Speech

Every speech ought to be put together like a living creature, with a body of its own, so as to be neither without head, nor without feet, but to have both a middle and extremities, described proportionately to each other and to the whole.

—Plato, *Phaedrus*

LEARNING OBJECTIVES

- To understand the steps required in preparing a speech

- To learn how to select a speech topic

- To utilize brainstorming techniques

- To determine your speech purpose

- To develop a central speech statement

- To create a preparation outline for your talk

- To list ways of opening and closing a speech

THE IMPORTANCE OF PREPARATION

Simon entered the speech class with his backpack slung casually over one shoulder. Eric, his classmate, asked anxiously, "What topic will you be speaking on today?"

With an air of false confidence in his voice, Simon replied, "'Drinking and Driving', but I haven't put much time or thought into my speech so I guess I'll be winging it."

When Simon received a failing grade for his talk, he was disappointed, yet his classmates were not surprised. "Winging it" will not suffice when it comes to public speaking. Some people are born with the gift of the gab and apply public speaking skills with great ease. Others find it a challenge. Even if speaking in front of an audience does not fill you with dread, if you fail to prepare adequately, then you prepare to fail. Bear in mind that you owe it to your audience to offer them respect and to demonstrate that you value their time and attention.

Remember public speaking is a skill that can be learned and mastered. There are concrete, specific steps you can take to ensure that you will present yourself and your ideas confidently and competently.

Below is a road map that outlines the preparation stages needed before delivering a speech:

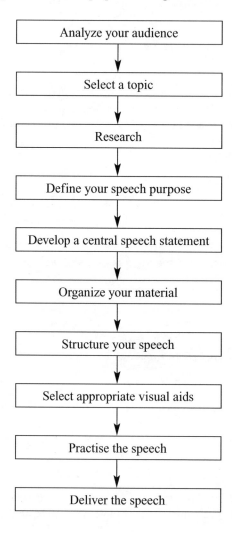

Analyzing your Audience

It is vital to do an audience analysis before selecting a topic and defining your purpose. (Refer back to the previous chapter to refresh your memory.) Naturally, you will want to present information that will provoke the interest of your listeners and hold their attention.

"Dating Guidelines for the Twenty-First Century" would be a more suitable topic for an audience of university and college students than a speech given on "Re-entering the Dating Game after Divorce." It is also far easier to choose a topic in which you are interested. For example, if the professor or teacher has asked the class to prepare a demonstrative speech, the student with an interest in the liquor industry might deliver a talk on "How Beer is Made," whereas someone interested in writing and penmanship might title a speech, "How to Analyze Handwriting."

Selecting the Topic

The first task the public speaker must accomplish is to select a topic. There are numerous subjects to choose from, such as your own personal interests, current events, controversial issues, travel, sports, music, education, health, problems, people, history, literature, hobbies, crime, theories, computers, events, processes, the environment, the media.

Sometimes a topic might be assigned to you, but in many public speaking classes you might be asked to choose your own topic for your speech.

You may be inspired by some of the subjects mentioned earlier, yet if you find that you are stuck and cannot come up with a suitable topic, try the following technique called "brainstorming."

1. Select one of the subjects listed above. Choose a subject that interests you, for example, Travel.
2. Write the subject at the top of a blank piece of paper.
3. Without judging or censoring your thoughts, write down your first association with that word. Then jot down the next association that comes to mind. Continue with this process until you have come up with six or seven points.

This is how your page may appear:

Travel

Space Travel

Travel by Car

Travel by Train

A Trip across the Canadian Rockies

Planning the Trip

Budgeting for the Trip

Accommodation

What you have done here is allowed for the free flow of your ideas. Here are a few simple Rules of Brainstorming:

1. Establish a time frame for brainstorming.
2. Aim for quantity not quality of ideas.
3. No evaluation or judgement is made.
4. Allow one idea to flow freely from another.

Now as you look at your brainstorming sheet filled with ideas, a particular topic will emerge. You will notice in this example on travel that "Travelling across the Canadian Rockies" could very well become your speech topic.

For more alternatives, refer to Chapter 4 for lists of potential speech topics.

Researching the Topic

As a university or college student you have learned how to research and you understand the importance of doing so in a timely and accurate manner. Allocate sufficient time for research and balance your time wisely so that it is evenly distributed between time for research, preparation, and practice. Often students can fall into the trap of spending too much time doing research and then find they are pressed for time when it comes down to putting all that research into a coherent, fluid speech structure.

There are four basic sources for information:

1. You, your knowledge, and experience
2. Printed sources
3. The World Wide Web
4. Interviews

You, Your Knowledge, and Experience   Begin your research with your own personal knowledge of the topic. You will derive credibility when you offer your own personal expertise and understanding of a subject. Remember *you* are a valuable source of information.

Printed Sources   *The Library*   Most libraries provide students with guided tours to help them become familiar with library research facilities. The library also offers access to periodicals, newspapers, specialized dictionaries, encyclopedias, quotation books, yearbooks, reference resources, and a variety of computer databases. Speak to a librarian for guidance when needed. You can even access library information from a computer with a modem. When your knowledge on a particular topic is limited, visit the library and take out two or three books on your topic, which will give you a good background to and overview of your topic.

College or University Bookstores   Campus bookstores can provide you with current textbooks on your topic. It would also be wise to purchase a set of reference books that should be on every public speaker's bookshelf, such as: *Bartlett's Familiar Quotations* by John Bartlett, *Bartlett's Book of Anecdotes*, the *Oxford Dictionary of Quotations,* and *Colombo's New Canadian Quotations.*

Newspapers   You can find the most up-to-date information from newspapers. Libraries will have the latest newspapers available and back copies of newspapers will be stored in your library on microfilm. Here is one way you can use a newspaper in your speech. If you are giving a speech on child abuse and a horrifying story appeared on the front page of *The Globe and Mail* on the morning you were due to deliver your talk, find a way to incorporate the report when you speak. You could hold up the newspaper at the outset of your talk and begin by saying, "The headlines of this morning's paper read, 'Worst case of child abuse horrifies hardened journalists.' This case tugged at our heartstrings as we read of the abuse that was inflicted upon James King by his ruthless stepmother. Today we will examine the subject of child abuse and discuss how pervasive it is in our so-called civilized society."

Newspapers are always a good source for quotes and stories.

Magazines, Pamphlets, and Brochures   Magazines will provide research material. Pamphlets and brochures will give a broad picture of a particular organization, subject, or product. *Maclean's* and *Time* magazines are two respected and authoritative news mediums. For example, the cover story of Time magazine, July 2000 was headlined "Should You Be a Vegetarian?". This would be a great resource if someone wanted to give a talk on "Becoming a Vegan." For a speech on "The World's Most Valuable Athletes," the student could be steered towards *Report on Business* magazine, which devoted its July 26, 2002 publication to sports issues. When doing research on "Maintaining a Healthy Heart," the Heart and Stroke Foundation could provide pamphlets and brochures on the topic. There are a few ways to access valuable information from magazines, pamphlets, and brochures and incorporate them into your speech. The *Reader's Guide to Periodical Literature* can usually be found in the reference section of the library.

The World Wide Web   Today's students are computer savvy and the Internet has become an indispensable resource. Not all the information on the Internet, however, is accurate or truthful, so use another source to check the validity of facts.

To perform a subject or keyword search, there are a number of search engines that will yield good results. Three such engines are google.com, alltheweb.com, and teoma.com. **Google.com** provides you with quick, focused results. **Alltheweb.com**, based in Norway, indexes over 2 billion pages, which are updated regularly. **Teoma.com** breaks queries into categories grouped by theme. Try them all and discover their differences and similarities. Visit **searchenginewatch.com** to find more information on new search sites.

Interviews   An individual who possesses intimate or expert knowledge of the subject you are talking about can provide in-depth, credible information that will add greatly to your speech. If you choose to conduct an interview in order to add an extra dimension to your talk, please refer to Chapter 14, which focuses on interviews, where you will find information on how to plan the interview, prepare your questions, conduct the interview, and do the follow-up.

As you proceed with your research, you may come across new alternative ideas or topics and then decide that you want to change the focus or purpose of your speech. This is a natural evolution. Sometimes you may be stumped when you find that there is very little information available on your topic. In that case, be flexible and choose another alternative. As you navigate through the wealth of material available to you, a new idea may trigger your fancy. Speak to your instructor should the need arise to change your subject. The exciting part of doing research is not the point of arrival but what you discover on the way. Enjoy this part of the journey.

Ideas for topics may pop into mind as you go about your daily activities. You may pass a newsstand when a newspaper headline stating, "Rock lyrics promote violence" attracts your attention. This leads you to think about composing a persuasive speech titled, "Offensive Lyrics in Music Should Be Censored."

The Internet, newsmagazine shows, current events, your family and friends, and discussions at school will provide additional resources when choosing a speech topic. Visit local bookstores and browse through the various sections, or go online to bookstores such as **chapters.indigo.ca** or **www.amazon.ca** for additional inspiration.

Once you have selected your topic, you then need to narrow it. A five-minute time limit for your speech will restrict what you have to say on a particular topic. If you choose to speak about crime, it would be wise to narrow your focus in order to do justice to your subject within the short time frame allotted for your talk. You may be very interested in the field of crime, but try to narrow that field until you come up with a topic such as, "Internet crime."

Defining your Speech Purpose

"It ain't where the puck is; it's where the puck will be." Wayne Gretzky, the famous Canadian hockey player, spoke these words that are as relevant to a hockey game as they are to developing a speech plan. Your purpose for speaking tells you where you want your puck to be.

Once you have chosen your topic, you need to determine what you want to achieve during your speech, that is, to establish your **general speech purpose.** We speak for one of three reasons: 1) to inform, 2) to persuade, or 3) to entertain. For the most part, you will be called upon to deliver informative or persuasive speeches in class.

The informative speech transfers knowledge from the speaker to the listener and increases their understanding while doing so. The persuasive speech encourages the listener to be convinced to take a particular action, change a belief, change an attitude, or change a point of view.

When we **inform**, we offer information to the listener. When we speak to **persuade**, our aim is to alter or reinforce the beliefs, attitudes, behaviour, or actions of the audience.

Once you have decided upon the general speech purpose, stating the intent of your speech, the next step is to craft a **specific speech purpose.** This will help clarify your speech goal and define what you wish to accomplish. A specific speech purpose will state precisely what you aim to achieve in your speech targeted to a particular audience. The following are some criteria for writing a specific speech purpose:

1. Confine the purpose statement to one main idea.
2. Word it from the audience's point of view.
3. Write it as an infinitive phrase, that is, begin the statement with the word "to."
4. Avoid being vague.
5. Use precision of language.
6. Be audience focused in order to meet their needs and expectations.
7. Your purpose should be attainable.

Here are examples of general purpose statements and specific purpose statements.

General purpose: To inform

Specific purpose: To inform the audience about what DNA is, where it is found, and how it is used in forensic science.

General purpose: To inform

Specific purpose: To inform the students about the five essential qualities a leader needs to lead effectively.

General purpose: To persuade

Specific purpose: To persuade the audience to continue to follow emerging technology projects despite the Internet boom and bust.

General purpose: To persuade

Specific purpose: To encourage the audience to adopt a healthy lifestyle through regular exercise and a sensible diet.

When formulating your purpose statement, measure it against the seven criteria.

EXERCISES

1. Choose a topic from the informative speech topics listed below. Select an audience. Write down a general speech purpose and a specific speech purpose observing the criteria for writing a speech.

   - Friendship
   - Crime
   - Travel
   - Vacations
   - Hobbies
   - Health and fitness
   - Organ transplants
   - Pollution
   - Sports
   - Inventions
   - Cloning
   - The media

2. Choose a topic from the persuasive speech topics listed below. Select an audience. Write down a general speech purpose and a specific speech purpose observing the criteria for writing a speech.

   - Cell phones should be banned in restaurants, theatres, and while driving a vehicle
   - Animal testing should end
   - The number of parking spaces on campus should be increased
   - Guns should be legalized
   - The legal drinking age should be raised
   - Physical education in school should be compulsory

3. Choose a topic from the informative speech topics listed below. Go through the brainstorming process in order to come up with four topics that relate to the original topic. For each topic, write down a general speech purpose and a specific speech purpose. Also, describe the audience for whom you have designed your speech.

   - Marriage
   - Global warming

- Chatrooms
- Famous scientists
- The cult of celebrity
- Recycling
- Birth control
- Terrorism
- The World Series
- Students

Developing a Central Speech Statement

Your central speech statement is a concise statement that focuses your speech and encapsulates your message. A **central speech statement** is sometimes called the thesis statement or the key message. It summarizes what you want to say in one sentence.

A central speech statement is phrased in a complete declarative sentence. For example, in a speech given by a student on "The Future of Banking," the student prepared the following:

Topic: The Future of Banking

Audience: MBA students, business leaders, and government officials

General Speech Purpose: To inform

Specific Speech Purpose: To inform the audience about the changing structure and strategies of the banking industry.

Central Speech Statement: Technology and competition are the two key drivers of change in the banking industry, both domestically and abroad.

In a persuasive speech titled, "The Flu Shot, Not the Flu" by student Sue Kelly, this is how she defined her speech purpose and central speech statement:

Topic: The flu shot

General Speech Purpose: To persuade

Specific Speech Purpose: To encourage the audience to get their flu shot.

Central Speech Statement: Influenza is, at best, a miserable illness of one to two weeks duration and, at worst, a life-threatening disease. Therefore, it makes sense to take advantage of health department offers of free vaccinations to all residents of our province.

Here is another example:

Topic: Academic education and its relevance to real life

Audience: University students

General Speech Purpose: To inform

Specific Speech Purpose: To identify and offer solutions to the deficiencies in the education system.

Central Speech Statement: Academic education should include courses on stress management, public speaking, teamwork, work environment policies and procedures, and money management.

EXERCISES

1. Write down a central speech statement for the informative speech topic you selected for Question 1 in the last exercise.
2. Write down a central speech statement for the persuasive speech topic you selected for Question 2 in the last exercise.

Organizing your Material

Once you have selected a topic, defined your speech purpose, and established your central speech statement, you now need to think about how to organize your speech so that the audience will receive the intended message.

The Preparation Outline

To help you access ideas and sub-topics for your speech, you can use the technique referred to as **idea webbing**. Start by drawing a circle in the centre of a blank sheet of paper. Write down the title of your talk in this circle. Now draw an arrow that connects from this central circle to another circle and write down one main idea in that circle. Keep repeating this process until you have a large circle in the centre of the page from which about four, five, or six arrows radiate and connect to other circles. In each of these circles additional main points are written. The idea of webbing in order to arrive at a preparation outline is shown below using the topic "The Four Ps of Public Speaking."

FIGURE 3.1	Idea Web

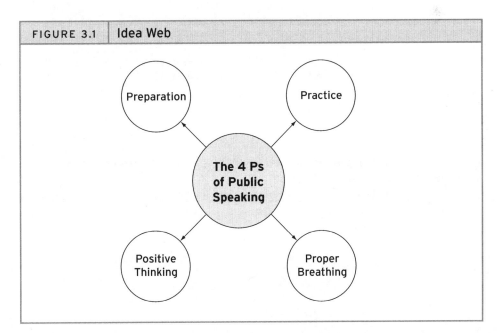

Now extend the circles further to expand upon the main points, adding sub-points and supporting material. The idea web should now look like this:

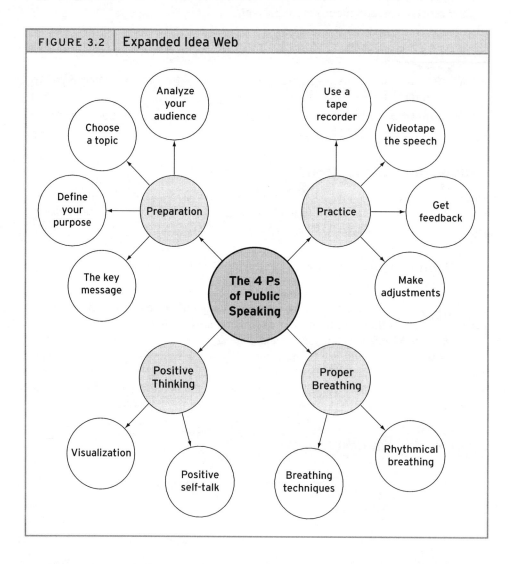

FIGURE 3.2 | **Expanded Idea Web**

Once the idea webbing is completed, an initial outline for your speech is the result. If a sub-point is unsuitable, simply eliminate it.

The next step is to put in order the main points for the topic "The Four Ps of Public Speaking." Here is the speech outline in point form. Notice how the idea web has been converted into a **speech outline**.

TOPIC: The Four Ps of Public Speaking
FIRST MAIN POINT: Preparing for the speech

(i) Choosing a topic

(ii) Analyzing your audience

(iii) Defining a specific speech purpose

(iv) The key message or central speech statement

SECOND MAIN POINT: Practising the speech

(i) Speaking the speech into a tape recorder

(ii) Videotaping the speech

(iii) Getting feedback from fellow students, family, and friends

(iv) Embracing the feedback and making adjustments

THIRD MAIN POINT: Positive thinking

(i) Visualizing success

(ii) Positive self-talk

FOURTH MAIN POINT: Proper breathing

(i) Breathing techniques

(ii) Rhythmical breathing

Now that you have discovered how relatively easy it is to access your own ideas through idea webbing and through developing a preparatory outline, we can now look at how to organize the speech.

STRUCTURING A SPEECH

Have you ever listened to a speaker and thought, "Where is the speaker heading? He sounds as if he is rambling and has no destination in mind." The listener needs the speaker to deliver a coherent, well-organized message to which he or she can relate.

There are three basic parts to a speech—the introduction, the body, and the conclusion. The purpose of the **introduction** is to grab the attention of the audience, to give them a reason to listen to you, to establish your credibility, and preview your topic. The purpose of the **body** is to supply the listener with concrete content, evidence, supporting material, or arguments. This is where you expand upon your purpose and develop your train of thought. The body of the talk is the segment where you provide the substance of your message. During the **conclusion** you drive home your message, ask for a call to action, if necessary, and provide a sense of completion.

Any good speech is like an airplane journey. You need a good take-off (this is your opening) to fly smoothly. Also of crucial importance is planning and executing a good landing (your closing to the speech). There are numerous options regarding how to open or close a speech.

Ways to Open a Speech

A good opening will capture the attention of the audience and make them want to continue listening. Here are ways in which you can open your talk. Notice how effectively the openings serve to capture your attention and focus on the information that follows.

Pose a Rhetorical Question   The speaker immediately captures the attention of the audience by using a question, as it provokes the listener to mentally answer the question.

> Have you ever felt really miserable? You were so tired you could hardly stand up. Your muscles were so sore and achy that you wanted to cry. Fever enveloped you, your head pounded, and you could not stop coughing. You were most likely suffering, and I do mean suffering, from influenza—a highly contagious respiratory infection otherwise know as the flu.
>
> Now, despite making you feel really miserable for one or two weeks, healthy adults usually recover uneventfully. However, influenza can be a serious disease and is responsible for approximately 2000 deaths in Canada alone. During the flu season, which runs from November to April, you have a one in six chance of contracting the flu.

Relate the Topic to the Audience   This speech was delivered to a group of students attending a public speaking class:

> I want to share a secret with you. It's my biggest fear—in public speaking—something I flee from like a postman from an angry dog, like a mischievous child from a swarm of bees, like a playboy from marriage, like a tourist in Pamplona from the charging bulls, like a teenager in his father's car, like a mouse from a cat, like a cat from a dog, like a fly from a frog. I think you know what it is...the pause.
>
> I do know the pause is important, even crucial. It's just that when I'm speaking, I forget to pause. Listen to a speech by a great speaker and notice the pause. John F. Kennedy, in his inaugural address, didn't say, "My fellow Americans ask not what your country can do for you but what you can do for your country." He said, "And so, my fellow Americans (pause), ask not what your country can do for you (pause), ask what you can do for your country.
>
> That is three pauses. It takes me four speeches to accumulate that number of pauses.

Students listening to this speech will be able to identify with the speaker immediately.

Tell an Anecdote   Elaine Humber, a clinical social worker, spoke at a conference on the topic, "The Benefit of Psychodynamic Understanding in Forensic Assessments." To the average listener, this could sound like an intimidating subject, so Elaine opened her speech with an anecdote to create interest and understanding.

Brian arrived on my floor last week—a 19-year-old, long gangly fellow with stringy, blond hair. The police brought him in wearing handcuffs and shackles. It tore my heart out to see him. He looked like my nephew. But he didn't seem alarmed at all. He was jovial, happy to be out of jail, and at home in the unit. I thought, "How is this possible? Whatever happened to him to allow him to see this experience as a positive one? Or does he? Could he be masking his pain and fear? And if so, what an expert he is at doing so.

So why is Brian important anyway? Why should we care? He's probably just a nasty little punk and it's good that he's locked up. Well, we should care, not only for Brian, but because there are so many like him. Our jails are full of Brians and the government is building bigger and bigger jails—warehouses. Is our society producing more people like him who need to be locked up? Is it a trend? If so, it's pretty scary.

Paint a Picture   A speech to raise money for The Society of the Blind began this way:

Imagine yourself in a blackout! You fumble about bumping into furniture as you search for that half-burned out candle you've misplaced. Darkness permeates your senses. There is no one around to help you in your time of need. The Society for the Blind needs you in their troubled times.

When you paint a picture with vivid words, the audience is immediately drawn into the picture.

List Examples   Here is an example of this technique:

They have rescued us from burning buildings, saved us from drowning and found us when we were lost. They've been our eyes when we couldn't see and our ears when we couldn't hear. During times of tragedy and loneliness, they've brought us comfort and been our most loyal and trusted friends. Just being in their presence lowers our blood pressure and helps us live longer, healthier lives.

Animals have given us all of this and much more.

Use A Quotation   Use the words of someone famous or noteworthy to attract attention. A presentation to a group of disillusioned investors could begin this way:

"Where is the wisdom we have lost in knowledge? Where is the knowledge we have lost in information?" Sixty-five years ago, the poet T.S. Elliot uttered these words. They are as relevant to us today as they were then. With all the glut of information that reaches us via newspapers, television, the Internet, business reports, and magazines, as investors we should have been able to make sensible investment decisions. Instead we have been swept way on the bubble of optimism without wisely assessing how dramatic the fall would be when the bubble burst. We've been exposed to lots of information, but wisdom has taken a back seat.

Today I will be presenting a sound strategy for investors who wish to take a back-to-basics approach in order to preserve their capital.

Open with an Action   A dentist once opened his talk with a nonverbal action. He walked up to the podium upon which was placed a glass of water, a toothbrush with toothpaste, and a large bowl. In silence, he proceeded to brush his teeth. After he had completed the task, he looked up at the audience and said, "What I have done before you today is a normal, healthy, daily act. What you are doing by putting that white, cylindrical stick in your mouth with regularity on the hour or half-hour is an unhealthy act. I am here to talk to you about the perils of smoking."

When the speaker, in this example, begins the speech with a nonverbal action, he quickly captures the attention of the audience. Once he has their attention, he then tells them he will give a talk, which will present an anti-smoking point of view. If the dentist had begun with the words, "I am here to talk to you about the perils of smoking," the listeners, who were all smokers, would clearly have adopted a defensive attitude. They would have tuned out the speaker and his message right at the outset. Since the speaker employed the technique of using an action to open his talk, it served his purpose of immediately creating a bond of familiarity with his audience, just by miming the simple everyday act of brushing his teeth.

An action works well when it serves your purpose and is pertinent. It works against you when it is used as a gimmick.

Open with Humour   When you ask someone to tell a joke to open a presentation, most people will respond: "I'm not funny. I can't tell a joke." However, when you say, "Well, tell me a humorous story," many will be able to reach into the recesses of their minds, recall a funny story, a funny occasion, a funny occurrence and be able to relate it to you. We often feel put on the line when asked to "be" funny, but remember that humour is universally enjoyed by the listener when the telling of it is well executed. One word of caution I'd like to issue is if you're not funny, do not try and be funny. It is very disheartening for a speaker to tell a funny story and then the story falls flat and no one laughs. On the other hand, when you deliver a humorous story or funny line and it is met with laughter, this certainly is a confidence builder and offers great encouragement.

We are a nation that has produced—and subsequently exported—many first-rate comedians such as Martin Short, Jim Carrey, and Howie Mandel. Naturally, we are not all comedians, but we can employ some of their techniques and words. If you are unable to generate humor in your talk, visit your local library, or the Internet to find a humorous quotation that is appropriate and relevant.

In the introduction to the great *Canadian Joke Book* (1976), Robert Shelley writes: "Humour is an integral part of a nation's history and of its culture. It reveals the character of its people and the kind of society in which they live better than any other barometer. It tells where they've been and where they're going. A simple joke, sometimes only a single line, can tell more about a country's government than volumes."

A well-crafted speech is like a beautiful rainbow. A speech to entertain that lacks the element of humour will be a few colours short of this rainbow.

When Stephen Lewis, Deputy Executive Director of UNICEF, opened his speech on "The Rise and Fall of Social Justice" in New York on March 24, 1998, he used humour:

> I want to thank John for so lucid and engaging and mercifully brief an introduction.
>
> I venture to this platform with some trepidation. I don't like these bright lights and dark platforms that are elevated. The last time I was on such a stage was a number of years ago at the Palais du Congres in Montreal, in

1990, and at the end of my remarks they turned off the light and I walked vigorously off the platform and into space. That did not surprise many of my friends who felt that I'd been walking into space most of my adult life.

Open with a Shared Experience   A speech of welcome was delivered at the national conference, Citizenship 2020/Citoyennete 2020, in October 2000. Desmond Morris, then director of McGill Institute for the Study of Canada, wrote the speech, "Twenty years from now, where will we be as a society?".

The address opened with the following words:

Citizenship in a country like Canada should be simple. We have a flag, a passport, a history, a constitution packed with rights, and a Supreme Court to uphold them. Canadian citizens speak their minds, challenge authority, even vote for their country's dissolution. Yet anyone knows that the citizenship in Canada is anything but clear. Many Canadians deplore their elected representatives, and resent their political institutions without understanding how they work.

This technique worked well as the listener, being Canadian, had a vested interest in focusing on the information that followed.

State the Purpose   State the purpose of your speech, outline the direction it will take, and the conclusion it will reach.

An informative speech on "Day Trading" begins this way:

Day trading is an activity that individuals participate in as they try to make money on the daily price movements of the stocks in the stock market. First, I will look at the reasons why day trading is possible and popular. Second, I'll offer some tips on how to establish a strategy for entering and exiting the market while taking into consideration the difficulties you might encounter. Finally, I will present some guidelines and advice for those of you who have time to follow the market, have that extra money to invest, and can stomach the risks that accompany this endeavour.

This method of opening a presentation is popular in business. It can also be used in conjunction with a question. For example, the particular speech above could begin with, "How many of you are actively involved in trading for your own portfolio?", and then continue with, "Day trading is an activity that individuals participate in…" In this way, you attract the audience's attention by posing a question first and then move on to outline the content of your talk.

Open with Poetry   In a speech on "Escapes," the speaker begins by reciting the opening verse of the poem *Mary's Farm*, written by Canadian poet, Bruce Meyer:

Mary's Farm

is seated atop a winding road
where hill crest almost touches clouds
and summer shadows all blow by
away from the city's crowds;

is a place remade, a place of ghosts,
of laughter's thirst and saddened wind
where old door hinges sing to time
because they've found a friend;

When deadlines loom and exams seem to be just around the corner, don't you
wish you could escape your obligations? A visit to Mary's farm might provide
the appropriate remedy. A week on a pink sandy beach watching the
turquoise surf ripple upon the shore might do the trick. A hiking trip though
the Canadian Rockies would be energizing and invigorating. The simple practice of embracing meditation as part of your daily routine could provide you
with the necessary escape you require.

Poetry appeals to the senses and quickly transports the audience to this magical haven
called *Mary's Farm*. The speaker then addresses the reality of the listener's situation
(examinations on the horizon), and offers suggestions for escape.

Open with a Startling Statement   The startling opening statement, in the following
example, serves to alert the listener to the dangers of crime. Since each listener could be a
potential victim, he or she will listen with greater interest.

One out of every four of you will become the victim of a crime. Most violent
crimes are committed at night. Summer is the time of year when more personal
victimization occurs. Today I would like to urge you not to become complacent
and careless during the carefree days of summer. Take the necessary precautions to ensure that you and your family are safe. Lock your front doors
while barbecuing in your backyard. Inform your neighbours that your home
will be vacant during your vacation. If you need to walk alone at night, do so
in well-lit areas. You can avoid becoming a victim of crime by taking these
three simple precautions.
    My presentation will offer you further tips and warnings to help foster
safety and security in your neighborhood.

Here's another example of a startling statement:

Tourists are more likely to be killed by falling coconuts than shark attacks!
Club Direct, a London travel insurance agency, says that 150 vacationers die
each year after being hit on the head by a coconut.

This statement would grab your attention and certainly you would listen with great
focus if you were planning to visit an island with tropical palm trees.

Ways to Conclude A Speech

Refer back to the analogy of the airplane journey being similar to the process of structuring a speech. Your opening has provided an effective "take-off" and your conclusion must
offer a "landing" conducted with precision. Pay particular attention to how you close your

speech. This is the segment where you clinch your argument, reinforce your purpose, and imprint your message. Your conclusion provides the final impression that you leave with your audience and it should be memorable, make an impact, and offer a sense of totality and completion.

Here are different ways in which you can close your talk:

A Call to Action   Louise Knox, a spokesperson for MADD, Mothers Against Drunk Driving, spoke on a topic titled, "Taking Back Our Road—A Strategy for Eliminating Impaired Driving," at the federal policy launch event, November 2001. The speech was a call for the federal government to take action and introduce new impaired driving legislation and to implement new measures to fight this crime and the deaths and injuries caused by impaired driving crashes. She closed her speech with a call to action.

> We have come to Ottawa today to point out, in no uncertain terms, that there is much more our federal government can do. We are here with the support of a vast majority of Canadians. Nine out of ten Canadians (90 percent) believe that driving under the influence of alcohol is a major highway safety problem. A majority of Canadians (55 percent) believe that governments are not doing enough to reduce impaired driving. Our research shows that Canada is lagging behind other countries in how we are dealing with impaired driving. MADD Canada is in the good company of our police community in calling for enhanced enforcement for impaired driving, and this morning the Canadian Police Association is present as a sign of its strong support.
>
> To conclude, MADD Canada is calling on the government to act and earnestly tackle this crime during this Parliament. Impaired driving affects far too many Canadians for the government not to act on these important, essential steps in providing the safety Canadians need on our roads. There is a real need for more effective laws in our country. The research is readily available. A working plan is here. From our perspective, the federal government has no excuse for delay—there are effective ways to reduce impaired driving in our country. Today, we urge the government to take up MADD Canada's initiatives in Taking Back Our Roads.

Paint a Picture of the Future   In a talk on "The Future of Banking," the speaker could say:

> How do I see the bank of the future? My prediction is that the consumer will be dealing with mega-banks, but there will still be a need for branches. Technological investment will continue to grow. What we don't know is how the consumer will accept new brands, what the rate of technological adaptation will be, and we cannot say with certainty what the regulatory environment will be. What we do know is that the banking industry is changing, both domestically and abroad. Technology and competition will be the two key drivers of that change. And finally, can the future of banking be simplified into a single model? I think not.

An Emotional Climax   A student speech that discussed the impact of the September 11 terrorist attack concluded like this:

As the story surrounding the World Trade Center and Pentagon attacks began to unfold, more words began to emerge that would evoke new meaning and significance.

Boxcutters, Al-Quaeda, Osama Bin Laden, Taliban.

I am so terribly saddened by the loss of humanity and the empty cavity, which was left by the collapse.

I have never been a fan of George W. Bush but somehow I felt comforted by the fact that Colin Powell, Dick Cheney, Donald Rumsfield, and Condoleezza Rice were at the helm.

I even feel good about John Ashcroft, the Attorney General, a religious zealot who holds contrary beliefs to mine.

Many of my liberal friends and I share the same views about Bush and were subsequently impressed with the leadership and resolve he demonstrated. George W. seemed to rise to the occasion.

For unknown reasons, I sense we would not have felt so reassured if it were Al Gore who was in charge this time.

Over the next few weeks, more new words became part of our collective psyche and lexicon.

Northern Alliance, Kandahar, Anthrax, Cipro.

I find myself addicted to NEWS radio—something I never listened to in the car prior to this event.

I ordered eight bottles of water for the cooler from Culligan.

I went to Costco and bought a package of flashlights and a 10-kilo bag of rice. I was ready for anything—and nothing—at the same time.

Since 9/11 I am more patient with others. I observe others being more patient and caring as well. This is a good thing. So where do we go from here? Certainly, things have changed. Air travel will certainly never be the same, but I'll never complain again about the line-up or the delays. I don't think we will ever feel safe—I mean truly safe from an attack of one sort or another.

And unfortunately, I do not think we will gain any real and meaningful sense of satisfaction from pummeling Afghanistan, capturing Al-Quaeda, or destroying Hussein in Iraq.

The genie is out of the bottle and it is not going back.

This speech, delivered in October 2001, one month after the terrorist attacks, riveted and moved the audience profoundly. It was a timely message delivered to an audience who were also struggling to make sense of their own personal emotions.

A Summary   A summary offers an effective way to recap your message by highlighting the key points in your speech. The summary also provides proof that you have met your objectives. Before summarizing, use a transitional phrase such as, "Let me summarize…" so that the audience is forewarned that you are approaching the end of your presentation. This will help focus their attention and keep them engaged.

In a speech on "Our Global Challenge," where the speaker has addressed the issues confronting the world's population, she ends by using the summarizing technique effectively.

We have spoken about the issue of urban air pollution, we have examined the importance of providing access to safe drinking water, and we have ascertained that we have renewable energy resources. We are making good progress in these three areas. Let's remind ourselves of our deficiencies. We need to redirect our efforts to the water shortages experienced by 40 percent of the world's population. We need to heighten the awareness of the damage done to our forests through the exploration by large corporations and above all, let's not forget about the food scarcity that plagues Africa and Asia.

Each one of us can play a part in making our world a kinder, gentler place, a world that garners our respect and ensures our long-term survival.

Tie the Ending Back to the Opening   This method creates a sense of unity and offers a sense of completion for the listener.

A student used this method when he spoke on "Kyoto and the Plot to Destroy Canadian Ice Hockey." He opens his speech with these words:

George Walker Bush isn't telling us the real reason why he rejects the Kyoto Protocol. His official statements about the agreement to slow global warming only confirm that there is a hidden agenda. That agenda is about ice hockey and it started long before these Olympics.

Americans don't like to be second best and our hockey-playing superiority annoys them. This is why they bought the Canadians, took over Tim Horton's, and introduced the glowing puck. But our competitive advantage is not about Habs, donuts, or biscuits. It took the attentive 43rd President of the United States to figure out that the climate gives us the edge.

Our country's frozen ponds and backyard rinks provide endless hours of practice and guarantee a steady supply of the world's best players—fellows like Gretzky, Lemieux, and Orr.

The speaker then proceeded to discuss the three official reasons the United States government gives for not ratifying Kyoto. He says that President Bush doubts the reality of global warming. Bush feels that Kyoto threatens the American people and its economy and that developing nations have not established their own reduction targets.

In his closing, the speaker returns to the subject of George Bush's "common-sense" approach and the subject of Canadian hockey. This ending ties the speech together very nicely.

George Bush's "common sense" approach has not been induced by one too many pucks to the head. His conduct furthers his ice hockey supremacy objective. It explains his refusal to ratify Kyoto despite the evidence and worldwide pressure. It also explains why U.S. greenhouse gas emissions keep increasing. The pace they set in the 1990s when emissions rose by 18 percent, bringing the American share of the world total to over one quarter, is being maintained.

Shinny hockey players across Canada, like street hockey players in Hamilton before them, must now unite—pick up the puck, and stop the plan to destroy Canadian hockey, and thereby save the planet.

A Quotation   A quotation that reinforces and encapsulates your message will add great impact when you close your speech.

Here is a good example from a speech titled, "The Authentic Canadian."

We cannot become inextricably entwined with the plans, ambitions, and hopes of our neighbours to the south. Let us embrace and remain faithful to our authentic Canadian identity. The words of Vincent Massey echo this sentiment: "When it is possible, of course, what we do should have a Canadian character. We should be ourselves, and the traveller, the tourist, the visitor, from wherever he comes, will respect us the more if we are. No one looks his best in someone else's clothes."

This quotation is apt and supports the speaker's proposition that Canadians maintain their unique, separate, and authentic identity.

Restate Your Key Message   In a speech entitled, "Women and Career: A Balancing Act," Yuree Soh highlighted the career obstacles and family problems that woman encountered in the work force. Her key message was reiterated when she closed the talk by saying:

Expecting women to have two full-time jobs is damaging for all of us. It is not the problem of some aliens from another planet. These women are our spouses, our mothers, our daughters, and our friends. This issue affects all of us, every one of us. We as a society need to face and conquer it. We must and we will.

You may choose to be creative and combine two techniques of closing. For example, you can combine a summary with a call to action. You could also repeat your key message and follow it with a quotation. These are suggestions to help you prepare a conclusion that will reach your audience and create a strong final impression.

EXERCISES

1. Select a topic from the following list:
    *   How to find a date
    *   How to exercise safely
    *   How to search the Internet
    *   How to deliver mouth-to-mouth resuscitation
    *   How to ski
    *   How to manage your time wisely
        a) Write down two different ways in which you could open a talk on the subject you have selected. Refer to the techniques of opening a speech method in this chapter.
        b) Write down two different ways in which you could conclude the talk on the topic you have selected.

2. You have been asked to deliver an informative speech. Choose a topic of interest to you and
    a) write down two different openings for the speech.
    b) Now write down two ways in which you could close that particular talk.

3. Examine the speeches in the final chapter of this book and identify the method each speaker used to open and close the speech.

4. Prepare an informative speech of your own choice. First go through the idea webbing process. Then prepare your outline.

5. Plato said: "Every discourse ought to be a living creature, having a body of its own and head and feet; there should be a middle, beginning, and end, adapted to one another and to the whole."

   Discuss this comment and relate why the "head" and "feet" of a speech are important.

6. Below is a list of topics. Choose six topics and prepare an opening and closing for each one.

   - Drug abuse
   - Freedom of speech
   - Tuition fees
   - My first day at college
   - Losing weight
   - A famous person I would like to meet
   - Rock music
   - The value of an education
   - Ozone depletion
   - World hunger
   - Jogging
   - Airline safety
   - A topic related to your major
   - Alternative medicine
   - The meaning of ethnicity
   - Nuclear war
   - Self-esteem
   - Crime prevention
   - Women in different societies
   - The generation gap
   - Suicide
   - UFOs
   - Censorship on the Internet
   - Canadian heroes

7. Visit the following Web site or "research launchpad" to find additional sources for topics. **www.researchpaper.com/directory.html**.

SUMMARY

In this chapter we looked at the process of preparing a presentation that begins with analyzing your audience and then selecting and shaping your topics to meet your audience's needs and expectations. Brainstorming is suggested as a method of choosing and narrowing your topic. Then conduct research at the library, from your own personal knowledge and experience, from newspapers, journals, magazines, pamphlets, interviews, or via a search on the World Wide Web.

A speaker begins his preparation by establishing a general speech purpose, a definitive speech purpose, and then develops a central speech statement, also known as the key message. Through idea webbing, the student learns to access his or her ideas and then create a speech outline, providing a road map and a sense of coherence.

We then discussed the importance of creating a good opening and closing for the talk and offered ways in which to do so.

SUGGESTED READING

Andrews, Robert. *Cassell Dictionary of Contemporary Quotations*. London: Cassell, 1996.

Braude, Jacob M. *Braude's Treasury of Wit and Humour*. Englewood Cliffs, NJ: Prentice-Hall, 1984.

Humes, James. *The Sir Winston Method*. New York: William Morrow and Company Inc., 1991.

Linver, Sandy. *Speak and Get Results*. New York: Fireside, 1994.

Safire, William. *Lend Me Your Ears, Great Speeches in History*. New York: W.W. Norton and Company Inc., 1992.

Spinrad, Leonard and Thelma Spinrad. *Complete Speaker's Almanac*. Englewood Cliffs, NJ. Prentice-Hall, 1964.

Wilder, Lilyan. *Talk Your Way to Success*. New York: Simon and Schuster, 1987.

REFERENCES

Colombo, John Robert. *Colombo's New Canadian Quotations*. Edmonton: Hurtig Publishers Ltd., 1987.

Corliss, Richard. "Should we all be vegetarians?" *Time* magazine (2002 July).

Daly, John and Judith Pereira. "Who's got game? The world's most valuable athletes." *Report on Business* (July 26, 2002).

Ehninger, Douglas, Bruce E. Gronbeck, Rae E. McKerrow, and Alan H. Monro. *Principles and Types of Speech Communication*. Glenview, IL: Scott Foresman, 1986.

Meyer, Bruce. *Anywhere*. Toronto: Exile Editions Ltd., 2000.

 ## WEBLINKS

World Wide Web Search Engines:

AltaVista
www.altavista.digital.com
This is a keyword search engine.

Excite
www.excite.com
This will perform keyword, concept, or topic searches.

Lycos
www.lycos.com
This site scans the Web in order to index sites. You can also search for maps, sound and picture files.

Google.com
www.google.com
Type in your topic and this engine will producer quick, focused results.

Alltheweb.com
www.alltheweb.com
Provides you with vast resources as it indexes over 2 billion pages that are regularly updated.

Teoma.com
www.teoma.com
This site breaks down its queries into categories grouped by theme.

Searchengine.com
www.searchengine.com
When you visit this site you will be given information on new search sites.

Hotbot
www.hotbot.com
Hotwired magazine sponsors this site which performs searches for multimedia files.

Infoseek
www.infoseek.com
This offers keyword searching functions and "Quickseek" which allows you to customize your search.

Internet site
thorplus.lib.purdue.edu/~techman/eval.html
This site addresses why we need to evaluate information on the Internet.

Interview | Silken Laumann

At every level of competition, rower Silken Laumann has excelled. A former World Champion and Olympic medallist, Laumann has also been named Canada's Outstanding Athlete. Since retiring from competitive rowing, Silken has become a sought-after dynamic, motivational speaker, sharing with others her path to success.

Q **Could you describe the attributes and qualities of a good speaker?**

A A good speaker speaks from their experience, whether that experience is an academic experience or it's actually what they've lived, seen, and believe. A good speaker makes a connection with the audience and doesn't put themselves above the audience. Often it's not because the speaker wants to put themselves above the audience; it's nerves that do that. A good speaker has given some thought to who their audience might be and where they might be professionally or personally. Passion is really important to me. I think if you don't really have it as a speaker, you know, why are you bothering? If you go in feeling that you really care about the people that you're speaking to and you hope that you can impact them, that's a good way to go into a presentation.

Q   **How do you prepare for a speech?**

A   I have a unique and eccentric ritual for getting prepared for a presentation. The first thing that I do is speak with the client and I usually try to have at least three people on the phone and through that conversation I get a good sense of the event I will be speaking at, what they're hoping to achieve in the event and where they are as a company. Are sales down? Are they up? Is there a certain objective that they have in their company? Is there a theme to the conference? By asking all those really basic questions I get a pretty good sense of what they want me to speak about and what their expectations of me are. I try to make sure that their expectations, what I'm going to deliver, and what I'm capable of delivering are equally matched. Sometimes you can get a client who thinks you can speak about a certain topic and really it's not your area of expertise. I don't mind stretching my area once in a while but it's better to stick with what you know.

Q   **Yes. It's more authentic, definitely.**

A   That's the first thing that I do and then I start to do some preliminary notes. From the conversation I write notes and I come up with probably half a dozen key points that the client wants me to speak

about. Then I start thinking about what stories would work for those points. I write them down in point form and think about them for a while. Then I try to weave a bit of a story line throughout the presentation. I tend to have a bit of a formatted story line in my presentations if I'm presenting about my experiences in sport, but I don't like getting stuck there. There are probably two or three stories that I always tell because they are so instrumental in my life and people would feel short-changed if I didn't tell them. One is the story of my accident and another is about the first day that I ever rowed and how I tipped the boat. There are a couple of stories that pretty well fit into almost any presentation because they're about overcoming challenge and believing in yourself. After that I do some cutting and pasting of old presentations and put it all together. Then I start speaking out loud. I'll practice the intro and think about how I'll introduce the topic. Then I'll move from one subject to another and see whether there's a logical connection and flow between the different topics that I'm speaking about. It's only really through speaking out loud that I can really imagine and practise. I can work and work on text but my medium is the spoken word, so I have to speak it. It's not as if I practise my presentation from beginning to end, but I practise it in stories and points. I probably spend upwards of ten to fifteen hours preparing for each presentation, which other speakers tell me, is a lot. But it's just the way I am.

Nervous energy has always been a factor for me. The more prepared I am, the more calm I feel. I speak in a conversational style. I have fun with it and lately I've been taking more risks in my presentations, not speaking from notes as heavily, and that's been really invigorating.

People prepare in a lot of different ways. I always say to my assistant, "Okay, I'm going to talk to myself right now, so just ignore me for the next couple of hours," and she just laughs. Sometimes I'll take something that I'm working on and I'll try it on someone and ask them, "What are you getting out of this?" and they'll say, "This is what I'm getting," and I'll say, "Oh, that's not what I meant at all." Or I'll say, "Okay, I'm on the right track."

Q   **Do you still use notes?**

A   Depending on how new the subject area is, I may do a full set of notes. I tend to use cue cards more. I leave them on a table and don't look at them. My cue cards are really my map. I just did a talk on the weekend to the Canadian Centre of Management Development and I was speaking about leadership in a way that I've never spoken before and there were certain connections that I wanted to make and certain bridges that I didn't want to forget. I walked over and looked at my cue cards twice.

Q   **Are you nervous before you're speaking?**

A   Absolutely.

Q   **Always?**

A   Always. There are a few speakers out there that don't get nervous, or say they don't get nervous, but no, I don't think I've ever not been nervous.

Q   **Is the ability to give an effective speech or presentation a crucial skill in the business and professional world?**

A   I think the ability to communicate is an essential skill and it's an enormous asset. It's an enormous asset when you need to express your perspective, and having the ability to do it verbally to a group is important.

Q   **So do you think students should spend more time polishing this skill?**

A   I think students should spend more time learning how to communicate. In my experience running a small business and working with different companies, a lot of grief and money is lost due to poor communication and misunderstandings. I think there's really something to be said for being able to pick up the phone and in a really polite and professional way, express your point of view or to be able to stand in front of a board and be able to express your passion for something and be convincing.

Q   **Are there any speaking habits that annoy you?**

A   Yes. It annoys me when politicians, during inaugurations or during really important events, speak strictly from notes. I understand why they do so but it still bothers me that they don't have better speaking skills. They don't look up at the end of a sentence; they're actually looking down. It bothers me because they are conveying the message that they don't care about the people they're speaking to. It's as if a real person isn't giving the presentation.

The other thing I find irritating is people who speak like ministers and preachers and get into a singsong rhythm. It's kind of my pet peeve. The way that you motivate people is by really inspiring them from your heart and your soul and your experiences. You encourage them and support them to find their own potential and their own strength. I don't think you do that by manipulating people and coming up with cute phrases.

Q   **What kind of voice do you like to listen to?**

A   I can tell you my favourite voice in the world is that of Shelagh Rogers. She has the most delightful voice. It always sounds like she's just about to burst either into song, laughter, or tears. She really has a very alive voice and she says she comes by it naturally. Her mother has the same kind of voice and there's something so comfortable, natural, lively, and engaging about her voice. She's definitely found her calling by doing radio. It's not necessarily a booming voice, just a natural voice.

Q What advice would you offer novice speakers?

A To always be yourself. I think that often when we begin speaking we have a perception that we have to have a lower voice or a more authoritative tone. But the best speakers are really able to be themselves in front of large groups in important moments. I think as human beings we are really drawn to that, that humanness in each one of us. I would say, be yourself. Nothing beats preparation in my mind. It doesn't mean memorizing everything but it does mean knowing your topic, knowing your audience, and being prepared for what you're going to say. Try to enjoy it. Try to add a little bit of fun. In my most recent presentation about Leadership I went right into the presentation, hardly introduced, and bang, gave them a very powerful message. My message was that our capacity to lead is bound by our passion for what we do and our love for the people we do it with. I never tell jokes but I have fun with my presentation. I've got some self-deprecating humour and I know enough to laugh at my own ridiculous weaknesses. We're all ridiculous, I guess, in our own ways.

Q Which public speakers have left an indelible impression on you?

A Rick Hansen, who's really a peer. I can relate so much to what he says and he speaks from the heart so he certainly leaves an impression. I would also say Martin Luther King and Nelson Mandela. Most recently I had the pleasure of listening to Nelson Mandela's new wife, Graca Machel. She spoke at the conference for war-affected children and I was captivated, not only with what she said, but the way that she presented it. She spoke passionately.

Q Who do you consider to be a great Canadian speaker?

A Rick Hansen is top of my list. I admire Rick so much as a person and he's also a mentor and I think that's what makes him special for me.

chapter four

Structuring Different Types of Speeches

If you do not know where you are going, every road will get you nowhere.

—Henry Kissinger, Scholar and former U.S. Secretary of State

LEARNING OBJECTIVES

- **To structure an informative talk**
- **To deliver a demonstrative speech**
- **To understand the general principles of persuasion**
- **To structure a persuasive speech**

In every walk of life, the ability to inform with clarity will serve you well. The simple act of giving directions, explaining how to make your favourite chili, reporting on your company's sales results, describing the plot of a film you have recently seen, or telling someone how to fight a parking ticket, requires the skill of being able to communicate information effectively. At school, you may be called upon to explain a concept, clarify a complex theory, describe a procedure or an event, offer an opinion or idea, and even present abstract information or principles.

The success of a speaker hinges upon a myriad of factors, one of the most important of which is the ability to prepare thoroughly by structuring a speech to achieve its purpose and to meet the audience's needs while doing so. To speak without having a definitive speech structure is like embarking upon a cross-country roadtrip without taking a map along for directions. This chapter offers structures for the informative speech, the demonstrative speech, and the persuasive speech—the three most common types of speeches.

THE INFORMATIVE SPEECH

When we inform, we offer information to the listener. The speaker acts as a teacher or lecturer who transfers knowledge, and facilitates understanding, as he or she explains, describes, reports, defines, or demonstrates something. For an informative speech, the speaker uses illustrations, evidence, examples, testimony, statistics, and visual aids as support during the speech.

The informative speech should follow this structure:

I. Introduction

    A. Get the audience's attention.

    B. Give the audience a reason to listen to you.

    C. Establish your credibility.

    D. Preview your purpose and topic.

II. Body

    A. First Main Point

        1. Sub-point

            a. Sub-sub-point

            b. Sub-sub-point

                i. Sub-sub-sub-point

                ii. Sub-sub-sub-point

        2. Sub-point

            a. Sub-sub-point

                i. Sub-sub-sub-point

                ii. Sub-sub-sub-point

            b. Sub-sub-point

    B. Second Main Point

        1. Sub-point

            a. Sub-sub-point

            b. Sub-sub-point

                i. Sub-sub-sub-point

                ii. Sub-sub-sub-point

    C. Third Main Point

        1. Sub-point

            a. Sub-sub-point

            b. Sub-sub-point

                i. Sub-sub-sub-point

                ii. Sub-sub-sub-point

III. Conclusion

Tips for Outlining a Speech

When preparing an outline, use a set of symbols that follows a consistent pattern. For the introduction, body, and conclusion, use Roman numerals I, II, and III.

Use capital letters for the main points (A, B, C). For sub-points, use small Roman numerals (i, ii, iii). When adding any sub-sub-points, use lower-case letters of the alphabet (a, b, c).

Also note that indentation should be used in the outline. This makes it clear where each new point begins and ends.

Here is an example of an informative speech given by a student, Paul Kilbank, applying the speech structure discussed above.

Title: "Business with Japan–It Can Positively Change Your Organization"

Specific Purpose: After listening to my speech, the audience will be able to consider their readiness for successfully doing business with Japan.

Attention-getter: Well, congratulations. Your products are very marketable, channels to the market are in place and now a major contract is expected. So after significant planning, effort, and expense–you're being rewarded with business in Japan...But are you ready?!

Sure, all the basics appear to be in place, but do you really understand your customer's expectations, motivations, and the pressures that are going to shape their behaviour? And will your organization be able to respond appropriately?

Importance: While it may have been the Marketing Four Ps that created this opportunity, it'll be your team behaviour that determines success or failure. And Japanese companies normally have much deeper supplier relationships, and that can create unexpected challenges for newcomers.

Your Qualifications: For the last 10 years, I've worked in product management and business development roles for the Japanese market. And during this period I've experienced many of these challenges and understand what is required to succeed.

Purpose: So the purpose of this evening's talk is to share with you four key questions that can help assess your readiness:

First Main Point: Is there a commitment from executives at the top level of the organization?

When the project starts from an unexpected sales order it is critical to have a pro-active executive involved.

Internal activities will be driven by managers, so it is key that the organization feels the strong involvement of a senior executive. This is particularly pertinent since Japanese customer expectations will differ from current practices, and the organization will likely resist change.

This executive will need to forge customer relationships at senior levels in order to open doors for managers. Otherwise, access to people and information may be rather difficult since they'll be unsure whether you're a friend or a foe.

A good example is Nortel Networks and their former Chairperson Ed Fitzgerald who invested significant time building relationships with NTT executives. He jokes about his time spent carrying Eskimo carving gifts to Japan. Yet this effort was important to show Nortel's commitment to the relationship.

So...Is there an executive losing sleep, worrying whether this business will be successful?

Second Main Point: Have cross-cultural employees been assigned?

Proper etiquette is important in any business environment and I don't want to downplay it. However, you're not going to destroy a relationship by wearing "toilet slippers" back into the main dining area. I can personally vouch that it will be embarrassing and you'll trigger much laughter in the smoking room later. But it won't diminish your authority, and more importantly, you haven't betrayed a trust to your customer.

However, making a commitment that can't be honoured, or expecting the Japanese company to perform an activity without confirming their agreement, are behaviours which can seriously damage the relationship.

This is why you should invest in skilled, cross-cultural employees who can manage the cultural gap. This interface is critical and goes well beyond language. It demands cultural awareness that can influence decision making, manage communication exchanges and explain mysterious logic. These employees need to be experts in their respective fields and they need to possess the authority to make reasonable commitments in a timely manner.

So...invest in cross-cultural employees to manage the day-to-day relationship to help avoid confusion or misinterpretations.

Third Main Point: Does the organization demand responsibility and accountability?

Trust is the lifeblood of relationships in Japanese business culture and, as a result, the Japanese make every effort to meet commitments, frequently well beyond what we might consider reasonable. For this reason, they are also very cautious before making a commitment, to ensure that (1) the expected outcome is very clear, and (2) their organization can execute it.

Compare our subway systems. In Toronto, the schedule is posted as "every two to three minutes during rush-hour," so people have a general idea about the service level to expect. In Tokyo, the schedule is posted as 6:03 p.m., 6:07 p.m., 6:11 p.m., and so on, in order that commuters have a very clear expected outcome and can easily confirm the reliability of the subway operator.

So let me ask you this? Which subway system does your business culture reflect? How do you ensure that products are shipped on schedule? Does that schedule mean next week or next Tuesday at 4:00 p.m.? Japanese customers will make promises to their customers and organize resources based on your promises. That takes significant effort and is a very public commitment for them.

Make sure that your people articulate clearly what they're going to do. Do it on time and get agreement that it has been done as promised.

Fourth Main Point: Do you strive for perfection?

Most Canadian companies today make an investment in ISO certification showing that the company has set procedures and that it follows them in practice. However, companies aren't under any obligation to improve these processes and frequently the cost of making changes is judged too high.

Now Japan tends to be very process-oriented, perhaps with the goal of achieving consistent and predictable outcomes. As a result, companies typically embrace a well-known concept called *kaizen* or continuous process improvement. This goes well beyond the manufacturing process and into the operational processes of almost all departments and almost all industries. Investing in these improvements is expected to increase quality, or decrease time, or reduce materials.

The Japanese will expect you to share their enthusiasm for improving processes. And even if product quality is lower than that which is ultimately needed, they will be tolerant if you can show that serious process improvements are being made. Now be careful. Powerful customers may insist on their right (contractual or otherwise) to impose process changes on suppliers. They fear dealing with the same problem again at extra cost, extra time, embarrassment, and inconvenience to their customer.

So, view problems as valuable clues to fix broken processes that are costing you money.

Conclusion: In conclusion, my overall message is, please assess your ability to manage the behavioural aspects of your Japanese customer relationship.

The first questions to consider are: "Do you have executive-level commitment?" and "Have cross-cultural employees been assigned?".

Both of these questions are relatively simple to address.

The last questions, however, are about corporate culture and are much more difficult to change: "Does the organization demand responsibility and accountability?" and "Do you strive for perfection?".

You can see how these issues will affect the relationship, and any initiatives to change the culture will benefit not only relationships with Japan but with any market in which you conduct business. It just happens that Japan is significantly more demanding in its relationships and may provide the initial motivation to trigger change.

Informative Speech Topics

Below is a list of possible topics for an informative speech:

Friendship	Acting	Fundamentalism
Crime	Evolution	Movies
Travel	Karaoke	Diets
Vacations	Photography	The Bible
Hobbies	Feminism	Famous crimes
Health and fitness	Divorce	Business in the twentieth
Organ transplants	Gambling	century
Pollution	Internet	Apartheid
Sports	World cultures	The Holocaust
Marriage customs	Stamp collecting	Suicide
Inventions	Dog training	Gay rights
Global warming	Cheating	Board games
Corporate greed	The World Series	Pierre Trudeau
Famous scientists	Dinosaurs	Louis Riel
The cult of celebrity	Leadership	Robert Bateman
The right to strike	Architecture	Wayne Gretzky
Child abuse	Missiles	Stephen Leacock
Elderly abuse	Censorship	Jim Carrey
AIDS	The wonders of the world	Marshall McLuhan
Genetic engineering	Racism	Frederick Banting
Healthcare	Surrogate mothers	Leonard Cohen
Capital punishment	Adoption	Neil Young
Abortion laws	Advertising	Billy Bishop
Refugees	Volcanoes	The future of our planet
Athletes and steroids	Karate	Leisure
Students and politics	Music	Dating
Humour	The stock market	The impact of technology
Sleep disorders	Scuba diving	in our lives
Drunk drivers	ESP	Planning for a successful
Teenage pregnancy	Etiquette	career
Homelessness	Psychics	Medical ethics
Peace	Heroes	Drug legalization
Astrology	Terrorism	The Heimlich manoeuvre
Slavery	Volunteerism	Airline safety
		Political correctness

Living in a small town	Review a favourite book	Hypnotism
Latchkey children	Study techniques	How to lead effectively
Farming	Grooming a pet	Don't judge a book by
Collecting baseball cards	Charity scams	its cover

THE DEMONSTRATIVE SPEECH

Another type of informative speech is the **demonstrative speech**. A demonstrative speech explains how to do something, or it describes how something works or operates. Apply the basic structure for an informative speech when doing your preparation.

When designing a demonstrative speech begin by giving a general overview of what you are about to present. Then break down the information into a series of steps that follow a clear, logical order.

Communicate concisely and use appropriate visual aids to assist understanding.

Here is an example of an outline for a demonstrative speech.

General Purpose: To inform

Specific Purpose: To demonstrate how to conduct an effective meeting

Central speech statement: An effective meeting results in increased productivity, better communication, and more efficient use of time.

Audience: Business students

I. How to prepare an agenda
   A. Produce a detailed agenda
      1. It acts as a structural basis for discussion
      2. It informs members about the topics to be discussed
      3. Decide on the subject matter and place the items in logical sequence
   B. Circulate the agenda
      1. Do this in a timely fashion
      2. Attach any pertinent reports or written briefs
   C. Chairing and conducting the meeting
      1. Define and convey a clear objective
      2. Establish a time limit
      3. Prepare a good introduction
      4. Control the discussion
      5. Clarify and summarize frequently
   D. Evaluate the meeting
      1. State what has been achieved
      2. Discuss the next steps
      3. Hand out meeting evaluation form

This speech describes a procedure and tells the listener how to accomplish something. In this example, there are four steps outlined by the speaker. It is not advisable to use more than five steps for a process speech.

Practise your speech exactly as you plan to deliver it, incorporating the use of your presentation aids to ensure that the physical demonstration does not exceed the time limit allotted to you. Remember to keep up the conversation or "banter" throughout your demonstration. Check, too, that everyone in the audience has a clear view of any object you may be showing. With a complicated demonstration, the audience may not be able to retain all the details you have provided, so include an internal summary after each step. You can close with a summary too.

FORM 4.1	Demonstrative Speech Planner

Topic: _____

Speech Purpose: _____

Specific Speech Purpose: _____

After hearing my speech, the audience will be able to: _____

Audience: _____

I. Introduction
   A. Attention getter:
   B. Preview:
      1. Overview of speech
      2. State importance of your message

II. Discussion
   A. First step:
      1. (example, illustration, technique, etc.)
      2.
   B. Second step:
      1.
      2.
   C. Third step:
      1.
      2.

III. Conclusion
   A. Summary
   B. Closing statement

DEMONSTRATIVE SPEECH TOPICS

Here are some topics for demonstrative speeches. They can also be called "How to…" speeches.

How to…

take a photograph	deal with difficult people	write a resume
wrestle	apply makeup	use PowerPoint
do a card trick	plant a perennial garden	create a Web site
prepare a romantic dinner	play the guitar	listen actively
make a Caesar salad	change a tire	perform a magic trick
design a deck	loose weight	make a good investment
select a lawyer	swing a golf club	perform foot reflexology
hang glide	start a book club	analyze handwriting
hypnotize someone		

FORM 4.2	**Evaluation of an Informative Speech**

Speaker's Name: _____

Date: _____

Topic: _____

Speech Purpose: _____

Evaluate the speech using the following scale:

1 = Excellent   2 = Very Good   3 = Average
4 = Fair   5 = Needs Improvement

INTRODUCTION   1   2   3   4   5

- Opens with good attention-getter
- Motivates audience to listen
- States qualifications
- States position and previews arguments

ORGANIZATION   1   2   3   4   5

- Uses clear logic
- Uses suitable pattern
- Employs transitions

FORM 4.2	Evaluation of an Informative Speech (continued)

SUPPORTING MATERIALS   1   2   3   4   5

- Uses appropriate verbal supports
  - –Quotations   –Explanations
  - –Comparisons   –Statistics
  - –Expert testimony   –Examples
- Uses effective visual supports

CONCLUSION   1   2   3   4   5

- Summarizes main ideas, recommendations, or position
- Asks for audience acceptance or action step
- Closes in memorable way

DELIVERY   1   2   3   4   5

- Well-projected
- Confident posture and movement
- Uses gestures or facial expression effectively
- Maintains direct eye contact
- Sounds dynamic yet conversational
- Uses notes efficiently

SUGGESTIONS FOR IMPROVEMENT

_____

_____

_____

_____

_____

_____

THE PERSUASIVE SPEECH

Speech is power: speech is to persuade, to convert, to compel.

—Ralph Waldo Emerson, poet, philosopher, essayist

Everyday we are exposed to messages that invite or encourage us to alter our point of view, change our behaviour, purchase something, or adopt a new idea. We encounter these messages via the radio, television, billboards, newspapers, or from family members, friends, authority figures, fellow students, salespeople, businesspeople, government officials, spiritual leaders, and activists. Sometimes the message reaches us on a subliminal level. For example, we are not even conscious that we are purchasing a Coke during intermission at the cinema simply because we just viewed a commercial for Coke on the screen. We have been persuaded to make a particular purchase as the advertiser of the Coke brand has encouraged us to take action.

Have you ever spoken these phrases, "He's a snake oil salesman," or "She's just trying to sell me on her product. Does she really think I'll be taken in by her?" We have grown increasingly distrustful of persuasive messages. People today are generally more cynical and skeptical of new ideas and unchartered territory. So your role as a persuasive speaker is a challenging one.

Persuasive messages and speeches urge the listener to do one of three things:

1. To take action.
2. To change or modify attitudes and opinions.
3. To have a belief or concept reinforced or confirmed.

The audience will trust a speaker who is ethical. Greville Janner, the British advocate said, "Advocacy is an art. Deception is evil." As a speaker, you are acting as an advocate when you persuade, so ensure that you use ethical proof, strong facts, and sound logic.

We want to hear from a speaker who is credible and believable. We trust a speaker who is fair, honest, and displays integrity. We trust a speaker who is an expert on the subject. We trust a speaker who has vast experience in a particular field and is capable of articulating his or her knowledge. A persuasive speaker is passionate and enthusiastic while still conveying a sense of being objective and open-minded.

EXERCISE

1. Divide students into pairs. Next, choose one of the scenarios below and use your powers of persuasion to obtain your objective.

   i) A tries to persuade B to attend a rock concert. B's interest lies in classical music.

   ii) B is the employer. A is the employee. A asks B for a raise.

   iii) A wants to stay at home and study for an upcoming examination. B tries to encourage A to spend the night bar-hopping.

2. Report back to the class. Describe the scenario, your method of persuasion, how it did or did not work, and how the person being persuaded reacted to you.

3. Choose another scenario and reverse roles.

4. Again, report back to the class.

You have just completed your first in-class exercise in persuasion. These types of situations occur daily and we don't give much thought when communicating in this fashion. We need to develop our ability to persuade in numerous situations such as these—you want your roommate to clear away his own dishes, you want your friend to join the student union, you need to ask for help on a school project, you want to persuade an employer to hire you, or you want to institute change. The list is endless.

In order to help you become more proficient in this area, consider the **general principles of persuasion.**

1. People are resistant to abrupt change, so in order to encourage the listener to change, do so gradually. For example: If Derrick has a fear of swimming because he fears drowning, initially you could encourage him to simply stand in ankle-deep water in the shallow end. Then you would proceed to encourage him to gradually move towards the deep end.

2. Persuasion should be tailored to the needs of the audience. For example, an audience of retirees will not be interested in a talk by a real estate agent on "Buying your first home," but they would be interested in a talk on "Getting a reverse mortgage on your home."

3. As you present your persuasive speech it should be clear that the benefits you are presenting outweigh the disadvantages. For example, civilians would be willing to give up certain liberties such as being searched at airports and borders, in order to combat terrorism and achieve greater security. Clearly the benefits in this example would overshadow the negative aspects.

4. You are more likely to convince your listeners if your message is congruent with their attitudes, beliefs, values, and behaviour. When the speaker gives information that contradicts or undermines these aspects, the listener becomes uncomfortable and will resist receiving the message.

How do you persuade your audience? Follow very similar steps to those suggested earlier in this chapter, plus add a few variations in structure.

1. Decide on a specific persuasive speech purpose.

2. Analyze your audience, their attitudes toward your topic, and the degree of persuasion that you need to use.

3. Establish a key message that you want the audience to accept or act upon.

4. Do your research.

5. Organize the talk.

6. Practise delivering the argument in a logical and persuasive manner.

7. Create speaker notes and visual aids.

8. Deliver the speech.

When structuring a persuasive speech, let's turn to the words of Aristotle (384-322 B.C.) who greatly influenced how we now structure a speech to persuade. He said, "Persuasion is achieved when the orator's speech is so spoken as to make us think him credible; when the speech stirs our emotions, when the speaker provides logical arguments."

We briefly touched on credibility, now let's give it a little more attention. When someone is credible, we believe in him or her. There are three stages of developing and establishing credibility.

Stage 1: Initial credibility
Before speaking, pay attention to the image conveyed through dress, posture, gestures, body language, and eye contact. Approach the podium energetically and establish eye contact with the audience before speaking.

Another way to reinforce your initial credibility is to write your own profile detailing your accomplishments and achievements. Offer this to the person who will be introducing you. It will set a favourable tone for you and help establish your credibility.

Stage 2: Acquired credibility
This is achieved during the course of your speech as you establish common ground with your audience, present a coherent, well-organized speech that is well-supported, one that demonstrates that you are well-informed and ethical.

Stage 3: Definitive credibility
This arrives at the conclusion of the speech. If there is a question and answer period, that is when definitive credibility is established. At this stage, aim to leave the audience with a positive impression and an enduring image. End with strength and good eye contact. Conduct the question and answer period with firm mastery.

To design an effective persuasive speech, you need to examine the different **kinds of appeals** used.

Successful persuasive speakers use these four patterns:

1. Logical Appeal
2. Psychological Appeal
3. Personal Appeal
4. Emotional Appeal

Logical Appeal

When you use a logical appeal you are using a formal system for making inferences which Aristotle called *logos*. You are using reasoning, which encourages the listener to reach a conclusion from the evidence presented. Examples, facts, statistics, expert opinion are forms of evidence that are used in persuasive speeches to lead the audience to adopt your argument or point of view.

The three popular types of reasoning that speakers often use to persuade are inductive, deductive, and causal reasoning.

Inductive reasoning is a method that begins first with the specifics and then proceeds towards a general conclusion. Begin with a specific case, viewpoint, or conclusion and then use inductive reasoning as a basis for reaching a general conclusion. For example:

Specifics:

- Eighty people were laid off from our company today since our company's profits dipped.
- Twenty people were laid off last week.
- Thirty people were laid off last month.

General conclusion: It appears as if our company is in financial trouble and needs to downsize its workforce to cut costs.

However, be cautious when using generalizations. If you talk about four corporate chief executive officers being crooks, you cannot generalize that all CEOs are crooks. You do not have sufficient evidence to arrive at that conclusion. Don't jump to a conclusion without providing evidence that is untainted, truthful, fair, and representative. Remember, reasoning is a process of drawing a conclusion from evidence and you need to ascertain that your reasoning is sound and appropriate for your speech.

Deductive reasoning involves reasoning from a general premise and then moving to specifics. When using deductive reasoning, first state your point and then give your logic, facts, and reason. The audience will ask themselves whether or not the argument makes sense, whether or not it is logical.

A student uses deductive reasoning when he or she follows this thought process:

General premise: This has been the hottest summer in Toronto in 53 years.

Specific premise: We had 40 days during which the temperature was above 30°C.

We had 19 nights during which the temperature was above 20°C.

The year 1959 was the last recorded date when this city had 43 days when the temperature was above 30°C.

Source: Environment Canada

When you present your persuasive speech and support it with this type of concrete evidence, it will be more effective, assuming your premise is sound.

In this example, the premise that this has been the hottest summer is true as it has been measured by Environment Canada. You have given supporting evidence. Therefore your audience would be inclined to adopt your conclusion.

Be on guard for flawed reasoning. For example, you might argue:

- Cats eat fish (premise).
- Michael eats fish (premise).
- Therefore, Michael is a cat (conclusion).

The conclusion is obviously wrong.

Causal reasoning is a process of reasoning that shows how events relate or link to each other, and then how the one event caused the other.

We use this form of reasoning fairly regularly. For example, you've just attended an all-night party where the liquor was freely available. The next day, after having had an excessive amount of beer at the party, you have a pounding headache. You say, "Because I overindulged in the free flowing booze last night, my head is throbbing." There is a clear relationship between the cause (the liquor) and the effect (your pounding headache).

Psychological Appeal

By placing your audience's needs, feelings, motives, and concerns front and centre, your psychological appeal will work. Many speakers place their own needs and wants at the forefront and forget the individuals to whom they are targeting their message. Consider your argument from the audience's viewpoint.

In order to better understand human needs, consider psychologist Abraham Maslow's (1908-1970) Hierarchy of Needs. Maslow believed that human beings are motivated by unsatisfied needs, and that before we satisfy our higher needs the basic ones need to be met first.

Imagine the Hierarchy of Needs as a pyramid, and at the bottom of the pyramid are **physiological needs**. These are our strongest needs and are composed of our need for air, food, water, sleep, sex, activity, and bodily comfort. If we were to be deprived of these, our basic needs, we could not survive.

In order to proceed upwards, towards the next level, our **safety needs**, the physiological needs must be met first. At the safety level, people need to feel freedom from danger and threat. They need to embrace what is familiar and what feels safe.

The third level of needs is **social needs**. This embodies the need for identification with others, the need to be accepted by others, the need to be wanted, the need for love, affection, and a sense of belonging. People join groups or organizations to feel part of something larger than them. For example, by joining the Civic Garden Centre Club, the isolated gardener feels a sense of belonging.

Level four is **self-esteem needs**. At this level we need to earn the respect of others and we need to gain self-respect. We need to earn prestige, success, and a good reputation. Achievements are very important at this stage. By having these needs taken care of, the individual will function well, feel valued, centred, and self-confident.

Self-actualization is at the top of the pyramid. At this level we aim to realize our potential. We search for peace, knowledge, creativity, independence, freedom from restraint, and aesthetic experiences. We need to know and to understand, to tackle the unknown, and to become what we are capable of becoming. Aesthetically, the individual has a higher need for taste and discrimination, and for symmetry, system, and structure. Very few people are at this level. You may find individuals on a sound economic and academic and spiritual footing functioning at this level of need. Perhaps a spiritual or a religious individual, like the Dalai Lama, operates on this plane.

Here is an example bearing Maslow's theory in mind. Assume the government decided to build a new superjail in the middle of a densely populated area. In presenting the idea to the public, the government representative would need to consider the concerns of the local inhabitants who oppose the idea. By taking Maslow's theory into account, the speaker would understand that his or her audience would have serious worries about their safety. When the official frames the persuasive appeal it would be important for him or her to offer the audience reassurance and a level of comfort to appease them. The speaker has to stress that the safety and security of the inhabitants would be a number one concern.

Personal Appeal

When a speaker is an authority or is a person who possesses influence or expert knowledge on a particular topic, he or she can use personal appeal in a persuasive speech. For example, Christopher Reeve, the actor who played the part of Superman in the movie of the same name, became paralyzed after falling off a horse. After years of intense physiotherapy and rehabilitation, he miraculously found that he began to experience sensation again.

Now, if he were delivering a persuasive speech to encourage people with spinal cord injuries to pursue a program of regular therapeutic massage and physiotherapy, he would be a credible speaker. He would speak from first-hand experience and the audience would be receptive to his personal appeal.

Emotional Appeal

An appeal that arouses emotions in the listeners can be effective in specific situations. Sometimes using logic and evidence may not be sufficient. The speaker may choose an emotional appeal to achieve his purpose. For example, if a mother wanted to encourage a child to pursue higher education, she might build in a fear factor when persuading her off-spring to follow this educational path. The mother might say, "If you do not attend college or university you are unlikely to become financially secure as an adult. A college or university education will provide you with the tools to compete in the ever-changing, challenging marketplace. You will be able to pursue a career that will enable you to become self-sufficient and secure. On the other hand, most teenagers who leave school early end up in mundane jobs that do not satisfy them. Give my advice some serious thought and choose the route that will help you realize your potential and ultimately lead to a rewarding life and lifestyle."

In making this emotional appeal, the speaker has discussed the consequences that would follow if the teenager chose not to go to college or university. The mother mentioned the consequences of not pursuing a higher education and then showed how, by adopting her suggestion, her teenager would encounter positive results or consequences.

Fallacious Reasoning   When presenting an argument or persuasive speech there are some reasoning fallacies to avoid. A fallacy is a flaw in reasoning which results in a misleading argument. A discerning audience will recognize the fallacies listed below.

1. *Ad hominem* **argument**. This is when the speaker attacks the person and their misfortunes or habits, and not the argument.

2. *Ad populum*. In this case, it is argued that since everyone holds the same belief or knows that something is right, it is therefore true or correct. This type of argument ignores the real issue by appealing to bias and passion. Here's an example to illustrate this. A teenager states "All the girls in my class have pierced their navels and inserted a gold ring. I want to be fashionable so I want one too." The parent might respond, "If everyone jumped off a cliff, would you?" The parent did not buy into the bandwagon fallacy that because everyone was doing it, it would be acceptable for her daughter to do it, too.

3. **Hasty generalizations are based on too few facts.** When this fallacy is used, the general conclusion is based on insufficient evidence and examples.

4. **Anecdotal evidence**. This is when the speaker uses a personal story to prove an argument. When using anecdotal evidence back it up with expert testimony and statistics to prove the point.

5. **Red herring fallacy**. This "red herring" originates from a story about a group of people who were being tracked by hounds. In order to throw the dogs off track, a red herring was dropped behind them. This resulted in the dogs going off on the wrong track,

because the scent of the herring confused them. Politicians are very adept at using the red herring fallacy when they do not want to address a particular issue.

6. **False authority**. This happens when a celebrity is called upon to endorse a product and yet is no expert on the product. When a popular basketball star endorses a toothpaste for a television spot, an intelligent listener might question whether the star is doing the commercial for the money, whether he actually gets wonderful results from this toothpaste, or whether he has naturally white teeth. It would be more convincing to have a professor of dentistry endorsing the product as he or she would be an expert authority on teeth.

7. **Non-sequitur fallacy**. This comes from the Latin word meaning, "does not follow." Here is a non-sequitur fallacy: "To keep in shape, Joan jogs three kilometres twice a week and takes a stretch class occasionally. Therefore Joan would be a perfect candidate to run in the Boston marathon." Or, "Bradley sings in the school choir, therefore Bradley would become a good conductor."

8. **Cardstacking fallacy**. This occurs when the speaker presents all the evidence on his or her side of an argument and ignores the evidence on the other side. The speaker therefore delivers a one-sided argument. To present a fair argument, acknowledge that another side exists. If you encouraged a group to follow a diet of only vegetables and presented the benefits of doing so, you ought to also mention that such a diet might be deficient in particular vitamins and minerals. In addition to advocating this diet, you could add that a multivitamin tablet would be a good supplement to take once a day.

9. **Taking evidence out of context**. For example, the play *King Lear* recently received a negative review in the press. The reviewer described it as "a mediocre production which, astonishingly, combined dismal acting ability by the lead star and moments of sheer brilliance from the supporting actress." The theatre company issues a press release the next day and extracts the words "moments of sheer brilliance" from the review. They use this phrase in their advertisement to entice patrons to see the production of *King Lear*. This type of reasoning is misleading.

10. **Circular reasoning**. In this situation, the speaker's argument never proves anything since it moves in a circle. The speaker simply restates the same thing in different terms. For example, "I like pasta because it's my favourite food."

If you make sure that your logic is sound and that there are no fallacies in your reasoning, people will find you believable.

STRUCTURING THE PERSUASIVE SPEECH

Now you are ready to structure your persuasive speech. Select your topic, determine your purpose, analyze your audience, and determine your key message. There are two types of structures that can be used. Choose the one that best serves your objectives.

The first structure offers a motivated sequence, which was developed in 1930 by Alan Monroe, a professor of Speech at Purdue University. This approach is comprised of five steps, the aim of which is to motivate the listener to be persuaded to adopt the speaker's point of view.

The Motivated Sequence

1. ATTENTION: Gain the attention of the audience and focus them on the main ideas of the speech. Refer back to the section on "Ways to Open a Speech" in Chapter 3.

2. NEED: Define your general problem and relate it to the needs of the audience. The audience must understand the need for change. Then illustrate the need by using examples, evidence, testimony, and statistics. Relate these to the needs, interests, and values of the audience.

3. SATISFACTION: Provide a solution to the problem. Do this by offering the following details:

   • The solution states how your action will meet the need discussed earlier

   • Your comprehensive plan

   • Demonstrate how your solution will work

   • Use strong evidence and supporting material

   • Raise objections you might anticipate and overcome the objections

4. VISUALIZATION: Increase the desire for your proposed solution by using vivid descriptions to paint pictures through the use of imagery. Show how the audience will benefit from your plan, how the future will look, how they will profit from a policy, or how an altered belief will bring about a positive result.

5. ACTION: Every persuasive speech should end with a call to action. You have created a desire, now tell the audience what you want them to do. For example, tell them to buy your product, vote for you as president of the student council, approve a policy change, or book a vacation. Use a direct appeal to achieve the desired action. Conclude on a strong note that convinces the audience to act based on the soundness of your proposal.

Here is a persuasive speech planned and delivered by Elaine Humber, MSW, ATTP.

A Speech to Persuade
Audience: Mental Health Professionals
The Value of a Developmental Perspective in Forensic Assessments

Attention: This story works well to capture attention and interest for two reasons. First, it is realistic because of its dramatic and vivid detail. Second, it brings a personal element directly to the topic.

Brian arrived in handcuffs and shackles last week—a gangly 19-year-old with stringy, blond hair. He was jovial and seemed at home in the unit at the psychiatric hospital. I thought, why is he not distressed? What has happened to allow him to see this experience as positive? Or does he?

Brian was arrested for shooting a pellet gun at road signs over the roofs of cars. Given his already lengthy criminal involvement, the courts were asking mental health professionals for advice in the form of a pre-sentence assessment. Brian's needs and society's protection had to be considered.

So why is Brian important? He is a pathological liar, antisocial, impulsive, lazy, and careless. From his criminal record it is clear that he has little regard for the law and should probably be locked up. But that's easy. Looking at the bigger picture we see that society is turning out lots like Brian. Our jails are full of them. Punishment is what Brian expects. His family, the schools, and the legal system have always been telling him he is bad. Would another report just confirm this?

A psychiatric diagnosis based on his thinking, behaviour, emotional expression, and symptoms describes what Brian is like and that, combined with a risk assessment, gives a good idea of what to expect from him in the future. I believe that this suffices to protect society, but it could reinforce a moralistic and self-righteous attitude towards Brian.

A "developmental perspective" would add a valuable dimension to the assessment as it considers the underlying reasons for Brian's thoughts and actions—how his mind developed as he grew up in his family and community. It would also afford a better understanding of his limitations and his capacity for change. The developmental perspective lends more respect and empathy to the client and it paves the way towards designing interventions and treatment plans more helpful to him and, ultimately, to society at large.

Solution: While stating both the importance and deficits of existing approaches, the speaker introduces the central idea as the solution—the need to understand the reasons for human behaviour.

The stages of psychological development are building blocks of the mind. A person cannot master one stage without having mastered the previous one. Also, to master the stages one must live in an atmosphere that supports that growth.

So, let us look at what Brian's parents had to offer him. His mother, Debbie, was on her own. She was a prostitute but was determined to make a life for herself and her baby. Brian's father died in prison when Brian was an infant. Debbie cared for her child but had poor parenting skills and no support. For example, she did not realize that when Brian slept for 12 hours straight as an infant there was something wrong.

Brian began having problems at age three. He was terrified of his angry, violent stepfather, Ron. He also thought Ron was his father until age nine when Ron, in a fit of rage, told him otherwise. Brian's most positive relationship was with his next stepfather, Carl. But this came to an end with Carl's sudden death when Brian was eleven. Throughout school Brian had learning difficulties, was disruptive, and had no friends. Legal troubles began at age thirteen, and for the past two years Brian has lived on the streets.

History and Elaboration: The speaker elaborates upon the central idea by explaining, through example, what a developmental perspective consists of. She describes the deficits in the client's environment throughout his formative years to show how it would have thwarted healthy development and to show why he needed to develop specific psychological coping strategies.

Aside from Brian's genetic makeup, which may be problematic in itself, one can see that his childhood environment was traumatic and seriously lacking. It was devoid of safety, security, stability, predictability, and protection, in spite of his mother's best efforts. He did not receive consistent nurturing so did not experience a deep connection with her, his only caregiver. For these reasons he did not develop an ability to form healthy relationships, a shared sense of humanity, empathy, compassion, or trust. His childhood relationships did not support his initiative or ability to solve problems and consequently, he did not develop a sense of worth. Lack of soothing and comforting resulted in a tendency to be overwhelmed by emotions and to act on impulse.

Any child who grows up in such an environment will have significant psychological problems. The child will embrace strategies to cope with trauma and deprivation and this, in turn, becomes a part of his personality. However, in adult life those strategies prove to be detrimental. Coping states become personality traits if employed long and often enough.

Visualization: Visualization of the individual's pain and suffering further persuades the audience of the critical need.

During the assessment process Brian behaved as a child. The staff was his family. His lies represented a fantasy world in which he was a loved son, brother, and partner, a worker, a successful and respected member of society—this was his defence against seeing himself as "a loser." He was overwhelmed on his birthday when one of the young nurses brought him a cake. He hid in his room for hours and didn't touch the cake. He explained to me later that he could not handle the situation because he was afraid he would cry. He had never had a birthday cake and could not imagine that a pretty girl thought he was anyone special. This confidence represented a break in his armour of cheery playfulness. Another glimpse into his pain was his longing for his mother to visit him.

Time reveals Brian's pain and fear. Given the deprivation and trauma of his childhood his character deficits are evident and his prospects are bleak. Many prisoners have experienced a childhood much like Brian's and have likewise developed poor coping skills.

Visualization: The solution is visualized as a reduction in suffering by means of providing an environment appropriate to clients' needs.

We can see that Brian, like so many others, needs to be in a secure, supportive setting with consistent but firm limits. Brian also needs meaningful activity and minimal turnover in staff to avoid repeated losses. On a broader scale we can see that appropriate support for, and intervention with, people like Brian and his family early on may have mitigated many of Brian's current difficulties

Action: This is what the audience needs to do to bring about the solution.

Whatever the past has lacked, however, to better help Brian and others in their current situation, we need to *understand* the value of a developmental perspective in forensic assessments. It is vital that we *include* this perspective as part of the evaluation process. A developmental perspective of an individual's behaviour does not condone it, but it counteracts the punitive, judgemental, moralistic attitude we encounter so often today.

(Brian is a fictional character.)

Here is an alternative structure you can use when you have a specific proposition that you want the audience to accept or believe. Use logic, evidence, and emotion to achieve your purpose.

The Structure for a Speech to Convince

1. Present a **history** of the problem. Discuss the events that preceded the problem and outline the importance of the topic.

2. Discuss the **effects** of the problem at the present time. Give illustrations, evidence, facts, proof, and examples to support your claims.

3. List the **causes** that brought about the effects. Again, use supporting evidence.

4. List possible **solutions** to solve the problem. Present alternatives and use supporting evidence, such as examples, facts, analogies, and illustrations.

5. Present **your solution** to the problem. Offer the evidence and reasons for choosing the solution or promoting a particular belief or idea.

6. Show how the audience will **benefit** from your proposal. For example, they will get a better education; increase their profits; obtain better access for the disabled.

7. Conclude your speech with a final statement supporting your solution/proposal. What **action** would you like the audience to take?

By this stage you know how to plan and structure a persuasive speech that is supported by solid research, strong evidence, and proof. When it comes to the delivery of this speech it is essential to speak with conviction and confidence. This will demonstrate your energy and solid commitment to your message. You now have a roadmap to assist you in delivering a successful persuasive speech.

Persuasive Speech Topics

Capital punishment should be instituted for individuals who murder police officers.

Sex education should not be taught in schools.

The number of police officers patrolling the streets should be increased.

The government should subsidize university and college education.

Gambling should be legalized.

Smokers who develop lung-related illnesses should be responsible for paying their own health-related costs.

Advertisements for alcohol and cigarettes should be banned.

Drug testing in the workplace should be mandatory.

Chief executive officers who break the law should be held criminally responsible.

Rapists should be castrated.

Become a volunteer.

Physical exercise is vital for good health.

Put an end to animal testing.

Place a limit on the amount of time you spend watching television.

More accommodation for the homeless should be provided in each city's budget.

The media is an unreliable source for accurate, impartial information.

Adult children should be responsible for the care of their elderly parents.

The cloning of humans should be forbidden.

Violence on television promotes violent behaviour.

Cell phones should be banned in restaurants, theatres, and while driving a vehicle.

It should be harder to get married and easier to get divorced.

All prospective parents should attend parenting classes.

Professional athletes are paid too much.

The problems in the Middle East will never be solved.

Prostitution should be legalized.

Young children should have supervised access to the Internet.

Condoms should be distributed at high schools, colleges, and universities.

Avoid tap water, drink bottled water.

Teen pregnancy can be avoided.

Steroid taking is rampant in sports.

FORM 4.3 | **Evaluation of Persuasive Speech**

Speaker's Name: _____

Date: _____

Topic: _____

Speech Purpose: _____

Evaluate the speech using the following scale:
1 = Excellent   2 = Very Good   3 = Average
4 = Fair   5 = Needs Improvement

INTRODUCTION	1	2	3	4	5

- Opens with good attention-getter
- Motivates audience to listen
- States qualifications
- States position and previews arguments

ORGANIZATION	1	2	3	4	5

- Includes clear and significant arguments
- Uses suitable pattern
- Employs transitions

FORM 4.3	Evaluation of Persuasive Speech (continued)

SUPPORTING MATERIALS 1 2 3 4 5

- Uses appropriate verbal supports
  - −Quotations   −Explanations
  - −Comparisons   −Statistics
  - −Expert testimony −Examples
- Uses effective visual supports

PERSUASIVENESS 1 2 3 4 5

- Relates to needs of listeners
- Uses appropriate evidence and logic
- Is a credible speaker

CONCLUSION 1 2 3 4 5

- Summarizes main ideas, recommendations, or position
- Asks for audience acceptance or action step
- Closes in memorable way

DELIVERY 1 2 3 4 5

- Well-projected
- Confident posture and movement
- Uses gestures or facial expression effectively
- Maintains direct eye contact
- Sounds dynamic yet conversational
- Uses notes efficiently

SUGGESTIONS FOR IMPROVEMENT

_____

_____

_____

_____

_____

_____

EXERCISES

1. What are the aims of persuasive messages?
2. What are the general principles of persuasion?
3. Explain what credibility means to you. Describe a speaker who you find to be credible and outline how this individual establishes his or her credibility.
4. Divide into pairs. Discuss the four types of persuasive appeals you can use in a persuasive speech. Then, independently, write down an example you would use for each type of appeal. Share your examples with your partner.
5. Name five fallacies in reasoning.
6. Refer to the list of persuasive speech topics. Choose one. Identify your target audience. Prepare an outline for your speech. Then develop it into a fully detailed, word for word speech. Practice delivering the speech. When assessing the effectiveness of your persuasive speech, use the evaluation sheet, which follows the list of topics.
7. Present a persuasive argument that supports or opposes these quotations by Shakespeare:

   a) Mend your speech a little,
      Lest you may mar your fortunes.
      King Lear

   b) All that glisters is not gold,
      Often have you heard that told.
      The Merchant of Venice

   c) Have more than thou showest,
      Speak less than thou knowest,
      Lend less than thou owest.
      King Lear

SUMMARY

This chapter presented methods to structure the informative speech, the demonstrative speech, and the persuasive speech. Tips for outlining a speech using a set of symbols in a consistent pattern are suggested. The student can use an evaluation form to assess his or her performance. Separate evaluation forms for the informative and the persuasive speech are included. The general principles of persuasion are discussed while taking into account the importance of establishing credibility as a speaker. The different types of appeals used by persuasive speakers are examined. They are the logical, psychological, personal, and emotional appeals. The student is encouraged to avoid using reasoning that is based on fallacy. The chapter concludes by defining ten types of fallacious reasoning.

SUGGESTED READING

Lucas, Stephen E. *The Art of Public Speaking*. New York: Random House, 1986.

Lusser Rico, Gabriele. *Writing the Natural Way*. New York: St. Martin's Press, 1983.

Miner, Margaret and Hugh Rawson. *A Dictionary of Quotations from Shakespeare*. New York: Penguin Books, 1992.

Ross, Raymond S. *The Speechmaking Process*. Massachusetts: Allyn and Bacon, 1998.

Tacey, William S. *Business and Professional Speaking*. Dubuque, Iowa: WM. C. Brown Publishers, 1983.

Walter, Otis M. *Speaking to Inform and Persuade*. New York: MacMillan Publishing Company Inc., 1982.

REFERENCES

Bettinghaus, Erwin P., and Michael J. Cody. *Persuasive Communication*, 4th ed. New York: Holt, Rinehart & Winston, 1987.

Maslow, Abraham H. A Theory of Human Motivation. *Motivation and Personality*. New York: Harper Collins, 1970.

Mayer, Robert. *Power Plays*. Toronto: Random House Canada, 1996.

Spence, Gerry. *How to Argue and Win Every Time*. New York: St. Martin's Press, 1995.

chapter five

Organizing a Speech

Speech finely framed delighteth the ears.

—Bible, Apocrypha

LEARNING OBJECTIVES

- To select an organizational pattern for your speech
- To list the five types of supporting material
- To explain how connectives are used in a speech

Lord Birkett, an eminent British judge, gave many insightful and telling comments on public speaking. The one quotation that is relevant here is, "I do not object to people looking at their watches when I am speaking. But I strongly object when they start shaking them to make certain they are still going."

An effective public speaker will give the listener a reason to listen to his or her message and inspire the listener to pay attention until he or she has completed his speech. Doesn't it bother you when you have to concentrate intensely and work hard to understand a speaker? Chances are you will turn your attention away if the speaker has not structured his message in a way that makes the speech easy to follow and digest.

Plan a well-organized speech so that you will never have to encounter an audience who are constantly looking at—and perhaps shaking—their watches.

Organization provides the listener with coherence, and a natural flow of ideas that are easy to follow and remember. It conveys relationships between ideas and concepts, promotes understanding, and adds to your credibility as a speaker. We are constantly organizing in our day-to-day lives. We plan our day on our Palm Pilots or in our agendas. We organize our closets to suit our lifestyle. We plan and organize vacations. Life would be slightly chaotic without a sense of order. An organizational approach is necessary in a speech since it gives our listeners a sense of order.

We know that a basic speech is composed of three parts: the introduction, the body, and the conclusion. The body of the speech is the most important segment. Generally speaking, the introduction should take up about 10 to 15 percent of the speaking time, the body comprises 75 to 80 percent of the speech, and the conclusion assumes 5 to 10 percent of the entire speech.

As you prepare the body of the talk you will:

1. Decide upon the key points that will support your speech purpose and reinforce your central speech statement
2. Make a note of your key points
3. Organize your main points by choosing an organizational pattern that is best suited to your purpose/objective
4. Include supporting evidence, examples, anecdotes, testimony, and statistics
5. Connect the elements of your speech by using transitions, signposts, and internal summaries

Once you have prepared your speech outline, select an organizational pattern to suit your material and your intention.

THE TOPICAL PATTERN

A topical pattern is used when the speaker divides the main topic into themes or sub-topics. Structure a speech using the topical pattern to discuss several ideas. This is a very popular method when key topics can be easily broken down into sub-topics.

Helen Simeon, director of public affairs for the Hospital for Sick Children, gives an annual talk to public relations students of Humber College and Ryerson University. She uses a topical arrangement and her preparation page looks like this:

Specific Purpose: To present an overview of the media relations role at the Hospital for Sick Children.

Central Idea: Media relations is only one element in the communications process.

Main Points:

1. Why the hospital is in the news
2. The communications philosophy of the department
3. The importance of understanding how the media work
4. Trends in news reporting

THE SPATIAL OR GEOGRAPHICAL PATTERN

A spatial pattern follows a particular direction based on space. Your main points are arranged from left to right, top to bottom, north to south, west to east, inside to outside. This pattern works well when an architect describes his plans, when you describe a journey, or when you examine the climatic regions of a country. For example:

Specific Purpose: To inform vacationers about the different regions to visit in Canada.

Central Idea: Canada is a vast land of incredible beauty and interest.

Main Points:

1. Atlantic Canada, comprised of New Brunswick, Prince Edward Island, Nova Scotia, and Newfoundland, has numerous cultural and historical points of interest as well as natural beauty.

2. Quebec offers a blend of French-Canadian culture and a well-preserved history.

3. Ontario, the most populated province in the centre of Canada, draws the largest number of visitors.

4. The Prairie Provinces, including Manitoba, Saskatchewan, and Alberta, boast spectacular landscapes and national parks.

5. British Columbia offers magnificent scenery, fine beaches, parks, skiing, and mountain trails for hiking.

6. Northern Canada, including Yukon, Northwest Territories, and Nunavut, is a unique destination.

THE CHRONOLOGICAL PATTERN

A chronological pattern structures the main points in a timeline. This pattern works effectively to describe a sequence of events or to describe a process. Here is an example of a speech that analyzes a process:

Specific Purpose: To describe the stages of the consulting process.

Central Idea: There is a method that needs to be followed in order to achieve the client's business goal.

Main Points:

Step 1: Gathering information to establish the needs and goals for the engagement

Step 2: Defining and exploring the problem

Step 3: Diagnosing the problem

Step 4: Recommending actions to be taken

Step 5: Implementing changes

Step 6: Evaluation of the news processes

Here is an example of a chronological order that follows a timeline:

Specific Purpose: To inform the listener about the origins and development of money.

Central Idea: Money, as we know it, may become an outdated form of currency.

Main Points:

1. Cattle, crops, and cowrie shells were the oldest form of money
2. The first base-metal coins were manufactured in China in 500 B.C.
3. Paper currency appeared in China in A.D. 806
4. Gold was made the standard of value in England in 1816
5. Evolution is towards electronic money in the 21st century

THE CAUSE AND EFFECT PATTERN

A cause and effect pattern first addresses the causes of the problem, an event or a condition, and then comments upon the effects thereof. This pattern is also known as a causal pattern.

Assume that your specific purpose is to persuade parents in encouraging their children to reduce their intake of snack food and to exercise more frequently. You would plan your talk as follows:

Specific Purpose: To persuade parents to encourage their overweight children to eat less junk food and increase the frequency of physical activity.

Central Idea: Each year 300 000 deaths occur due to poor diet and lack of exercise.

Main Points:

1. Obesity can be caused by poor eating habits, lack of exercise, depression, stress, family history of obesity, medical illness, personal problems, or low self-esteem.
2. Obesity can lead to diabetes, high blood pressure, risk of heart disease, lack of sleep, and breathing problems.

THE PROBLEM-SOLUTION PATTERN

A problem-solution pattern first presents the problem and then offers a solution to it. This method is often used in persuasive speeches. Let us revamp the speech purpose from the previous example and use a problem-solution approach.

Specific Purpose: To persuade parents of obese children to diminish the health risks that result from obesity by managing and treating this condition.

Central Idea: To prevent obesity from becoming a lifelong struggle, enroll your child in a weight-management program.

Problem: Statistics Canada (1994-1999) reports that obesity in children is on the rise and is emerging as a growing problem.

Solution:

1. Parents and family physicians can take an active role
2. Conduct a medical evaluation
3. Develop a comprehensive treatment plan involving healthy eating, regular exercise, and parental involvement
4. Include behaviour modification
5. Attend a support group such as Weight Watchers or Overeaters Anonymous

SUPPORTING MATERIAL

A good public speaker will use supporting material to reinforce the speaker's credibility and point of view. When used in a masterful way, the listener will become immersed in the speaker's message. If you bake a dry, tasteless sponge cake it will be edible, but when you add the sugar, the spice, the rich ingredients, and the topping, how much tastier the treat becomes! When you use supporting material with skill, you can raise the level of your speech from an average to an exceptional one.

You can use a variety of supporting materials, such as:

1. Statistics
2. Quotations
3. Testimony
4. Examples
5. Narration
6. Definitions

Statistics

> *He uses statistics as a drunken man uses lamp-posts—for support rather than for illumination.*
>
> —Andrew Lang, *Scottish poet 1844-1912*

Statistics can corroborate your message and enlighten. Use them, as Andrew Lang says, "to illuminate" and not bore the audience.

Louise Knox, spokesperson for Mothers Against Drunk Driving, used statistics with great impact when she offered recommendations to the government at the Federal policy launch event in November of 2001.

MADD Canada is also recommending the government amend the *Criminal Code* to lower the federal blood alcohol concentration (BAC) legal limit from 0.08 percent to 0.05 percent. We are asking for this amendment because our current BAC limit is not deterring people from drinking and driving. In Canada, there are an estimated 12.5 million impaired driving trips made annually, with tens of thousands of impaired drivers on the roads each night. It has been estimated that only one in every 445 impaired driving trips in Canada results in a criminal charge. The fact is that too many Canadians are drinking too much and then driving.

Another disturbing reality in Canada today is that it is common practice not to charge a drinking driver unless his or her BAC is above 0.10 percent. So, what does this mean about those drinking drivers on the road? To stay within the current limit, a man weighing 91 kilograms can drink almost six beers, or more than a bottle of wine, in two hours and drive without being criminally charged with impaired driving. A 57-kilogram woman can drink three beers in two hours and get behind a wheel of a car and drive, relatively comfortable that she would not be criminally charged.

In this example, the statistics help to clarify the speaker's ideas. By relating the statistic to the 91-kilogram man and the 57-kilogram woman, the speaker establishes a frame of reference for the listener.

Have you ever become bored when a speaker spouts forth a list of "boring" statistics? The key for the speaker here is to include statistics that are relevant and meaningful and eliminate any that are unnecessary. Members of the audience do not retain figures with great ease so it would be helpful, if using a lot of figures and statistics, to represent them visually in graphic form. This will aid retention. When using statistics, let the listener know the source of your information and if it is not self-evident, explain what the statistics mean to the audience. Audiences today have become cynical when it comes to statistics as they can be easily falsified. Offer your listener assurance by presenting the source of your statistics as a reliable one.

In addition, you can mention the size of the population from which the statistics were derived. One last word about statistics. When you mention figures, round them off. Instead of saying, "Sales increased by 25.25 percent," rather say, "Sales increased by more than 25 percent." Precision of measurement is very important to people like accountants, actuaries, scientists, and architects, so present the listeners with accurate, detailed figures in the form of a handout. That's where you can note: "Sales figures rose 25.25 percent."

Quotations

A quotation can offer an endorsement of your message and make the speech memorable. When using a quotation, make sure that you give credit to the author.

A talk on "The Importance of Perseverance" could open in this way:

"You never conquer the mountain. You only conquer yourself." Jim Whittaker, the first American to climb Mt. Everest, spoke these words, reinforcing the idea that when we strive for something we have to confront and know ourselves, our limitations, our strengths, and our ambitions. With heightened self-awareness we also need to embrace the one quality that a winner always possesses and that is perseverance. Babe Ruth struck out 1330 times on his way to hitting 714 home runs. Imagine if he had allowed the 1330 strikes to defeat him. He would not have been inducted into the Baseball Hall of Fame.

Testimony

When a lawyer defends a criminal, he or she frequently calls in an expert to provide testimony to assist in the defense of the client. If you want to persuade an audience to support your point of view, the opinion of an expert will be valuable.

During a child abuse case where a young girl was physically scarred, a teacher who saw evidence of black and blue welts and bruises on the child's legs was called into court to offer lay testimony. Someone who offers lay testimony may not be an expert but he or she can offer a first-hand account of an event or situation simply by having witnessed it personally. This type of testimony can be very powerful and persuasive.

When you decide to use testimony always identify your sources and ascertain that the expert you are quoting has the required expertise and that the authorities you quote are unbiased. Today, athletes are often called upon to endorse a product. For example, a tennis star might promote a new line of hair colour products. Would you regard that tennis player as an expert on hair colour? Perhaps a qualified hair colourist with 15 years of experience in working with different brands of hair products would offer more convincing testimony.

Examples

When you use an example in a speech it provides a concrete element that adds interest and clarity to a point you wish to make. In a speech on "Posture," a student used an example that is attributed to Eleanor Roosevelt.

The first impression one forms of a speaker is based upon a visual judgement. Always assume erect posture as you enter the speaking area. When Eleanor Roosevelt, wife of President Roosevelt, was asked how she managed to maintain her sense of serenity while under duress, she responded by saving, "I wear my invisible crown." Well, if that is a good enough image to inspire her, why not envision that you are wearing an invisible crown when walking up to the podium. Eleanor Roosevelt used that image to handle stress. You can apply it to your posture.

Assume that you are introducing a new member to your book club and you want to present her as a person of intelligence who could contribute a lot to the discussions. You might say, "Joanne is a recent arts graduate from the University of British Columbia. She is an avid reader who has been actively involved in introducing literature to underprivileged students. She helped institute reading clubs and book discussions in low-income schools and this, in turn, helped students to expand their horizons and develop a genuine love of the written word."

Examples can be brief, factual, humorous, serious, or detailed. Be sure that they are always relevant and pertinent.

A longer example is often referred to as an **illustration**. An illustration will often make an abstract idea become concrete. When talking about eating disorders, you might use an illustration to help the audience understand and perhaps identify with these illnesses.

My beautiful, vivacious daughter was disappearing before my eyes. Her obsession with being a perfectionist became disturbing. Downy hair began appearing on her face and arms. Her skin developed a pale anemic pallor and she was in a perpetual state of depression. Her ability to concentrate and think clearly became impaired. Food became anathema to her as her fear of gaining weight intensified. One evening, I entered Helen's bathroom and found her vomiting uncontrollably. I opened the bathroom cabinet and found it lined with diuretics and laxatives. The time had come for active intervention, as all my deep suspicions seemed to come true. Helen was a victim of anorexia nervosa. She was in dire need of help. I did not want my daughter to be one of the 15 percent of sufferers who die from this dreadful eating disorder.

This illustration offers vivid detail as the speaker tells a compelling story based on personal experience.

Narration

Everyone loves a well-told story or narrative. Narrative can be used to explain, to persuade, or to demonstrate examples of excellence. You can include a story about yourself, a famous person, or an average individual. Always demonstrate the connection between your story and the point you are making in your speech. Use dialogue to add further interest.

For a speech on "Overcoming Adversity," a student began with a narrative that attracted the attention of the audience:

> If you're looking for inspiration, you don't have to look any further than cyclist Lance Armstrong, of the United States. He was diagnosed with cancer after he won his first Tour de France, arguably the toughest sporting event in the world today. Doctors gave him a three percent chance of survival. Not only did he survive, he went on to win the next four straight Tours, and he fathered three children....It's a classic example of mind over matter.
>
> After reading his autobiography, I said to myself, "If Lance Armstrong can overcome a life threatening experience like cancer, I really have very little to complain about, in my life."
>
> In my mind, Lance Armstrong, is without a doubt, one of the most inspirational figures in the world of sport today. Over the next few minutes I'd like to talk to you about overcoming adversity, and all that you can accomplish when you put your mind to it.

Definitions

When it is essential, use a definition, and make sure that the audience understands the meaning of the definition. Dictionaries will define words by classification. The *Oxford English Dictionary* and *Webster's Collegiate* are reputable dictionaries that will furnish you with definitions.

If you are addressing a group of high-school physical education students and you want to suggest an alternative form of exercise called Pilates, you need to offer a definition of Pilates. A speech on the subject might begin in this way:

> Jogging, skiing, hiking, yoga, walking! You've all taken part in these physical activities. If you want to improve your posture and lengthen and strengthen your muscles without adding bulk, try Pilates. Pilates is a method of exercise

that offers a non-stress approach to better posture, and stronger, leaner muscles. It improves flexibility and co-ordination. With its emphasis on correct breathing, it leaves participants feeling revitalized. It is a complete approach to developing body awareness and an easy physicality in day-to-day life.

CONNECTIVES

Even though you have prepared and organized your material, remember that most listeners will not pay attention to your speech 100 percent of the time. Minds tend to wander and it is the speaker's job to keep the listener focused. You can do this by using connectives in your speech. A connective offers a link between one idea and another. It shows how one thought relates to another. There are four effective connectives that will help the audience follow your train of thought:

1. Signposts
2. Verbal Transitions
3. Previews
4. Internal Summaries

Signposts

Signposts take the form of brief statements and indicate the direction the speaker is going. For example:

> The first issue we'll address is …
>
> The second issue is …
>
> And the third and final issue is …

Verbal Transitions

A verbal transition offers a bridge between ideas and helps create a fluid movement from an earlier idea to a new one. Use a transition when moving from the introduction to the body of the speech and use one again when moving from the body to the conclusion. Additional transitions can also be added between main points.

Here are some examples of transitional words and phrases.

> Now we'll examine …
>
> The next point will provide you with …
>
> If questions like this intrigue you …
>
> Let's look at this from another perspective …
>
> Now, consider this …
>
> To show you what we mean …
>
> In other words …
>
> Therefore …

In addition …

Let's move along and analyze why …

Here is the most significant result …

So, where do we go from here? …

We have examined … now let's look at …

We have discovered the causes of the problem, now let us explore the possible solutions …

However, you need to consider …

Now, let's take into account the following …

In summary…

In conclusion …

You can also use a pause, silence, movement, or offer a vocal change such as increasing the volume you use. These devices are called **nonverbal transitions**.

Previews

"Come and I'll tell you something" tickles the ear.

African proverb

A preview states what is to follow. An **initial preview** is often used during the introductory section of a speech. An **internal preview** is used during the balance of the speech. When a speaker offers an **internal preview**, it helps the audience to anticipate the information that is about to be presented.

A psychologist began a speech on "Assertiveness" by describing the four behaviour types. Once the speaker had completed that portion of the discussion, she then provided an internal preview of the next segment of her talk. "Now that you understand the four behaviour types, I will show you techniques to become more assertive so that you will stay in control of your feelings, confront an issue with another person, and stand your ground."

Internal Summaries

When you have been speaking for an extended period of time, or if you have presented complicated information, an internal summary will reinforce your main points for the audience. The internal summary restates your main points before you move onto the next segment of your speech. This type of summary aids recall, reinforces ideas, and helps the listener follow the sequential ideas you present.

In a demonstrative speech offered to novice golfers, James Randolf, the golf pro, has just taught the novices the name and function of each golf club. Before moving on to teach specific golfing techniques, James delivers an internal summary:

As we mentioned, 14 clubs are allowed in a golf bag, including the putter. It is the distance from the position of the golf ball to the hole that determines the club the golfer will select. The object of the game is to get the ball in the hole with the fewest number of strokes. Now that you have grasped those basics, we will move along and discuss the techniques of putting and hitting the ball out of the rough.

Use these four connectives to add fluidity to your talk so that the audience's attention is riveted on your message.

EXERCISES

1. Name five types of structural patterns you can use when designing a speech.
2. What type of pattern would you use for the following topics:

- Climate in Africa
- How to reduce road rage
- Famous explorers
- The history of tyrants
- Inflation

3. Visit the History channel archive of speeches **www.historychannel.com/speeches. index.html** or **www.stanfordplus.com/education/inspirationals/speeches.php.** Select a famous speech and listen to it. Find examples of supporting material used by the speaker such as quotations, testimony, examples, narration, definitions, and statistics. Share your findings with your classmates.

4. Form into groups of four. Each member of the group will search the Internet for a Canadian speech. Print out a transcript of the speech for each member of your group. For the speech that you have selected, identify all the signposts, transitions, internal previews, and internal summaries used by the speaker. One at a time, each student will summarize the content of the speech he or she has chosen and then point out the connectives the speaker has used.

5. Visit **gos.sbc.edu/**, which displays women's speeches from around the world. Select a particular speech, which you find effective. Get into pairs. Give your partner a copy of the speech you have chosen. Discuss the structure of the speech, how the speech opened and concluded, and how connectives were used. Tell your partner why this speech impressed you and how it achieved its effectiveness.

SUMMARY

This chapter discussed the five types of organizational patterns used in speeches: the topical pattern, the spatial or geographical pattern, the chronological pattern, the cause and effect pattern, and the problem-solution pattern. We then discussed and illustrated the variety of supporting materials a good public speaker could use, such as: statistics, quotations, testimony, examples, narration, and definitions. To link the content together, the student is encouraged to use connectives such as signposts, transitions, and previews and internal summaries.

SUGGESTED READING

Bartlett, John. *Bartlett's Familiar Quotations by John Bartlett*. Toronto: Little, Brown & Company, 1980.

Colombo, John Robert. *Colombo's New Canadian Quotations*. Edmonton: Hurtig Publishers, 1987.

Fadiman, Clifton. *The Little Brown Book of Anecdotes*. Toronto: Little, Brown & Company, 1995.

The Reader's Guide to Periodical Literature

REFERENCES

Statistics Canada. National Longitudinal Survey on Children and Youth: Childhood Obesity, 1994-1999.

| Interview | **Dr. Robert Buckman** |

Dr. Robert Buckman is a medical oncologist, a Professor in the Department of Medicine at the University of Toronto, a television broadcaster, and a leading clinical researcher in communications theory.

Q **My first question is: Which public speakers have left an indelible impression on you?**

A Very, very important question! Always the ones that have, as it were, lifted my pulse rate and left me totally excited. They were people talking about a very complicated area and making me a map of the area so that I understood the general layout of the subject, which I could then remember. Now the one speaker that I probably will remember every single word of–this would probably bore your audience out of their minds–but it was a guy talking about the way cancers—primary cancers—probably control the spread of their secondaries. This is a man who is now world-famous, named Judah Folkman. I heard him about seven or eight years ago giving a talk about his work, stretching back over twenty years, and at the end of it I under-

stood material that I had never understood before. It was absolutely astounding and I remember that very distinctly.

Q **Now, in terms of Canadians, is there somebody that you think is a strong speaker?**

A Actually, there are two now that I think about. The first one is the television broadcaster, Pamela Wallin. She spoke at a debate at which I was the moderator, and it was one of those debates in which you had to argue against your own position; it was "Journalism is the lowest profession," the lowest profession of all. She had to argue in favour of that motion, of course, as a journalist. She was absolutely brilliant. She had written it beautifully and written it to be spoken, and she was absolutely wonderful. What was so joyous about her talk was that she took a lot of risks. But it was very clear, after the first couple of minutes, that she knew exactly what she was doing so that the more risky it became, the more the audience rejoiced—so they were laughing with relief and joy as well. It was fabulous!

The other really good speaker, who is a terrific guy, is Bob Rae. He plays with the audience and he also takes risks. He would take a risk, then tell the audience that he's taking a risk, which enrolls them and recruits them, and brings them back on board. Both speakers are enormously enjoyable.

Q **What do you think are the attributes of a good speaker?**

A Okay, number one: it is essential that you are not too nervous when you get up there. Number two: (which relates to number one) you have to know where you're going with every point that you want to make. Number three: you have to be sensitive to how you're doing as you go along. Number four: (which is the essence of number three) you *have* to acknowledge what is happening between you and the audience. If they fail to laugh when you intended them to laugh and it is quite obvious that you intended them to laugh, you have to say something like, "That's funny, that went well at rehearsal" or, "I'm on my own with this one," or "Obviously that didn't tickle you, but my agent said it was quite good," or something like that. You know, "It worked very well at the matinee." If they laugh unexpectedly when you were saying something serious, you say something along the lines of, "Obviously you're ahead of me here because you see something funny in this and I thought it was quite serious, but we'll move on, we'll move on." You must acknowledge what goes on between you and the audience. Acknowledgement is the absolute key. And then the fifth and final one is the famous university rule: "Tell 'em what you're going to tell 'em, tell 'em and then tell 'em you've told them."

Q **What started your addiction to speaking—was it the love of an audience interaction?**

A We haven't got time for me to discuss this in detail! No, I guess, to be liked and to be accepted and then to know that you've done the job well. What I do nowadays is much more difficult because I'm teaching communication skills. I'm talking about dying, I'm talking about cancer, I'm talking about complementary medicine-these are all very, very difficult subjects to talk about. I find that when I'm, as it were, feeling my way with an audience and exploring a new area, and particularly in the question period, it is absolutely ecstatic! I love that.

Q **How do you prepare for a speech?**

A In my cases, most of the speeches I enjoy giving are on medical topics to do with cancer research or something like that. I first prepare a set of slides. I mean, I may use them many times but I can't give the speech until I've done the slides. I have a few rules, one of which is that if you're talking for an hour, eight slides are plenty unless you have major pictures. What you want are the seven or eight points that are really important which the audience will remember. The slides are just to show the audience that you've done your homework and you're not making it up. I cannot possibly give a talk unless I know the seven or eight main points. Then I think it's very important that I have some idea of how I'm going to illustrate the points.

Q **How much time do you spend preparing?**

A All my life—in the sense that when I'm giving a talk, I'm talking about what I do as a cancer doctor or a researcher or a cancer communicator, so it's very difficult to say how much individual time I take to prepare. But it is very important that you have the main points. When I'm doing a new talk that I've never done before, I'm usually a little bit nervous about it, so I write the seven or eight main points down on a 3x5 card and I carry it. Even if I don't take it out.

Q   **Okay, the next one is–and this is for the students–is the ability to give an effective speech or presentation a crucial skill in the business and professional world?**

A   Being able to explain? Yes. Being able to explain publicly. For the vast majority of us, your success, as it were, depends on your ability to change other people's mind. So explaining is it. You've *got* to be able to explain yourself and that means you've got to think about what is the crux of what you want to say.

Q   **Are there any speaking habits that annoy you?**

A   Yes. I once did a presentation on this about 20 years ago. I call it "duplex presentation" where the speaker flashes the slide up and then says *exactly* the same words that appear on the slide. Just have a few words on the slide to remind the audience while you talk about the important issues.

Q   **Let's look at the vocal element. A dull, monotonous voice can** hamper the effective delivery of a speech. What kind of voice do you like to listen to?

A   The speaker must be *really* sensitive in terms of speed. The important thing is not the timbre of the voice but sensitivity. I mean, there are comedians who specialize in a monotone presentation but they know when they're working and they know when they're not.

Q   **Irving Layton, the Canadian poet, said: "An aphorism should be like a burr: sting, stick, and leave a little soreness afterwards." How important is it to use aphorisms, quotations, and anecdotes in a speech?**

A   Oh, my own personal rule is: only use quotations as something to fill out and support totally. I think the same is true of an aphorism, unless you're making it up yourself. That's absolutely fine. But anecdotes to me, they've got to be personal; "This happened to me…" If somebody wants to talk to you about tolerance, for example, then you've got to find an anecdote that resonates with the listener.

Q   **What advice would you give to novice speakers?**

A   Start somewhere where the pain of failure is not too bad. Start somewhere where you can fail relatively safely and work your way up. It takes a long time.

chapter six

Spoken Language
and Stylistic Devices

.

Eloquence is the power to translate a truth into language perfectly intelligible to a person to whom you speak.

—Ralph Waldo Emerson

LEARNING OBJECTIVES

- To learn about the techniques and devices that can be used to add colour to your speech

- To identify 14 different stylistic devices that can be utilized when crafting your speech

- To offer concrete examples of each type of device

- To present exercises to test your knowledge

We use language to stimulate the audience to action, to enchant, to entertain, to inform, to transport the listener to new uncharted realms, and above all, to convey our message accurately and appropriately. Vivid language makes the speech compelling and colourful.

When you think of quotable quotes by famous people, which lines reverberate in your ear? Do you think of, "Ask not what your country can do for you, ask what you can do for your country" by J.F. Kennedy, or "We have nothing to fear but fear itself" by Franklin D. Roosevelt? Or do you recall the widely quoted aphorism by Pierre Trudeau, "There's no place for the state in the bedrooms of the nation."? Even Clinton's line, "I did not have sex with that woman, Monica Lewinsky" has now become a sound bite for television and will be recalled for decades to come.

A well-turned phrase remains embedded in our minds. S.I. Hayakwa in *Language in Thought and Action* says, "Like snakes under the influence of a snake charmer's flute, we are swayed by the musical phrases of the verbal hypnotist." To capture and retain the attention of our audience, we need to become a "verbal hypnotist."

As you embark upon the process of preparing a speech, bear in mind that the talk is meant to be heard. If we wrote the way we spoke, would anyone read us? If we spoke the way we wrote, would anyone listen? As you plan the talk, listen to it with your audience's ears. (See yourself with your audience's eyes.) Aim for a conversational style, which will enable you to talk **to** the audience, not **at** them.

Mark Twain knew the importance of precision of language. He said, "A powerful agent is the right word. Whenever we come upon one of these intensely right words, the resulting effect is physical as well as spiritual." Pepper your speech with colourful language and the precise word.

With the advent of e-mail and the use of technology as a means to communicate, scant attention is being given to the beauty of language and accuracy of expression. Speed is what seems to count in this form of communication. Those who cannot spell can draw on the convenience of spell-check to disguise their weakness. However, nothing will compensate for the deficiency of being unable to structure and craft a talk with care, competence, and clarity.

There are numerous techniques for you to employ in your speech writing. Once you have planned your talk thoroughly, go back through your content and see where you can enhance and enrich your message by using some of the following stylistic devices.

STYLISTIC DEVICES

Alliteration

Alliteration is the repetition of the same consonant sound in words or syllables succeeding each other at close intervals. Here are some examples of alliteration:

In 1985 Mario Cuomo, the articulate former mayor of New York City, said, "You campaign in **poetry**, you govern in **prose**."

J.F. Kennedy at Amherst College in 1963 proclaimed, "When **power** leads man toward arrogance, **poetry** reminds him of his limitations."

The plosive *p* consonant reaches our eardrum gently, yet with impact.

When Adrienne Clarkson, the Governor General, delivered the Eulogy for Canada's Unknown Soldier in Ottawa on May 28, 2000, she coined the alliterative phrase "smithy of sacrifice." In closing the eulogy she said, "The wars fought by Canadians in the twentieth century were not fought for the purpose of uniting Canada, but the country was forged in the **smithy** of **sacrifice**. We will not forget them."

René Lévesque, in his 1980 "We are Quebecers" speech to members of the French National Assembly repeated the d and n sounds, "This is what **defeat** broke up, but it did not manage to **dispel** the **dream**. It was a dream, which, though **normally** unacknowledged, was strong enough to **nourish**, even today, a **national** identity and a **national** idea that only **numerical** weakness and total isolation prevented us from realizing."

Trudeau was a dynamic, passionate speaker and he recognized the power that alliteration had in a speech. In Montreal in 1969, he said: "Don't **drop** out, **drop** in. Don't **cop** out, **complete**. Don't **exit**, **excel**."

At the National Newspaper Awards Dinner, 1972, Trudeau used alliteration again when he spoke about Canada, saying, "**Canada** is not a **country** for the **cold** of heart or for the **cold** of feet."

Jean Monty, Chairman and CEO of BCE Inc., addressed the Empire Club of Canada in Toronto in September 2000 about the expanding communications industry. In this extract he used alliteration, "That's why we can pretty safely say that **data** will be **dominant**…and the Internet will continue to **drive** change in the way we communicate with each other and interact with information in the future."

The repetition of the *d* consonant gives greater emphasis to the importance of data in the future.

The American president, Franklin D. Roosevelt said, "The truth is **found** when men are **free** to pursue it."

The soft, fricative *f* gives us the feeling of freedom.

John Turner, a past Prime Minister of Canada, was questioned about the fate of Canadians under the terms of the Free Trade agreement. Using the *h* sound for his alliterative sentence, he said, "We will not only be **harmonized**, we will be **homogenized**, and we will be **hosed**." He also used a little humour when he incorporated the word "hosed" in this quote that appeared in the Montreal *Gazette* on June 14, 1988.

Use alliteration judiciously to avoid overuse. We do not want the audience to focus on our technique, but rather on the reception of the message.

Assonance

Assonance is the repetition of vowel sounds. Remember we are writing for the ear and this is a good device to employ when writing your talk. Speak the following sentence aloud and notice how the oh sound slows down your speech:

The **low moans** and **groans** were heard **o**ver and **o**ver.

The following sentence combines alliteration, where the letter *b* is repeated, and assonance, where the oo sound is repeated:

The **blue moon bewitches**.

This paints a vivid picture and evokes a mood.

Antithesis

Antithesis is when two parallel but contrasting ideas are contained in one sentence. Politicians frequently employ this technique for dramatic effect.

Kennedy used antithesis masterfully in his 1961 inaugural address, "If a free society cannot help the many who are poor, it cannot save the few who are rich."

He did so again, when he said, "Let us never negotiate out of fear, but let us never fear to negotiate."

In Abraham Lincoln's second inaugural address, he used the phrase, "With malice toward none, with charity for all…"

Trudeau used antithesis during the October Crisis Proclamation in October 16, 1970, "Those who would have divided us will have united us."

By using antithesis, Trudeau stresses the importance of unity for Canada. When you want to emphasize a key idea, use antithesis.

Repetition

Repetition is a powerful device to use in speech writing. It reinforces a theme, as we hear in the "I have a dream" speech by Martin Luther King. Repetition helps the listener stay on track as it offers a rhythm to which we respond.

Chief Dan George, the elected chief of the Co-Salish Indians, used the technique of repetition in his lament for Confederation Speech in 1967. He repeats the phrase "I have known you" three times in the second paragraph of the speech:

> How long have I known you, Oh Canada? A hundred years? Yes, a hundred years. And many, many seelarum more. And today, when you celebrate your hundred years, Oh Canada, I am sad for all the Indian people throughout the land."
>
> For I have known you when your forests were mine; when they gave me my meat and my clothing. I have known you in your streams and rivers where your fish flashed and danced in the sun, where the waters said come, come, and eat of my abundance. I have known you in the freedom of your winds. And my spirit, like the winds, once roamed your good lands.

This use of repetition gives us a sense of historical connection to the land and waters of Canada. This technique serves as a device to unite the listener and the speaker.

In the final paragraph of his speech, he repeats "shall" and "I shall":

> I shall see our young braves and our chiefs sitting in the houses of law and government, ruling and being ruled by the knowledge and freedoms of our great land. So shall we shatter the barriers of our isolation. So shall the next hundred years be the greatest in the proud history of our tribes and nations.

The repetition of "so shall" gives a sense of hope and endurance.

Brian Mulroney, an ex-prime minister, commented on news reports about Marcel Masse's alleged irregular campaign spending and used repetition in his response. He said, "I think people have to recognize that it happens in families, it happens in marriages, it happens in business, it happens in trade unions, it happens in government."

He appears to be justifying the excess spending by using the phrase "it happens" repeatedly.

In Sir Winston Churchill's "I have nothing to offer but blood, toil, tears and sweat" address in London on May 13, 1940, his speech swayed the crowds and the repetition of the word "victory" impacted and uplifted the listeners profoundly: "You ask, what is our aim? I can answer in one word: Victory. Victory at all costs, victory in spite of all terror, victory however long and hard the road may be; for without victory, there is no survival."

In his address to the Empire Club of Canada in September 2000, Jean Monty, chairman and CEO of BCE Inc., let the words "Great Expectations" echo throughout his speech. Here is how he used this technique to great effect. He opened his speech in the following way:

> GREAT EXPECTATIONS...when I first heard the theme of this conference—three things came to mind: ... maternity clothes... Charles Dickens... and the "GREAT EXPECTATIONS" we all share for this exciting, expanding communications industry.
>
> Dickens' *Great Expectations* was written during 1860 and 1861.
>
> So what? Well, let's look at what else was happening around the world just then.

Analogy

Analogy is a comparison between two things that are normally unlike each other.

When Churchill addressed the Canadian Parliament in Ottawa on December 30, 1941, his speech became known as the "Some Chicken! Some Neck" speech. Churchill compared the Nazis to "gangs of bandits" and described how England has been likened to a chicken:

> There will be no halting or half measures. There will be no compromise or parley. These gangs of bandits have sought to darken the light of the world, have sought to stand between the common people of all the lands, and their march forward into their inheritance. They shall, themselves, be cast into the pit of death and shame and only when the earth has been cleansed and purged of their crimes and of their villainies will we turn from the task which they have forced upon us—a task which we were reluctant to undertake, but which we shall now most faithfully and punctiliously discharge.
>
> When I warned them that Britain would fight on alone whatever they did, their generals told their Prime Minister and his divided cabinet, "In three weeks, England will have her neck wrung like a chicken." Some chicken! Some neck!

Here is what Edward L. Greenspan Q.C., a well-known legal mind in Canada, said about analogy (Barnard, 1996):

> It helps people know precisely what you mean; for instance a cabbie told Justice Berger of the U.S. Supreme Court: "Putting people in prison is like putting clothes in the wash without any soap. The clothes get wet but no dirt comes out."

When a speaker uses analogy, the listener often grasps the meaning with greater ease.

Metaphors

Metaphors are implied comparisons. Used in a presentation or talk, metaphors leave a powerful visual imprint on the listener.

Trudeau, speaking at the National Press Club in Washington in 1969, was referring to the United States of America when saying:

> Living next to you is in some ways like sleeping with an elephant; no matter how friendly and even-tempered is the beast—if I may call it that—one is affected by every twitch and grunt. Even a friendly nuzzling can sometimes lead to frightening consequences.

This metaphor emphasizes the size of our powerful neighbour in a way that simple description would not capture.

In November 1959, Premier Joseph R. Smallwood of Newfoundland used the metaphor of a barracuda when he described the International Woodworkers of America. He said, "But the I.W.A. is the barracuda of the trade unions of Canada…a savage shark of a union…able, extremely able, extremely clever, with enormous ability and experience. They can do a better job of brainwashing than anybody, and they are absolutely unscrupulous."

Simile

Similes make direct comparisons, using the words "like" or "as."

Churchill used reptiles as his favourite simile. He referred to the Nazis as follows: "The Nazis are like boa constrictors that first befoul their victim with the filthy spray of their propaganda before they engorge it."

Onomatopoeia

Onomatopoeia is the use of words that sound like their meaning, e.g., buzz, zoom, swish, crunch, crackle, hum.

The listener's senses are engaged when a speaker uses onomatopoeia. For example, here is a sentence using the words "crackling" and "buzzing":

The stillness of the autumn morning was broken by the crackling of the newly lit fire and the buzzing of the bees departing for a warmer climate.

Asyndeton

Asyndeton occurs when the conjunctions between linked sentences are omitted and when used, the speech becomes more forceful and has more impact.

Using asyndeton, Brian Mulroney spoke to members of the Economic Club of New York in December 1984, and described the importance of maintaining good relations between Canada and the United States. He said: "President Kennedy once described the relationship between our two countries in this way: 'Geography made us neighbours, history made us friends, economics made us partners, and necessity has made us allies.'"

John F. Kennedy also used this device when he said, "...we shall pay any price, bear any burden, meet any hardship, support any friend or oppose any foe to assure the survival and the success of liberty." (John F. Kennedy, "Inaugural Address", Washington DC, January 1961)

In November 1959, Premier Joseph R. Smallwood spoke using asyndeton:

I think sincerely, if you were to take a secret ballot vote in Newfoundland today, except for a few cranks, a few malcontents, a few crackpots (and we have a fair share of these in Newfoundland) I doubt that more than a hundred in all of Newfoundland would vote against union with Canada.

Hyperbole

Hyperbole is an exaggerated statement used to draw attention to a situation or problem.

Saddam Hussein coined the phrase: "The mother of all wars." He used this form of exaggeration as a scare tactic to instill fear.

Personification

Personification is when an animal, object, or concept is given human characteristics, feelings or qualities.

Pierre Trudeau, during the October Crisis Proclamation on October 16 1970, used personification in this way, "Violence, unhappily, is no stranger to this decade." George Bush personified his nation in this way, "Ours is a nation that has shed the blood of war and cried the tears of depression."

Rhyme

We all respond innately to **rhyme** and rhythm, beginning with our exposure to nursery rhymes as children. Listening to rhyme as adults affects us at a deep level.

When the lawyer Johnny Cochrane defended O.J. Simpson at his trial for the murder of his wife, Nicole Simpson, and her friend, Ron Goldman, he used the now famous line "if it doesn't fit, you must acquit." O.J. Simpson was asked, during the course of the trial, to try on a glove left at the crime scene. When he tried it on, it was too small for him. Johnny Cochrane made effective use of rhyme during his closing arguments using the words "fit" and "acquit."

Anecdote

An **anecdote** is a short story that is interesting, amusing, or biographical.

Everyone loves the well-told story, an anecdote. In fact, I would strongly urge you to include an anecdote in every speech. Begin collecting stories you like and place them in an "Anecdote File." When next you are called upon to deliver a talk, search through your story file for an appropriate anecdote that will serve to explain, illustrate, or simply entertain your audience. Here are two amusing anecdotes:

Churchill, the masterful orator, was the subject of many anecdotes. Here are a few personal favourites. Churchill had few illusions about his effectiveness as a speaker. One of his friends once said to him: "Aren't you impressed to see ten thousand people gathered to hear you speak?" Sir Winston responded: "No—because ten times as many would come to see me hanged."

When Sir David McNee, who headed the crack London Metropolitan Police Force, addressed the Canadian Association of Chiefs of Police, he gave an example of British police humour by quoting the following parody of a Metropolitan Police examination question:

> You are on patrol when an explosion occurs on the next street. Upon investigation you find a large hole and an overturned van lying nearby. Inside the van there is a strong smell of alcohol. Both occupants, a man and a woman, are injured. You know he is an unlicensed driver and his passenger is the wife of your inspector. A motorist stops to offer assistance and you recognize him as a felon wanted for armed robbery. Suddenly, another man runs out of a nearby house shouting that his wife is expecting a baby and that the shock of the explosion has brought the birth imminent. At that moment you hear someone crying for help, having been blown into an adjacent canal by the explosion. He cannot swim. Describe in a few words what you would do.

Sir David then said that one of his bright young officers was alleged to have given this problem some thought. The officer picked up his pen and wrote, "Remove uniform and mingle with the crowd."–International Fire Fighter. You can visit **www.legendsmagazine. net/11/police.htm** to read this amusing anecdote. If you were speaking to a group of law enforcement officers you could incorporate it.

Poetry

Poetry provides a vast resource for the presenter. Poetry has been described as the best words in the best order. So when you can "borrow" from the some of the best poetry and use it to enhance your presentation, do so.

If you were giving a presentation on Birds of North America and a description of the eagle was required, you could open the talk as follows:

> He clasps the crag with hookèd hands:
> Close to the sun in lonely lands,
> Ringed with the azure world, he stands.
>
> The wrinkled sea beneath him crawls;
> He watches from his mountain walls,
> And like a thunderbolt he falls.
>
> Can you guess which bird Alfred Lord Tennyson refers to in this poem? If you guessed correctly you would have said, *The Eagle*. Well, today my presentation to the Ornithological Society will be on this majestic bird, the eagle.

Tennyson's imagery is so vivid that we can picture the bird in our mind's eye. He incorporates alliteration when he uses the "c" consonant in "clasps the crag" and the "h" consonant in "hooked hands." Descriptive adjectives like "azure" and "wrinkled" also enhance the picture. When you read this poem aloud, you will notice how the rhyme scheme works so well. The first and second stanzas are each composed of only three lines. The three lines in Stanza One all end with the same rhyming sounds: "hands," "lands," and "sands". Stanza Two follows the same pattern. This time the rhyming words are crawls, walls, and falls. A lovely cadence is provided for the listener's ear because the poet employs this technique. The poem seduces the listener who now wants to listen further. The speaker then poses a question, "Can you guess which bird Alfred Lord Tennyson refers to in this poem?" Now the audience becomes engaged further since they are stimulated to answer the question in their minds.

If you want to lead, motivate, or inspire a team, use poetry to do the job.

In a eulogy I delivered for a friend of mine, who passed away in the prime of his life, I quoted from Thomas Grey's *Elegy Written in a Country Churchyard*. I wanted to convey that my friend's life was terminated prematurely and that he was unable to reveal all the innate talent that would forever lie dormant. I read this verse from the eulogy, which summed up that idea:

> Full many a gem of purest ray serene
> The dark unfathomed caves of ocean bear:
> Full many a flower is born to blush unseen,
> And waste its sweetness on the desert air.
>
> Our friend Stephen's life was snuffed out before he was able to blossom, before he was able to reach his fullest potential and shine like the purest gem he was.

Six-time NBA champion Phil Jackson, who coached the Chicago Bulls and the Los Angeles Lakers professional basketball teams, inspired his team by reading from *The Law of the Jungle*, a Rudyard Kipling poem:

Now this is the Law of the Jungle—
    As old and as true as the sky;
And the Wolf that shall keep it may prosper,
    But the Wolf that shall break it must die.
As the creeper that girdles the tree-trunk
    The Law runneth forward and back—
But the strength of the Pack is the Wolf,
    And strength of the Wolf is the Pack.

The image of the wolf is a very powerful one and, by implication, the basketball player could identify with the wolf and recognize that to succeed, he needs to acknowledge that he is part of a team, just as the wolf is part of the pack.

Phil Jackson knew and used the power of poetry to motivate and stimulate his team. As a student who will be called upon to present at college or at university and ultimately in the working environment, remember poetry can lend punch and pizzazz to your presentation. As you come across examples of poetry that are meaningful to you, take note of them for future reference and use.

Historical References

To give the audience a sense of time, an historic reference will often anchor your speech. If, for example, you are delivering your speech on November 22, you might begin it this way:

Today is November 22, 2003. November 22 is a date of great significance. In 1497, Vasco da Gama, the Portuguese explorer, became the first individual to sail around the Cape of Good Hope en route to India. In 1942, Mt. St. Helens in Washington erupted for the first time. On this date in 1917, The National Hockey League was established. In 1963, John F. Kennedy, the 35th President of the United States of America was assassinated in Dallas. On November 22, 1977, the Concorde, the world's first supersonic airliner, began regular service to New York City.

Why do I list all those events that are of importance to civilization? Why do I need to tell you that it was on November 22, 1890, that Charles De Gaulle, President of France, was born? Well, November 22, 1976, was my birthdate. Today, I stand before you to present the genealogy of my family. I am proud to be associated, even in some remote way, with these famous figures and these noteworthy events.

By using historical data, you let the audience feel that matters of important significance are being discussed, and the audience will listen to you more attentively. They will also recognize some of the events mentioned and this will create a sense of familiarity for them.

Edward L. Greenspan, Q.C., Canada's noted criminal lawyer and author, spoke to the Empire Club on November 19, 1987, on "The Role of the Defence Counsel in Canadian Society." He made an historical reference in his opening:

Thank you for the kind introduction. I can now die and hopefully go to heaven. I have spoken everywhere over the years but never at The Empire Club and The Empire Club is "Carnegie Hall." I have now made it in the big city. I even joined The Empire Club five years ago hoping you would notice me. I don't even mind that I am the 2521st speaker you have had in your 84-year history. Or that you waited so long to invite me. I am here and nobody can take this away from me.

Greenspan, in mentioning that he is the 2521st speaker in the 84-year history of the Empire Club, lets the members know that he has a respect for the club and its long history. He conveys his pride at being asked to address the club when he says, "Or that you waited so long to invite me. I am here and nobody can take this away from me."

When planning a presentation entitled "The Value of Persistence," you may research famous people who demonstrated this attribute. You could look at Thomas Edison who discovered there were 157 ways that didn't work in developing the light bulb. Read up on Helen Keller who persevered and finally became a beacon of light to others who are blind. You may decide to use Abraham Lincoln as an example of perseverance. The presentation could begin like this:

Which historical figure experienced the following challenges?

At age 22 he failed in business

23 he was defeated in his run for the legislature

24 he failed again in business

25 he was elected to the Legislature

26 his sweetheart died

27 he had a nervous breakdown

29 he was defeated for Speaker

31 he was defeated for Elector

34 he was defeated for Congress

37 he was elected to Congress

39 he was defeated for Congress

46 he was defeated for Senate

47 he was defeated for Vice President

49 he was defeated for Senate

51 he was elected President of the United States of America

It was Abraham Lincoln. He was a man of great determination who said, "Always bear in mind that your own resolution to succeed is more important than any other one thing." He certainly lived by the maxim he coined.

You can access this kind of information by using the Internet. Log on to **www.idea-bank.com**, type in the day and month you need, and a long list of interesting facts will come up.

Ruth W. Gregory's *Anniversaries and Holidays* is another good resource.

If you use historical references and relate them to current events or your present situation, you will convey knowledge and creativity, while capturing the interest of your audience.

Biblical References

The device of using "old" language and relating it to the present can make a big impact. Using words from the Bible, the Torah, or the Koran can add to your credibility and offers a sense of timelessness.

In a presentation on "Creating Balance in Our Lives," a speaker might quote the following from Exodus 35:2.27:

> Six days shall work be done, but on the seventh day you shall have a holy Sabbath of solemn rest to the Lord; whosoever does any work on it shall be put to death.

The speaker goes on to say:

> In our modern, harried lives, we certainly do not find enough hours in a day to complete our personal and professional tasks. The modern housewife/mother/ breadwinner faces enormous barriers to creating leisure time for herself. The Bible advocates a day of rest. This is a sound idea. We need respite from endless work. We need a day to recharge our worn-down batteries. We need a day to restore our dwindling energy supply. Do this for your mental and emotional security and sanity. Today, the threat of death, which the Bible mentions, is not a factor in our decision making. But to neglect yourself in favour of your work will lead to inevitable personal decline.

By using this biblical quote at the opening, we are quoting from a reliable and revered source. Quoting a higher authority adds credence to your key message. Not only are you encouraging your audience to find balance in their lives, but the Bible, a resource that is meaningful to so many people, supports your argument.

Here's another example of using a biblical reference.

A Canadian soldier returns from the war in Afghanistan and is asked to share his experiences with his local community. He speaks of the hardships he has endured and says:

> As a Canadian thrust into battle, I have witnessed heartache. I have witnessed the heartbreak of a child torn viciously from his mother's embrace, a child forced to witness the beating of his mother simply because she violated the Taliban decree which forbids women from talking to any male who is not a member of her family. I have witnessed the vacant stares of the Afghan child whose belly is hollow and distended. I have seen children under the age of 10, toiling endlessly making rugs, for the meagre pay of 50 cents per day.

> I have been a stranger in a strange land. In this world of strangers I learned a valuable lesson. No matter what our nationality, our race, religion, or sex is, we are all cut from the same cloth. We are all part of the larger fabric called mankind.
>
> As Canadians, we need to be aware of our limited, myopic view of the world. The continued hardship of the Afghanistan people and the Afghan women, in particular, needs be eased and we can all play a part in helping that ideal come to fruition. We, as Canadians, are blessed with a high standard of living. We need to distribute some of our wealth to aid and assist those less fortunate than ourselves. For after all, we would not want the words of Psalm 49: 1-20 to haunt us and echo down the corridors of time. The Bible says, "A man who has riches without understanding is like the beasts that perish." Let us not stand by while others perish. Let us help them prosper.

This soldier aims to stir up an emotional response from the audience. He uses the biblical quote, "A man who has riches without understanding is like the beasts that perish," to encourage the listeners to assist the cause of the Afghan people. For after all, they would not want to identify themselves with beasts that perish.

I'd like to make reference to a speech delivered in 1914 by our own William L. Mackenzie King. In this excerpt from his speech on "Culture and Religion," Mackenzie King embraces two stylistic devices—historical and biblical references. The biblical reference he employs here is not necessarily a direct quotation from any religious source, but rather, King uses God's name to support his point:

> With the Greek, let us measure our contribution to civilization in what we give to humanities. With the Hebrew, let us believe that God continues to work through the centuries and that He may work for continents as well as men. With the founder of our faith, let us believe that all life is sacred and all human life but the reflected image of the divine.

Remember that the device you select should be in keeping with the occasion, the purpose of your presentation, and the audience for whom it is intended. Use common sense. It would not be sound judgement to make constant biblical references when your audience is a group of atheists.

EXERCISES

1. Define each of the following words:
   - Assonance
   - Antithesis
   - Repetition
   - Analogy
   - Metaphor
   - Simile
   - Onomatopoeia

- Asyndeton
- Hyperbole
- Personification
- Rhyme
- Anecdote

2. Find or write an example to illustrate each device:
   - Assonance
   - Antithesis
   - Repetition
   - Analogy
   - Metaphor
   - Simile
   - Onomatopoeia
   - Asyndeton
   - Hyperbole
   - Personification
   - Rhyme
   - Anecdote
   - Biblical quotation

3. Name the device used in the following phrases:

   Ask not what your country can do for you, ask what you can do for your country.
   —J.F. Kennedy

   Virtue has never been as respectable as money.
   —Mark Twain

   Only those who dare to fail greatly can ever achieve greatly.
   —Robert F. Kennedy

   Necessity is the mother of invention.
   —Plato

   Wise men talk because they have something to say; fools, because they have to say something.
   —Plato

   The mistake a lot of politicians make is in forgetting they've been appointed and thinking they've been anointed.
   —Mrs. Claude Pepper

   A pinch of probably is worth a pound of perhaps.
   —James Thurber

   One small step for man, one giant leap for mankind.
   —Neil Armstrong

   A man's life is dyed the colour of his imagination.
   —Marcus Aurelius

Let us have faith that right makes might; and in that faith, let us, to the end, dare to do our duty as we understand it.

—Abraham Lincoln

The real danger of our technological age is not so much that machines will begin to think like men, but that men will begin to think like machines.

—Sidney J. Harris

We must dream of an aristocracy of achievement arising out of a democracy of opportunity.
—Thomas Jefferson

We cannot expect to make everyone our friend, but we can try to make no one our enemy.
—Richard M. Nixon

I once picked up a small girl who was wandering the street, lost. Hunger was written all over her face. Who knows how long it had been since she had eaten anything! I offered her a piece of bread. The little one started eating it, crumb by crumb. I told her, "Eat, eat the bread! Aren't you hungry?" She looked at me and said, "I am just afraid that when I run out of bread, I'll still be hungry."
—Mother Theresa

In the developed countries there is a poverty of intimacy, a poverty of spirit, of loneliness, of lack of love. There is no greater sickness in the world today than that one.
—Mother Theresa

I would rather have Roosevelt in a wheelchair than Reagan on a horse.
—Jesse Jackson

I stand before you today, the representative of a family in grief, in a country in mourning before a world in shock.
—Earl Spencer

4. Make a list of possible topics that would be enhanced by the use of an historical reference.

5. Read the following extract from a speech made by Joey Smallwood.

    (a) Make a note of all the speech and language devices that Smallwood used in constructing his talk.

    (b) In class, share your insights and observations. Discuss how successfully these techniques were used. Did they contribute towards the overall effectiveness of the appeal?

The following is an extract of a speech by Joey Smallwood, derived from a radio archive dating from January 23, 1948, after the Newfoundland National Convention. In this speech, Smallwood spoke to sway public opinion to embrace the idea of confederation with Canada.

I wish to choose my words carefully. I want my words to express exactly what I mean. I say that never in history, in this or any country, was any handful of people so looted, so plundered as our people have been since this late war broke out. It was in many cases cold, calculated plunder. If Major Cashin would talk about the plunder by those firms instead of talking about the plunder of the public chest, he would do more good for the people of Newfoundland. They took all the profits the traffic would bear, and all the government would let them take, and in may cases a lot more than the government would allow them to take. I have never heard or read of a handful of people whose pockets were so shamelessly looted as were the pockets of our Newfoundland people during the war. While their sons were offering their very lives for the brave new world they were promised, they themselves were attacked by a looting, monopolistic plutocracy here in Newfoundland.

I will tell you what this late war has done to our country. It has strengthened and solidified our new rich. It has put great fortunes into the hands of some who did not have them before the war, and it has doubled the fortunes of those who did have them before the war. It has drawn the reins of monopoly closer, it has fastened the chains of class domination more securely upon the masses of our people. Our struggling masses have managed to renew the wallpaper in their homes; they have managed to get together a bit more furniture and household utensils, to paint their houses, and generally to do a bit of replenishing. Those of them whose families were not large, and who were not quite so far down when the war broke out, have even managed to lay aside a little modest savings. But the great majority of our people are fast falling back to where they were before the war broke out, back into the same shameful old rut of poverty and insecurity. It has widened the gulf between the people and their economic masters. If the poor have not become absolutely poorer, it certainly cannot be said that the rich have not become richer, for they have become richer. The gulf between them has widened and deepened. And of few countries in this world today can the poet's words be more truly spoken:

Ill fares the land, to hastening ills a prey

Where wealth accumulates, and men decay.

This has got to stop. I know our Newfoundland people. I am one of them. I am blood of their blood, bone of their bone, soul of their soul. I am descended from a family that has lived in Newfoundland for over 150 years. My ancestors were fishermen, farmers, shopkeepers, manufacturers, skilled workmen, and artisans. I have dug deep into my country's history, and in so doing I have paid special attention to the story of our people's labours, their battles against nature and against injustice, the story of their endless search for a square deal. I have travelled my country, north, east, south, and west, into a thousand of the thirteen hundred settlements in it. I have been closely and intimately associated with our people. I have fished with the fishermen, logged with the loggers; I have gone down underground with the miners; held trade union meetings right inside the paper mills. I was never so close to our toilers as during those years of the dole, and always, so long as I live, I will remember those years of the dole, and always, so long as I live, I will remember those friends of mine, those toilers who were stricken down by beri-beri, those children who felt the pinch of hunger. I saw the heartbreak in the eyes of patient mothers who had not enough to give their little ones. I saw the baffled, sullen rage of fishermen whose greatest toil and endurance could not provide their families with enough to eat or wear. I attended meetings of the unemployed here in St. John's, but who was I to refuse their invitation to go and speak to them? I saw them in their despairing hundreds waiting around the street corners, waiting for the jobs that never turned up, and around the dole office, and helped to gather second-hand clothes to distribute to those who were half-naked, not for a day or a week or a year, but all through the Depression, I saw them, and I swore an oath to myself that never would I be a party to allowing such things to come back to our people again. I would never be a party to any form of government that would make us know that thing again, and that's why I became a confederate. I became a confederate and discovered that confederation would give our people a half-decent chance in life, and wipe away some of the worst obstacles in their life, and remove some of the millstones that hung around their necks.

They don't expect riches, but only the widest opportunity, by the toil of their hand, to earn an honest living. They have no extravagant ambition to become millionaires, but they do ache for common justice in their own land.

When wilt Thou save the people?
O God of mercy, when?
    Not kings alone, but nations!
Not thrones alone, but men!
    Flowers of Thy heart, O God, are they;
Let them not pass, like weeds, away,
    Their heritage a sunless day.
God save the people!

    Shall crime bring crime for ever,
Strength aiding still the strong?
    Is it Thy will, O Father,
That man shall toil for wrong?
    "No", say Thy mountains; "No", Thy skies;
Man's clouded sun shall brightly rise,
    And songs ascend instead of sighs,
God save the people!

    When wilt Thou save the people?
O God of mercy, when?
    The people, Lord, the people!
Not thrones and crowns, but men!
    God save the people; Thine they are,
Thy children, as Thine angels fair;
    From vice, oppression, and despair,
God save the people!

Mr. Chairman:
Order, please. There is too much noise altogether.

Mr. Smallwood:

Sir, I call upon every member of this Convention to vote for this motion. I call
upon even the bitterest anti-confederate here to vote for it. Hate all confederation all you like. That is your privilege, but do not vote to deny our people of
Newfoundland their rights to decide the matter.

   We here in this Convention have not been given the right to decide what
form of government this country shall have, the people have been given that
right, and they will exercise their right in the referendum.

6. Read through the following excerpts and write down the stylistic devices used. We
   can learn from all nations and all cultures, so a cross-section of extracts is included.
   Write your comments down as follows:

The device _____ is used when the speaker says _____.

   (a) Here is an extract from a translation of the French version of Bloc Québécois
       Leader Lucien Bouchard's speech delivered on October 25, 1995.

       What's going on tonight? Haven't we just heard the same Prime
       Minister talk about a wind of change? Evoking the recognition of
       Quebec as a distinct society and the return of its veto?
          So what is it then, just a few days before the vote, with a
       decision imminent, that makes Mr. Chrétien scrap his strategy and
       discussion? The answer is simple: It's the more and more serious
       possibility of a Yes. In other words, it's not a wind of change that's
       blowing over Ottawa, but a wind of panic....If only the anticipation
       of a Yes, just the possibility of a Yes, makes Ottawa's stubbornness
       waver this much, then just imagine the political impact that a Yes
       will give us, the Yes of a people, the Yes of solidarity.
          These changes that Mr. Chrétien is talking about so suddenly,
       they're not credible... Mr. Chrétien's distinct society, we're familiar
       with it, it's the one that doesn't mean anything. For him, Quebec is
       distinct but equal to the other provinces.

   (b) Nkosi Johnson, a brave young AIDS-stricken man, battled the illness for 12
       years until he finally succumbed to it. He campaigned to raise the aware-
       ness of AIDS. At the International AIDS conference in Durban, South
       Africa, he said, "We are all human beings. We have hands. We have feet.
       We can talk. We have needs just like everyone else. Don't be afraid of us.
       We are all the same."

   (c) Here is a segment of the famous speech by the Right Honourable Sir
       Wilfrid Laurier, delivered January 18, 1904, at the first annual banquet of
       The Canadian Club of Ottawa:

       The more I advance in life—and I am no longer a young man—the
       more I thank Providence that my birth took place in this fair land
       of Canada. Canada has been modest in its history, although its
       history has been heroic in many ways. But its history, in my

estimation, is only commencing. It is commencing in this century. The nineteenth century was the century of the United States. I think we can claim that it is Canada that shall fill the twentieth century. I cannot hope that I shall see much of the development which the future has in store for my country, but whenever my eyes shall close to the light it is my wish—nay, it is my hope—that they close upon a Canada united in all its elements, united in every particular, every element cherishing the tradition of its past, and all uniting in cherishing still more hope for the future.

7. Write an anecdote using at least three different devices within your story.

SUMMARY

This chapter examines how to enhance a speech by using stylistic devices to add colour and vibrancy to your message. The speaker is encouraged to use alliteration, assonance, antithesis, repetition, analogy, metaphors, similes, onomatopoeia, asyndeton, hyperbole, personification, rhyme, anecdotes, poetry, historical references, and biblical references. Examples of each of these techniques are given. Famous speakers embrace these techniques and the student is advised to start his or her own collection of anecdotes and stylistic devices.

As mentioned at the outset of this section, begin your personal collection of anecdotes today. Collect them from newspapers, magazines, books, friends, and real life incidents to provide you with a rich resource.

Take note of the words of Lord Birkett, who said, "It is lucidity that makes speech enjoyable to the hearer; it is grace of speech that makes the spoken word memorable; and grace and lucidity come only from the observance of the primary rules and the willingness to take pains."

So take pains, apply the above-mentioned stylistic devices to create an original, interesting speech that will delight, capture, and hold the attention of your audience.

SUGGESTED READING

Colombo, J.R. *Colombo's New Canadian Quotations*. Edmonton: Hurtig Publishers, 1987.

Hamilton, R. & D. Shields. *The Dictionary of Canadian Quotations and Phrases*. Toronto: McClelland and Stewart, 1979.

Hayakawa, S.I. *Language in Thought and Action*. Surrey: George Allen & Unwin Ltd., 1973.

MacArthur, B. *The Penguin Book of Twentieth-Century Speeches*. Toronto: Penguin Books, 1999.

Rohler, L. & Cook, R. *Great Speeches for Criticism and Analysis*. Greenwood: Alistair Press, 2001.

Safire, William. *Lend Me Your Ears: Great Speeches in History*. New York: W.W. Norton & Company, 1992.

Torricelli, R. & A. Carroll. *In Our Own Words*. New York: Kodansha America Inc., 1999.

REFERENCES

The Koran

The Torah

The Holy Bible, Revised Standard Version

The Holy Bible, King James Version

Barnard, Sandie. *Speaking Our Minds*. Scarborough, ON: Prentice-Hall Canada Inc.,1996.

Gregory, Ruth W. *Anniversaries and Holidays, 3rd ed*. Chicago: American Library Association, 1975.

WEBLINKS

www.idea-bank.com
Idea Bank

goon.stg.brown.edu/bible_browser/pbeasy.Shtml
Bible Reference

Interview | # Diane Francis

Diane Francis has been editor of *The Financial Post* since 1991, and currently contributes a monthly column to Canada's *Maclean's* magazine. She is a well-known author of a number of books and is nationally recognized for her insightful journalism and thought-provoking speeches.

Q Diane, which public speakers have left an indelible impression on you?

A   Well, going back early on in my life, Abba Eban, former Prime Minister of Israel, at the UN Security Council during a time of crisis. It was absolutely spellbinding. Bill Clinton: I've seen him three times in person, most recently in [Davos] World Economic Forum, absolutely magnificent speaker... inclusive, warm, funny, witty.

Q What do you regard as the attributes and qualities of a good speaker?

A   Like a good journalist or entertainer, a good speaker has to know who his or her audience is and what they're interested in. Do not talk down to them. To me, speaking engagements are very similar to writing columns. Over my career I was writing a column for *Maclean's*, for the *Sun* newspaper chain, and for the *Financial Post*, so I was doing material in totally different styles, totally different vocabulary levels, and just fine-tuning it so that it met the needs of the audience. You also have to be engaged and humorous whenever possible. If you're in a situation, which I always love–Q&As—then you have to be empathetic and listen, and try not to talk over people. I've seen rudeness on the podium, "cutesiness," and self-indulgence. Self-indulgence is, I think, one of the biggest failings. I think the vast majority of human beings are terrified of a mike and of public speaking. I think there have been studies that say 90 percent of humanity thinks public speaking is a near-death experience.

Q **Can you share with me your first speaking experience?**

A I did a lot of performances as a child. I've been speaking out all my life so, to me, it's just a commercialized version of my personality. That is to say, I was on Student Council. I was always a schoolyard lawyer defending the less fortunate from the bullies, and speaking up for the students against teachers. I did a lot of acting. I've always been in front of people.

Q **How do you prepare for a speech? What is your process?**

A Well, I have to talk to the organizers of the event to know who is in the audience, their areas of interests, their sensitivities, and what, if anything, they specifically want me to comment on. This phone call is very important. I debrief them and then I have multiples—lots of different speeches, structures, and skeletons—and I flesh them out depending on the audience. I use basically the same structure for most of my speeches….Speakers should keep in mind that people listen selectively. If you're in front of an audience for an hour or half an hour, they will remember what's important for them to remember and they will forget the rest….It starts with a phone call to understand the audience and then my job is to take my knowledge base and download it to them in a palatable, entertaining form.

Q **Oh, I like that. How much time do you spend preparing?**

A Very little. I speak from notes. I never have a text. I don't like lapel mikes. I like a podium where I can refer to my notes.

Q **Do you experience nervousness before a talk?**

A An edge… yes, always.

Q **Do you think that the ability to give an effective speech or presentation is a crucial skill in the business and professional world?**

A I know most of the CEOs and prominent business people in Canada and a number of them abroad in the United States. My observation is that if there is one personality characteristic that seems to be common to all of them–and some may have started as foresters, some may have started as petroleum engineers or geologists or financial analysts or CFAs or insurance underwriters–the ones that get to the very top have an ability, like myself, an aptitude for digesting a huge knowledge base and downloading it in a palatable, entertaining, insightful form to whatever audience. That could be to employees, to investors, to suppliers, to customers. CEOs are incredibly concrete thinkers and concrete speakers. They don't repeat themselves, they don't get lost in jargon—they just cut right through in a very incisive, insightful way…One of the most remarkable human beings I've ever met and seen a lot of is Bill Gates of Microsoft…Gates is twice a genius because he's a business organizational genius. He's created a single enterprise and numerous systems that deploy the technical people. So he has a foot in both camps. You don't have to agree with what he says but he is a very, very articulate man.

Q   **Are there any speech habits that annoy you?**

A   Well, if anybody is hesitant, it's just excruciating…Bad grammar or crudeness, insensitivity, and inappropriate remarks are all very annoying. Anger is annoying—but passion is great. Some people don't know the difference on the podium and I have sometimes crossed a line in a Q&A where I got angry instead of passionate about what I believed in.

Q   **Ralph Waldo Emerson said: "It is a luxury to be understood." How do you ensure that a diverse audience understands your message?**

A   I recently debated in New York City with Naomi Klein, author of *No Logo*…I spent a couple of hours skim-reading her book, anticipated all of her major points, and wrote them down. I had structured my viewpoint to be inclusive of her major points. It works in a debate, and it works with an adverse audience. One of the lessons that I learned early on in writing feature magazine articles is that you state your thesis and immediately afterward, you state the opposing view. You then destroy the opposing view—and in the process, you get the reader. This is how I write columns and this is what you do with the audience. You anticipate where they're coming from.

Q   **My last question is: What advice would you offer to novice speakers? We have students coming to college and university who are very bright academically, but they're fearful of oral expression.**

A   Obviously, number one: preparation. Preparation, preparation, preparation. Spencer Tracy was asked, "What's the important thing in acting?" He said, "Memorizing your lines." The most unnerving thing is to be up there and not know your lines. It's disastrous. It can be rehearsing in front of a mirror for hours. If you're going to do any public speaking, you have got to rehearse; you've got to be prepared and know your lines, and anticipate things going wrong and be able to know how to handle it. That can include heckling, that can include indifference—you've just got to do it. So preparation is number one. I think when you're prepared, it's no problem.

Visual Aids and Your Environment

Things seen are mightier than things heard

—Alfred Lord Tennyson

LEARNING OBJECTIVES

- To discuss the use of visual aids

- To understand the benefits of using visual aids to assist comprehension and listener recall

- To describe the different types of audio-visual aids available to help you communicate your message

- To offer guidelines for incorporating visual aids in your presentation

Most presentations benefit immeasurably from the use of visual aids, for, as the old adage says: A picture is worth a thousand words. According to Albert Mehrabian, a professor of psychology at UCLA, 55 percent of your message impacts the audience nonverbally. The effective use of visual aids can enhance your presentation and aid in the recall of your message.

Visual aids corroborate, demonstrate, elucidate, clarify, and explain. When visuals are added to a presentation, then understanding and communication is enhanced. Visuals should be used as an adjunct to a presentation, to illustrate, and support statements or conclusions. They allow your audience to follow your rationale.

Notice that the word "adjunct" is used here. Today we hear many students say, "I can use PowerPoint therefore I can present." They then proceed to design a very intricate presentation using all the bells and whistles that the computer software provides. Sound effects are added, words fly in from various directions, too many slides are used, and overall, the audience becomes visually overloaded. The presenter may not have the skills to shape, articulate, and deliver a strong verbal message, yet he believes he is a good presenter simply because he is technologically adept. His thinking is flawed.

A good presenter will use a visual aid:

- To impact
- To emphasize
- To stimulate the imagination
- To aid comprehension
- To arouse interest
- To explain new concepts
- To get audience involvement
- To assist visualization
- To corroborate
- To reinforce the message

Your visuals are not your entire message, unless you are a mime artist. Visual support aids your presentation. Use them wisely, selectively, and effectively. There is an old Chinese proverb that says: "I hear and I forget. I see and I remember. I do and I understand." Educational researchers suggest that 83 percent of our learning occurs through seeing, 11 percent through hearing, 3.5 percent through smelling, 1 percent through tasting, and 1.5 percent through touching. We should therefore take our cue from this proverb and these figures, and use visual aids in our presentation. The presentation should begin with a clearly defined purpose, a key message, a solid structure, and knowledge of your audience and the physical setting. The addition of visuals will follow.

Today you have at your disposal a wide array of visual aids. There are two basic types of visual aids: standard visual aids and visual aids that rely on technology or electronics.

Standard visual aids include:

Flipcharts

Chalkboards and whiteboards

Models

Objects

Handouts

Maps

Photographs

Posters

Electronic or technology aids include:

Overhead projectors

Video recordings

Audio recordings

Graphs

Computer generated presentations

STANDARD VISUAL AIDS

When you want to keep things simple and familiar, use a flipchart. It is an aid that does not rely on electricity or technology and is therefore a reliable and dependable medium for a presentation.

Flipcharts work well in a small group setting or a classroom where everyone can see the information you place on the chart. It will not be an effective medium to use in a large auditorium where people in the back row are far removed from your visual.

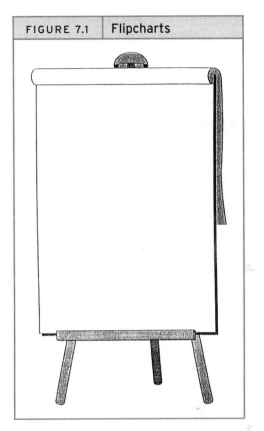

FIGURE 7.1 | Flipcharts

Benefits of using Flipcharts

1. You can prepare your flipcharts in advance.

2. It provides you with flexibility since you can add additional information at the last minute.

3. You can include contributions offered by audience members when your presentation is interactive.

4. For the technically unskilled presenter, the flipchart offers a viable alternative to visually reinforce the message.

5. On its own, the flipchart is easy to transport.

6. It is not a costly medium.

7. Colour can be added with ease. A palette of different hues can be added with coloured markers.

8. Details written on the flipchart can be removed and recorded for distribution to audience members or participants at a later time.

9. It is easy to use.

Disadvantages of the Flipchart

1. If the speaker's handwriting is not clear and bold, the notes will be difficult to read.

2. Frequently, too much information is crammed onto one sheet.

3. Many classrooms or auditoriums are not equipped with the stands or easels to accommodate flipcharts.

4. The easel supporting the chart is not sturdy, so when you write on the flipchart during the presentation, it could tumble to the floor. Check the steadiness of the easel prior to the presentation.

Take into consideration the pros and cons of using a flipchart. Once you make the decision to use one, follow these guidelines:

1. Prepare the flipchart in advance.

2. Have a variety of coloured markers available for use. Check that they are in working order and have not run out of ink.

3. Use large lettering so that people in the back row can see. Sit in the last row to check that all your information can be seen with ease.

4. Position the chart so that all members of the audience have an unobstructed view of it.

5. The first page of the chart should be blank. The reason for this is so that when you begin your presentation the listeners are solely focused on you, the presenter. This way, they do not have to split their attention between you and the information on the flipchart.

6. The second page can be the title page that displays the topic of your presentation.

7. Keep one idea or topic per page.

8. Ideally, have six lines of information per sheet. If you must include seven lines, do not exceed that number. The rule is, use only six to seven lines of information per slide or chart.

9. Sometimes flipchart pages will bleed ink from the front page onto the page behind it. When they do, it would be a good idea to find this out beforehand and make the decision to leave a blank sheet between pages to solve the problem. This bleeding occurs when you use regular markers as opposed to flipchart markers.

10. If you choose not to fill in all the details on the chart ahead of time, you can just write the headline of the topic on the chart. Then lightly in pencil, write down what you plan to add in later. These penciled notes will be a memory-jogger for you and will be invisible to the audience from a distance. For example, in a presentation on colour blindness, you may want to elicit participation from the audience by placing the following question at the top of one page, "What are the causes of colour blindness?". You can have the causes written down in pencil at the side of the chart for your personal reference, and you can list them in marker as you need.

11. For visual variety, use different coloured markers when you introduce different topics. Avoid using yellow, pale pink, and pale orange as these colours are hard to see from a distance.

12. For letter size, observe this rule: A 2.5 centimetre letter can be read from 11 metres. If you are sitting 22 metres back, lettering should be 5 centimetres in size. You never want to make the viewer strain to read your message.

13. Write your verbal transition from Page One to Page Two in pencil at the bottom of Page One of the flipchart. This will be your cue to remind you of the next topic you will be discussing, which appears on the following flipchart page.

13. Headlines can appear in block letters, but for the rest of the text, use upper and lower case lettering for ease of reading.

14. Do not turn your back on the audience while speaking. When writing on the flipchart, stand to the side of it. Always face the audience when speaking. So write first, then speak.

15. When you flip the page over, do so neatly. Little things such as sloppiness can irritate the audience. Let the page hang over the top of the easel in a smooth line.

The Chalkboard and Whiteboard

Many of the above-mentioned rules apply to these two visual mediums. The chalkboard is available to all students whereas the whiteboard is often more difficult to obtain. The objective of using both of these, however, is the same: to add visual impact to the presentation.

The chalkboard and whiteboard offer flexibility as you can erase, modify, and add new information spontaneously. The presenter should practise writing on this medium in advance of the presentation to ensure that the writing is bold, clear, and appears in a straight line. Visit the classroom ahead of time to write information on the board. In professions such as teaching, individuals have to practise blackboard writing in order to write neatly and in a straight line.

Write in a methodical fashion so that when you discuss your first item, it appears on the left side of the board and as you speak about Item Two, you progress to writing from the left to the right side of the board. It can be difficult to retain information if the speaker produces a diagram on the right side of the board, then gives a list of topics in the middle of the board and then writes on the left side of the board. There is no logical visual flow of information. Most people read from left to right, so plan for your visual information to observe this pattern.

Don't forget, too, to make sure that there is enough chalk available. For the whiteboard, you will need markers that are not indelible. Use water-based markers. You will also need a whiteboard eraser.

If you plan on using a graph or diagram, visit the presentation venue early on to give yourself enough time to draw the artwork on the board. If the audience needs to copy the illustration, allow sufficient "pause" time for them to do so. Alternatively, you could photocopy enough copies of your illustration and pass them out to members of the audience at the end of your presentation.

One final pointer here: avoid fidgeting with the chalk or marker as this becomes a distracting gesture.

Models and Objects

Any visual should add to and enhance your presentation. Sometimes words may not be enough and it becomes necessary to use a model, object, or handout to increase understanding and aid visualization. Within three to five seconds, an audience should grasp your message when you display an object. Using words to describe that object will take much longer. A visual has instant impact. Research has shown that we remember 2 percent of what we hear, 30 percent of what we see, and 50 percent of what we see and hear.

Models and objects are sometimes the perfect visual aid to use. If you were giving a demonstrative talk on wine tasting, you would need to bring a wineglass, an opener, and a bottle of wine to effectively add clarity to your talk.

A talk on the anatomy of the body would also have more impact if you brought along a model of a skeleton and a copy of a textbook such as *Gray's Anatomy* to show the class.

You could appeal to the senses of smell, touch, and sight if you spoke about, "How Perfumes are made." Your visual aids may be a variety of perfume bottles, and you could pass around the bottles so that audience members may smell the different notes in a perfume. The listener becomes actively engaged by seeing and touching the bottle, and smelling the aroma.

An architect could employ both models and scale designs to show to a potential client. A drawing may not suffice when enticing a new client or selling a visual concept.

Could you imagine someone trying to do a cooking demonstration without showing the ingredients or the cooking utensils?

You, too, can be your best visual aid. If your presentation is on, "How to achieve a black belt in Karate," you may dress the part in your white *gi* with your black *obi*. To add impact and entertainment value, you might also demonstrate some advanced Karate moves. Appropriate facial expression and body movement will assist you in conveying your message effectively while you demonstrate stances, kicks, punches, sweeps, and blocks.

Here are two pointers to consider when selecting a model as a visual aid: (1) make sure that it is large enough for the group to see; (2) do not pass an object around while you are talking. This becomes distracting and frequently encourages audience members to talk to each other while they pass the object from one person to the next.

Handouts

When using handouts, inform the audience prior to the presentation that you will be using handouts and state when you will be giving them out. For example, if you are an auditor and you are presenting the results of your audit to your client, there will be financial detail involved. It will not be possible to give all this information on overheads or on PowerPoint. You might begin your presentation with an executive summary that is projected onto a screen. You will then deliver your comments and proceed to give out the more detailed handouts of the report. With this scenario, it is recommended that you open your presentation by saying something like, "I will begin this morning's presentation with an executive summary of the audit done for company ABC. Following the comments we, your auditors, have to offer, I will distribute handouts of our report to you. We will then go through the details together."

This method works when you want active participation with your audience. Yet if you distribute the handout prior to your talk, you can rest assured that your listeners will be flipping ahead through the report while you are delivering your presentation. They will not be focused on what you are saying, but will be jumping ahead of you to find the information they find relevant.

The timing of the distribution of the handouts rests with you. There is a comfort factor you can offer the audience when you let them know at the outset that they will be receiving a handout or copy of your talk at the end of your presentation. During your introduction you can say, "At the end of my presentation you will receive a detailed handout, so it will not be necessary to take notes."

People like to be given a take-away. Always put your name, e-mail address, work address (if applicable), and phone number on the back page of the handout. For a business presentation, you would also include the name of the corporation or firm for which you are working. Handouts should always look professionally produced.

Guidelines for Handouts

1. Ahead of time, choose someone to distribute the handouts for you.

2. Include all important take-away points on the handout.

3. If using PowerPoint, print a copy of the slides on handouts. Leave room on the pages for participants to make notes.

4. Handouts should contain bullet points, graphics, graphs, and charts to add visual interest.

5. Use letter-size paper that can be easily placed in a binder.

6. Number the pages of the handouts.

Maps, Photographs, and Posters

A visiting student from South Korea gave a detailed informative talk on the differences between North and South Korea. The presentation was fascinating, yet the map she used to show the location of Korea was lacking in focus. She displayed a map that showed all the countries in close proximity to Korea. The countries of Japan, China, and Taiwan were clearly labelled. No label was attached to Korea. This was an unfortunate oversight and caused the audience difficulty in directing their focus. It would have been a good idea for the student to create a map that was black and white, and have Korea coloured in a strong red. The audience would have known where Korea is placed geographically.

Ensure that when you use maps, posters, or photographs, the dimension of your aid is suitable for the environment and the group size.

In a courtroom setting, photographs are blown up for all the jurors to see. An enlarged photograph of a victim at a crime scene can offer greater impact when the prosecutor wants to paint a vivid picture for the court.

When a surgeon is teaching at medical school and giving a lecture to students on "Reconstructive Surgery," photographs showing the patient before and after surgery are worth a thousand words.

A commercial artist addressing students at an art college on "Design for the Motion Picture Industry" would find that by using an assortment of posters, he or she could contrast styles and visual elements and point out what would work in a design.

When considering the use of maps, posters, and photographs, ask yourself the following:

1. Are they large enough for everyone to see?

2. Are they clear enough?

3. Do they add or detract from my message?

4. Do they add focus to my presentation?

5. Is the physical setting conducive to this type of visual aid?

6. Do these visual aids comprehension?

ELECTRONIC AND TECHNOLOGICAL AIDS

The Overhead Projector

Many professors and teachers find numerous advantages in using the overhead projector as their visual aid of choice. They can be used in both large and small rooms, and they are easy to operate. Overheads can also be used in a fully lit room, enabling the speaker to maintain eye contact with the audience. As well, it does not take a huge investment of time to produce overheads; you can even create them while you are delivering your talk. Overheads can essentially become your notes; they can guide you through your presentation.

Before using an overhead projector, as with all other equipment, it is important to check that the projector is in good working order. There is an on/off button to turn the machine on and off. There is an arm shaped like an "L". Attached to this arm is a large circular button you can rotate in order to focus the transparencies. Make sure that the bulb of the projector is functioning properly. You will often find that there are two bulbs in the projector. When the first bulb fails, simply slide the bar on the front of the machine across, so that the second bulb kicks in. As a secondary precaution, bring along a spare bulb and know how to change it. Familiarize yourself with the machine and know how it functions.

A **transparency** is placed on the overhead machine and the image on the transparency is projected in an enlarged form onto a screen placed behind the projector. The transparency, also known as an acetate or overhead, is a transparent sheet that resembles a fine plastic film. The transparency is easy to produce. After you type the information on your computer, you can download your presentation from your computer, and print the information onto inkjet transparencies. These acetates, or ones created with a laser printer, produce excellent results. If you do not have a printer, you can take the hardcopies of your slides to a local photocopy shop and ask them to reproduce the slides as overhead transparencies. If you are pressed for time, you could write directly onto the overheads with indelible markers. This look may not be as polished as computer-generated fonts and graphics, but it will provide you with visual support for your presentation.

In an ideal setting, the screen is placed at a 45° angle to the audience at the front of the room with the overhead

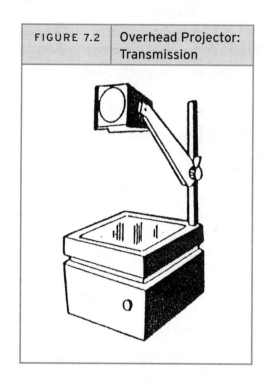

FIGURE 7.2 | Overhead Projector: Transmission

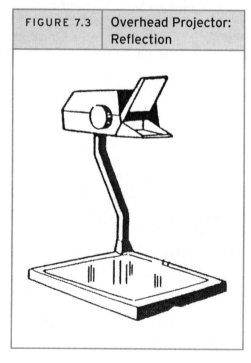

FIGURE 7.3 | Overhead Projector: Reflection

projector a few feet away from it. With this layout everyone has an unobstructed view of your visuals. Traditionally the overhead projector is typically placed in the centre of the room. This position often blocks the view of certain members of the audience. If you have no choice with regards to the placement of the machine, before you begin your presentation, ask the audience, "Can everyone see the screen? If you cannot, please find a seat that provides you with a clear vantage point." Never make your listeners work or strain to receive your message.

Enter the room prior to your talk. Place your first overhead on the screen, focus it, and turn it off. You are then ready to begin and won't have to fiddle around with the acetate and focus button in front of the audience. Align the transparency so that it fits into the frame of the screen and ensure that the image is projected high enough so that everyone can see.

Guidelines for the use of Slides and Transparencies

1. Each slide should convey one idea.

2. Keep the typeface simple. Do not mix more than two typefaces in order to avoid the slide becoming gimmicky and unfocused.

3. Use no more than six or seven lines of information per transparency.

4. The headline can appear in capital letters, but for the body of the text, use upper and lower case for easy reading and better retention.

5. Be consistent with your format. You may choose to display your material in a landscape style, horizontally, or portrait style, vertically. The horizontal format is often easier to work with.

6. If you have finished discussing a particular topic, turn off the overhead projector so that the focus of the attention returns to you. When you need your next overhead, turn on the projector again. Be advised that too much clicking of the on/off button can irritate or distract your audience.

7. Place each overhead in a border or cardboard frame. These can be purchased from office supply stores. Tape the overhead to the border and then number each overhead in the top right-hand corner. The border serves a double purpose. It makes handling the transparencies easy, and enables you to write extra notes for yourself on the borders. In this way, your overheads become your speech notes.

8. Do not talk to the screen. Keep your body language open, directing your words and eye contact to the audience.

9. For visual variety, do not produce a show that only has bullet points. Use a mixture of graphs, graphics, maps, photographs (which are easily downloaded from your computer and printed onto an overhead), and bullet points. Cartoons, where appropriate, can be very effective when reproduced on an overhead.

10. Use a font size that is easy to read. Do not use a font size lower than 30 points. For headlines you can use 48- or 50-point size.

11. Use colour for emphasis and variety.

12. Tape the extension cord of the overhead projector to the floor to avoid tripping over any loose wires.

13. Use a pointer to gesture towards important points. Be careful not to hit the screen when using the pointer. Also do not fiddle with the pointer unnecessarily by opening and closing it.

14. Check that there are no typing errors on your transparencies. Give your overheads to an objective classmate who can examine them with fresh eyes. Spell-check and grammar-check are adequate, but not perfect.

15. Before you close your talk, turn off the projector so that you, the speaker, become the focal point again. Move out from behind the overhead projector and deliver your closing line in front of the machine so that there is no physical barrier between you and your listeners.

Videotapes and Audiotapes

You can enliven a presentation by using video or audiotape. When you use either a video or audiotape as part of your presentation, make certain that the equipment you are using works efficiently. Visit the venue early and check the equipment. Cue up the tape and adjust the volume according to the size of the room. When the room fills up with people you might find that they act as sound absorbers, so you will have to adjust the volume level once everyone is seated.

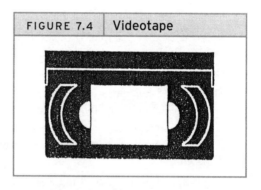

FIGURE 7.4   Videotape

Always introduce the video or audiotape. Explain your purpose for using it and talk about its significance to your project or presentation. You can create your own videos and incorporate them as supporting evidence or use them to paint an authentic scenario for the audience. In corporations, videos are used to promote the company vision, to train, and to market products. Students may use video or audio when they interview experts and want to share their research with the audience in a concrete way.

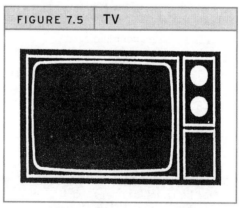

FIGURE 7.5   TV

Here's another way in which a student may use video. A student teacher may decide to film children during an art therapy class and use the film later to prove how this form of therapy can be helpful for children who are not verbally articulate. The film should show how this therapy could help the child to express his or her pain and hurt via the medium of art.

If you were giving a talk on, "What it takes to become an Olympic athlete," nothing would be more powerful than to use videotape showing various athletes crossing the finish line. The audio segment of the tape would let the audience hear the roar of the crowd in the background and the excitement conveyed by the commentator's voice. In a presentation on "The Impact of Voice on your Message," you could begin your talk by playing an audiotape of famous speakers' voices. Ask the audience to listen closely. Tell them that once the recording is over, you will ask them to try and identify the voices of the speakers.

The use of the tape-recorder and the VCR can heighten audience interest and involvement in your message, so use them when relevant and appropriate.

Graphs

Graphs help to make information concrete. A graph is a symbolic diagram that shows, pictorially, how various parts of the whole relate to each other, or how they relate across time. When you need to use statistics or show trends, graphs help the viewer see this in a more concrete vein.

There are four basic types of graphs.

The Pie Graph   In the pie graph, the circle is divided into segments and percentages are shown. In the chart below, we see Professor Mehrabian's study of the impact of the three components that contribute to a presentation.

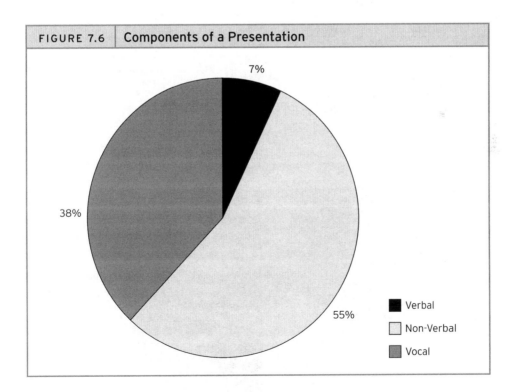

FIGURE 7.6 | **Components of a Presentation**

7%

38%

55%

■ Verbal
□ Non-Verbal
■ Vocal

Below are examples of ineffective and effective pie charts.

FIGURE 7.7	Ineffective Pie Chart

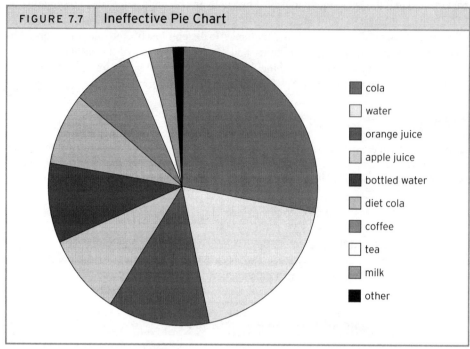

FIGURE 7.8	Effective Pie Chart

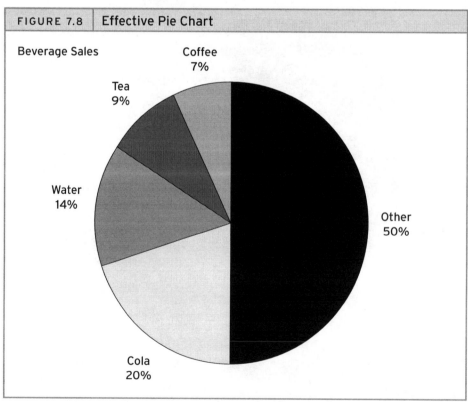

There is no title in Figure 7.7 and frequent cross-referencing is required between the actual chart and the legend.

Figure 7.8, the effective pie chart, clearly labels the data and the segments.

These graphs can be designed with ease when you use such programs as Microsoft's PowerPoint.

The Bar Graph   If you want to compare statistics, illustrate relationships, or show growth or decline in revenues, you may choose a bar graph to do so. It is hard for an audience to retain figures if they are not visually represented.

Below you will find examples of ineffective and effective bar graphs.

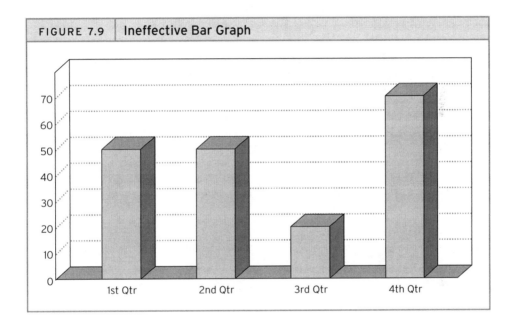

FIGURE 7.9 | **Ineffective Bar Graph**

You can see that Figure 7.9 does not include a title; and if we look at the third quarter, from where do we take our measurement? The top of the square or the lower line of the square? Use two-dimensional graphs to avoid confusion for the viewer when interpreting your information.

Figure 7.10, the effective bar graph, is clearly titled and is a two-dimensional representation. We can easily gauge the sales for each quarter.

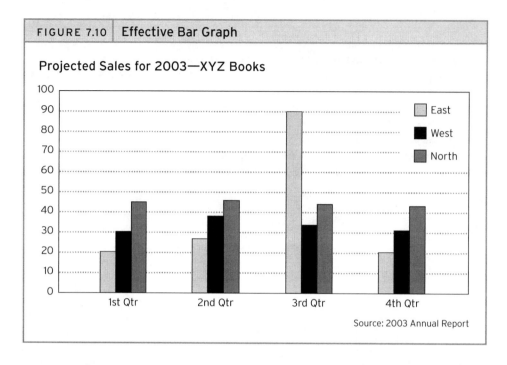

FIGURE 7.10 | Effective Bar Graph

Projected Sales for 2003—XYZ Books

Source: 2003 Annual Report

The Line Graph A line graph shows the relationship between two or more variables. They are often used to show trends over time.

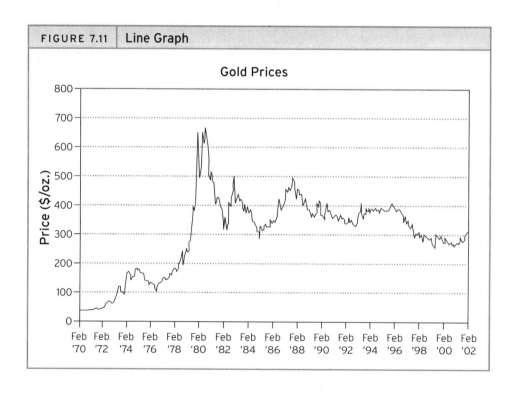

FIGURE 7.11 | Line Graph

Gold Prices

The Picture Graph   With a picture graph you use pictures instead of bars or lines. The pictures or symbols indicate the figures, values, or size you wish to represent.

FIGURE 7.12	Picture Graph

Estimated Pet Population in Canada*

*Each symbol represents 500,000

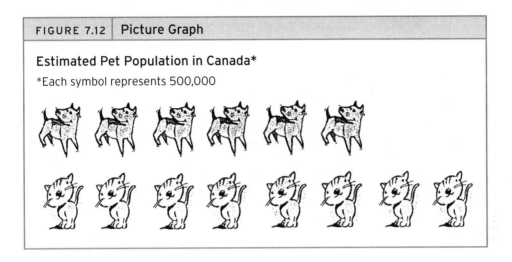

The graph above uses symbols to represent the pet population statistics. It is estimated that there is a population of three million dogs and four million cats in Canada.

The Computer-Generated Presentation

The most popular visual medium used today in business and academic circles is the computer-generated presentation. Presenters who use this form of slide presentation are typically considered to be more credible and professional.

When you decide to use a computer-generated presentation, you need to ask yourself the following questions:

- Will this visual aid enhance or detract from my message?
- Is this the appropriate medium to use in this particular environment with this particular audience?
- Do I possess the technical know-how and time to design a slide show that is well structured, easy to read, and visually attractive?
- Will my visual aid clarify information for the audience and thereby promote understanding?
- Can I use the technology with ease and confidence while I am presenting?

The computer-generated slide presentation is often referred to as a PowerPoint presentation. What is PowerPoint? It is a complete presentation graphics software program that provides you with the tools to create professional-looking presentations. With this software, you can create slides, overheads, outline pages, speakers' notes, and handouts.

Presentation Software   The most common presentation software program in use today is Microsoft PowerPoint. There are other programs available such as:

- Harvard Graphics Advance Presentations
- Corel Presentations 10
- Astound Presentation 8.0
- Apple Computer Appleworks 6.2
- ThinkFree Think Show 1.5
- CodeBlazer Technologies Upresent

Each software program offers different options and features. Select the one that suits your unique needs. To create a presentation that is compelling, you can contact the Microsoft Press division. They offer how-to books that teach you about all the capabilities of the PowerPoint software. Learning about the technical aspects of creating a slideshow goes beyond the scope of this textbook, so if you plan on using PowerPoint, it is recommended that you spend the time learning the technical skills necessary to create a slide show. As technology advances, presenters are offered far more choice when deciding which visual aid to select to enhance their presentations. As the presentation landscape transforms, it is important to stay current and embrace new products if they serve your presentation purpose.

Above all, consider that no PowerPoint presentation will save you if you have not prepared a thoroughly researched, well-structured talk, which delivers a pertinent message to a clearly defined audience. Prepare your oral component with great attention to detail and the visual component will both complement and enhance it.

Hardware   To produce a computer-generated presentation you need specific hardware. Save your presentation on a zip disk or a CD and bring it with you to your talk. You need to bring, or arrange to have, a laptop computer onto which you can load your saved presentation. The computer needs to be connected to a high-resolution data projector that will project the image onto a screen. Some of the industry leaders who produce solid quality, high-tech projectors are Epson, Nec, and Sony. Functions and features vary on each data projector so, prior to the presentation, familiarize yourself with the type you will be using. A remote mouse/clicker will enable you to change slides while standing at a distance from the computer, and thereby provide you with the ability to move across the platform with ease. If you do not have a remote clicker, you will need to remain within close range of your computer in order to change your slides. Alternatively, you can solicit the help of a classmate or colleague to forward the slides for you. Practise together prior to the presentation and give your assistant the cues that will tell him or her when you require a slide change.

When dealing with audio-visual equipment, Murphy's Law frequently seems to rear its ugly head. Anything that can go wrong will go wrong. It even happened to Microsoft when Bill Gates unveiled his new Microsoft 2000 software operating system in full view of the international media and his technical equipment failed. His PowerPoint show could not be projected. This could happen to you, so have a back-up plan. Make overheads of your presentation and take them with you in case you encounter technical problems. Also make certain that there is an overhead projector available to you. Here is one extra precaution you can take: before your talk, load your presentation onto the computer's hard drive and make a back-up copy of the presentation on disk.

The following is a checklist for you to use prior to the presentation:

- Laptop computer with an applicable CD-ROM drive or ZIP drive
- Mouse
- A spare disk with your saved presentation
- A pointer
- Overheads of your presentation
- Overhead projector
- Remote mouse/clicker
- Batteries (for any remote devices)
- Table for the computer
- Paper copy of your slides
- Location of light switches

Dos and Don'ts for Creating Digital Slides

Many of the same rules for overheads apply here.

Fonts

- Choose a font that is easy to read and one that matches the style and tone of your message. Times New Roman and Arial are simple, clean typefaces.
- Never mix more than two fonts per slide.
- Fonts should be large enough for the individual in the back row to read. As mentioned earlier, 30-point size offers comfortable viewing. Headlines can be in 48-point size.
- For headlines, you can use all upper-case lettering, if you choose. For the body of the slide, use upper- and lower-case letters.

Bullet Points

- Have no more than six bullet points per slide.
- Keep to six words per bullet point.
- When bullet points enter, let them do so from the same direction. Choose to have the bullet points enter from left to right or from south to north. Choose one way or the other. It is easier for the audience to follow this formation.

Design

- Choose a background colour that contrasts with your text and keep the same colour scheme throughout the slide show. A strong background colour is royal blue; for the text, white or yellow is effective.
- Show consistency in design and format. Use the same font and the same size titles or headings throughout.
- Avoid using a background that overpowers the message you are conveying on the slide. The background should be subtle.

- Title each slide.
- Place key information in the upper left corner, since the eye is drawn to this position first.
- In a business presentation, include the company logo on each page. Place it in the same position on each slide. The lower right-hand corner is a good placement spot for a logo.
- Leave space around your text. This makes it easy to read.
- Only use animation and sounds when they accent or add something distinctive.
- Do not use "tired" clipart: The clipart included in your software program has been used and seen over and over again by most audiences. You can purchase CDs that contain a wide choice of graphics to use creatively in your slide show.

Projection and Lighting

- After you have designed your presentation, project it via a data projector onto a screen. Sometimes the colours you have chosen alter when they are projected. You may also notice that bullet points turn into arrows when different projectors are used.
- Check the lighting. Try not to deliver in a totally darkened room. The speaker should always be visible. Begin the presentation with the lights turned on so that you, the speaker, are the initial focal point. Dim the lights for the slide show and turn on the lights again before you deliver your closing line. In this way, the audience's attention is redirected towards you once more.

Offer the viewer visual variety by using a mixture of graphics, bullet points, graphs, maps, photographs, and/or cartoons. However, avoid visual "overkill." Slides should not be used as a gimmick; rather they must enhance your presentation.

Colour   When you use colour in slide shows, the choice of colour should have eye-appeal and match the intention of your message. Use only two or three colours per slide, otherwise the overall look can appear garish. Have one dominant colour and the other colours should be of a paler hue. If you overuse strong, vivid colours they can tire the audience. Use natural colours to which your listener can respond.

First decide on the image and impression you want to convey. Then choose a background colour that matches your intention. Choose a text colour that provides contrast. For example, if you were creating a presentation for the Toronto Dominion Bank, you could select a green background and your text could be in white. These are the bank's signature colours. If you chose red as your background for this task, the viewer might associate the colour red with debt.

The colour of choice for most business presentations is a royal blue background with white, lemon, or pale turquoise text. This colour combination makes for easy reading.

When you select a background colour ensure that there is sufficient contrast with the text. Avoid these colour combinations: black/blue, brown/green, and blue/purple. Some individuals with colour blindness cannot distinguish detail when confronted with a red/green contrast.

When you want to draw attention to an important segment in your talk use a brighter colour that highlights this information.

Table 7.1 is a chart showing how we tend to perceive colour. Choose a colour scheme that matches your presentation objective.

TABLE 7.1	Colour and Perception
Blue	dignified, cool, calm, trustworthy
Red	passionate, exiting, stimulating; indicates danger or financial loss
Green	tranquil, eloquent; shows growth
Yellow	lively, happy; attracts attention
Purple	royal, artistic, creative, unique
Brown	gloomy
Burgundy	rich, exotic
White	winter, peace, purity, sterility
Black	elegance, night, evil, wealth

A black slide can also be used when you want to talk without an accompanying slide. It is also a good idea to place a black slide at the beginning and end of your presentation.

Ten Tips for Practising and Using Your Visual Aid

1. Check that all of your equipment is working efficiently.
2. Arrange the placement of your visuals and check the seating arrangement.
3. Talk to the audience, rather than to the screen or your object.
4. Do not place yourself in front of the projector; the material will be projected onto you instead of the screen.
5. Use a pointer to focus the attention on the point you are addressing. Hold the pointer in your left hand.

   NOTE: To avoid fidgeting with the pointer, place it down on the table or podium when you are not using it. Also make certain that you do not "whack" the screen when pointing.
6. Stand to the left of the screen since the audience reads from left to right.
7. When displaying an object, reach it towards the audience and move it across the room slowly.
8. Run through the entire presentation while using your slides so that you become familiar with the order of the slides.
9. Practise changing the bulb of the overhead projector.
10. When you show a graph or chart on an overhead or slide, first explain to the audience what they are looking at (refer to bar chart earlier in the chapter). You can say, for example, "Here we see a graph of the sales of our organization for the last four quarters. The horizontal axis represents the quarters, and the vertical axis indicates the dollar amount." Then give your message: "If we look at the fourth quarter we see a sharp decline in sales and we need to reverse this decline." If you begin with your message first, the audience will be preoccupied with trying to figure out the legend on your graph, and will not be listening to your explanation.

THE SPEAKING ENVIRONMENT

When you prepare your presentation aids, keep in mind the physical layout of the room in which you will be delivering your talk. Visit the venue to assess its suitability. If you have permission, you can alter the layout of the room to suit your needs. A theatre-style auditorium is suitable for large audiences, while a classroom set-up or U-shaped seating arrangement creates an environment that works well for educational purposes. In a college or university setting, you are not often given a great degree of flexibility with regard to changing and rearranging the seating. If this is the case, you will need to adapt to your environment and ensure that everyone can see both you and your presentation aids. If you are delivering to a small group seated around a meeting table, the presentation can be formal or informal. You may choose to stand or sit while presenting. However, the presenter becomes more of a focal point when he or she stands while delivering the talk. If you will be speaking from a raised platform or stage, practise walking up to the stage energetically. If you will be standing at a lectern, then stand behind it and experience how it feels to look out at the audience from that vantage point. If you are using a **standing microphone**, it needs to be placed six inches away from your mouth. Do not test the microphone in front of your audience. Do this beforehand. Sometimes you may use a **lavaliere** microphone. A lavaliere microphone is a small rectangular black box with a microphone attached to it. To use it effectively, hook the box into your waistband, and clip the microphone onto your lapel. A word of caution: Remember to turn the microphone off once you have finished speaking. You would not want any of your private conversations to be accidentally broadcast over the speaker system.

Speaker's Checklist: Key Questions

The following is a checklist to help you with your environmental planning:

- Have I familiarized myself with the speaking environment?
- Will I be speaking from a lectern?
- Is there a light on the lectern so that I can read my notes?
- Will I be using a microphone? Will it be a lavaliere, handheld, or upright microphone?
- Where will I place my visual equipment?
- Do I know how to operate all the equipment?
- Will the entire audience be able to see me from their seats?
- Have I cleared the stage of any props, flipcharts, or visual aids used by a previous speaker?
- Where are the electrical outlets and the light switches?

EXERCISES

1. Alfred Lord Tennyson said, "Things seen are mightier than things heard." Discuss the truths and falsities of such a statement.
2. Name the visuals that fall under the category of standard visual aids.
3. Which visual aids are electronically or technologically based?

4. What are the advantages of using a flipchart, whiteboard, and chalkboard?

5. Suggest five topics that would benefit from the use of models, objects, and handouts. Name the topic and describe how you would use your presentation aid.

6. When using an overhead projector what are the guidelines to which you should adhere?

7. When addressing an audience of businesspeople, what type of visual aids would be most effective?

8. Prepare a visual that illustrates the following: At the time of writing this book, there have been eight Canadians who have flown in space on various missions:

   In 1984, Marc Garneau was the first Canadian in space. He returned to space in 1996 and again in 2000 with Missions STS-97.

   In 1992, Roberta Bondar became the first woman in space.

   In 1992, Steve MacLean went on Mission STS-52.

   In 1995, Chris Hadfield was the first Canadian to visit Mir space station. Hadfield returned to space in 2001 and became the first Canadian to walk in space.

   In 1996, Robert Thirsk embarked on Mission STS-78.

   In 1997, Bjarni Tryggvason embarked on Mission STS-85.

   In 1998, Dave Williams embarked on Mission STS-90.

   In 1999, Julie Payette, on Mission STS-96, was the first Canadian to visit the International Space Station.

9. Design a visual to illustrate the Seven Ages of Humankind from William Shakespeare's *As You Like It* (II.vii.139):

   > All the world's a stage,
   > And all the men and women merely players;
   > They have their exits and their entrances,
   > And one man in his time plays many parts,
   > His acts being seven ages. At first, the infant,
   > Mewling and puking in the nurse's arms.
   > Then the whining schoolboy, with his satchel
   > And shining morning face, creeping like snail
   > Unwillingly to school. And then the lover,
   > Sighing like furnace, with a woeful ballad
   > Full of strange oaths and bearded like the pard,
   > Jealous in honor, sudden and quick in quarrel,
   > Seeking the bubble reputation
   > Even in the cannon's mouth. And then the justice,
   > In fair round belly with good capon lined,
   > With eyes severe and beard of formal cut,
   > Full of wise saws and modern instances;
   > And so he plays his part. The sixth age shifts

Into the lean and slippered pantaloon,

With spectacles on nose and pouch on side;

His youthful hose, well sav'd, a world too wide

For his shrunk shank, and his big manly voice,

Turning again toward childish treble, pipes

And whistles in his sound. Last scene of all,

That ends this strange eventful history,

Is second childishness and mere oblivion,

Sans teeth, sans eyes, sans everything.

10. Use the Internet to research the results of the Winter Olympic Games in 2002. Create a chart to show the top gold medal winners and indicate the country each winner represented. Now present your findings to the class using the chart you created.

11. Prepare a picture graph by researching the following data:

   a. Visit the following Web site: **www.statcan.ca/english/Pgdb/People/Population**. Gather information on the population of each province in Canada. Prepare a bar graph showing the population of Canada. Include a title on your slide.

   b. Visit the following Web site: **www.statcan.ca/english/Pgdb/State/Justice/ legal02.htm**. Create a bar chart to capture how crime decreased in Canada from 1996 to 2000. Create a title for the slide.

12. An article was published in the *American Journal of Public Health* on "Morbidity and Mortality Attributable to Alcohol, Tobacco, and Illicit Drug Use in Canada." Written by Eric Single, Linda Robsojn, Jurgen Rehnm, and Xiaodi, the article presents the results of a study designed to estimate mortality and morbidity attributed to alcohol, tobacco, and illicit drugs.

   Here are the results: In 1992, 33 498 deaths and 208 095 hospitalizations were attributable to tobacco, 6701 deaths and 86 076 hospitalizations were attributable to alcohol, and 732 deaths and 7095 hospitalizations were due to illicit drugs.

   Create two picture graphs. One will illustrate the deaths and the second one will illustrate the hospitalization. Title each graph.

13. The twenty-first century has been called occularcentric. What does this word mean? List the visual aids that you could use when giving a talk on "Global Warming" and bear in mind that your audience is largely occularcentric.

14. Take a presentation that you have previously delivered. Create new aids to add impact and interest to that presentation. Use at least two types of presentation aids.

SUMMARY

This chapter demonstrates how visuals can add impact and clarification to a presentation. You have been reminded that 55 percent of your message impacts non-verbally. We have examined the use of standard visual aids, which include flipcharts, maps, photographs, and posters. You too can be your best visual aid. We have looked at aids that are dependent upon electronics or technology: overhead projector, video and audio recordings, computer-generated presentations, and presentation software. The chapter has addressed pros and cons of using a particular medium and offered guidelines for the use of the numerous aids. You have also been reminded that the environment in which you speak impacts your presentation.

The chapter includes checklists and suggestions for you to use prior to the presentation that will help you prepare thoroughly. In terms of preparing slides, take into account the use of fonts, bullet points, design, lighting, and colour. It is advisable to practice with your aid so that you increase your proficiency and confidence. A good visual aid is clearly visible and will focus the attention of the audience. All elements of your visuals should complement your presentation objective, your message, and your spoken delivery.

SUGGESTED READING

Brown, Alan. *Power Pitches: How to Produce Winning Presentations using Charts, Slides, Video and Multimedia.* New York: Irwin Professional Publications, 1997.

Zelanzny, Gene. *Say It with Charts: The Executive's Guide to Visual Communication*. New York: McGraw-Hill Professional, 2001.

REFERENCES

American Journal of Public Health. (1999 March). Vol. 89, No.3.

Vogel, D.R., G.W. Dickson, and J.A Lehman. *Persuasion and the Role of Visual Presentation Support: The UM/3M Study.* St. Paul, MN: 3M General Offices, 1986. 1–20.

WEBLINKS

Presentations

216.156.235.253
Advanced Presentation Products: Tips and Tricks.

www.corel.com
Corel Presentations allow you to create different types of business presentations.

mspress.microsoft.com/office2000/learning.htm#powerpoint
Microsoft Press offers publications to learn how to use PowerPoint.

www.presentations.com
www.powerpointers.com
www.presentersuniversity.com/courses/cs_visualaids.cfm
www.actden.com/pp/
PowerPoint in the classroom.

instein.csuri.edu/tutorials/csc101/powerpoint/ppt.html
PowerPoint tutorial.

Fonts:

www.itcfonts.com/
www.1001freefonts.com/fontfiles/ffonts3.html
www.arts-letters.com/freefont100/freefont.html
www.fontfile.com

Colour:

www.designsense-cd.com/productinfo.html#color
www.myth.com/color/meaning.html-2k
www.3m.com/meetingnetwork/presentations/pmag_visualsstudy.html-48k

Eight Things to Know About Designing Presentations

by Jeffrey P. Hemmelgarn

1. Content is king. Just as form follows function, design follows content. Visual models and graphic metaphors are most effective when they support and clarify the speaker's message. Graphic design bells-and-whistles can exert a powerful influence on a viewing audience, so let's make sure that we're focused visually on what it is that we're orally communicating.

2. Know your audience. Each audience has their own likes and dislikes. Whether professional or cultural, each audience has their own language, tastes, and preferences. When giving your presentation, be aware of the jargon, exclusive information, and images that you use and how each may affect your audience. If they can't understand or identify with you, they will most likely not listen.

3. Balancing what we want to say and what the audience can remember. Sometimes we say too much, offer too much detail because we are passionate and excited about our topic. Bear in mind that our audience can remember only so much information, so many details, and what we want them to remember most are those special nuggets of information that we have identified on their behalf. When condensing presentation materials, ask yourself, "What's the one key point that I want them to know about this presentation point, slide, or topic?"— everything else is filler.

4. First impressions matter. Your presentation should give the audience the impression that you care about your topic. It should look like you deserve whatever it is that you're asking from your audience, i.e., attention, respect, or money. In that spirit, don't wait to the last minute to identify a graphic designer to help build your presentation.

   Rush jobs often result in sloppy or misaligned representations of the content and lack of visual aesthetics; furthermore, rush jobs may be interpreted as a lack of respect for both the content and your audience.

5. Priming the audience's mind. Setting the tone and scope of your presentation will influence the mood and receptivity of your audience. When planning your presentation, let the audience's perspective influence your delivery. If the audience cannot relate to the topic, they will not retain the information. With the audience in mind, ask yourself these questions in the planning stages of your presentation:

   "Why does it matter to me?" "Why should I listen and retain this information?" "What do you want me to do with this information?"

6. It's all in the flow. The "Problem–Solution" method of presenting a new product or idea is always a safe choice. We call it a "Visual Metaphor." First, you visually represent the current situation, the problem, within a visual model. Then you layer a visual representation of your product or idea, the solution, on top of the problem visual. In this manner, your audience will see how your solution changes or enhances the current situation. Follow up with some credibility points, financials, success history, and strategic partners.

7. Learning the image. When visually presenting an idea, the audience must first understand the visual metaphor before they can understand what it represents. Keep the visuals simple and clear so that the audience can get right to understanding your message. A visual metaphor that is both familiar to the audience and applicable to your topic will be the most effective for your content.

8. Technology for technology's sake doesn't matter; it's the business value that technology enables that matters. You can't match ROI [return on investment] to technology unless a business value is identified. Technology enables business solutions. When presenting your technology to an investing or decision-making audience, err on the side of marketing know-how, not engineering expertise.

Jeffrey P. Hemmelgarn is a principal and co-founder of Creative Presentation Resources, LLC. CPR is a San Francisco-based visual communication agency that specializes in developing multimedia presentations, HTML E-mail campaigns, and interactive product demonstrations for both live and online audiences. 1-415-284-0202 **www.ineedcpr.com**.

chapter eight

Vocal Mastery

It ain't whatcha say, it's the way howcha say it.

—Louis Armstrong, jazz musician

LEARNING OBJECTIVES

- To become aware of the importance of a well-modulated, clear, well-projected voice for public speaking

- To analyze your own voice

- To learn the characteristics of a good voice

- To provide the student with practical exercises to develop vocal mastery

When was the last time you looked in the mirror? It was probably this morning. Each morning we evaluate ourselves visually. We ponder silently: "How is my hair looking?" "Is this style of dress appropriate for university or college life?" "Will Marla like my new jacket?" We think about how others see us. We are concerned about our visual image.

We know that the first impression we form of someone is a visual one. The second impression is formed when that individual contradicts the first impression and we say to ourselves, "I made an external judgement on David because of his shabby appearance, yet when he opened his mouth to speak, I was amazed at how articulate and well-spoken he was."

VOICE AND SPEECH

The power of eloquence accompanied by a resonant, well-modulated voice is enormous. According to Albert Mehrabian, a professor of psychology at UCLA, the vocal element of a presentation (how we sound) accounts for 38 percent of the impact made during a presentation. The verbal (the words and content) accounts for 7 percent and the non-verbal element for 55 percent. As public speakers, we need to pay considerably more attention to how we sound.

Successful public figures recognize the vital role voice and speech play in conveying their message effectively and successfully. From Martin Luther King and John F. Kennedy to Pierre Trudeau and Bill Clinton, it can be seen how well-framed speech and a well-modulated voice are valued. William Gladstone, the nineteenth-century British Prime Minister said, "Many a professional now in obscurity might have risen to the highest ranks if he had been far-seeing enough to train his voice and body as well as his mind."

We live in a fitness conscious era. We are concerned with a fit mind and a fit body. Can we allocate the time for vocal fitness? Can we afford not to?

Our vocal goal is to convey information so that the audience receives it effortlessly. The effort of listening to a voice that is raspy, monotonous, high-pitched, or unclear detracts from the speaker's message. The speaker who makes us strain to receive his information because he speaks softly, loses authority. To listen to machine-gun delivery is exhausting. Have you encountered a voice that droned on like a buzzsaw? It is hard to focus on the message when the voice impacts us in such a negative way.

Roz Comins, British voice expert and co-ordinator of the Voice Care Network UK, explains that "every voice is unique and is affected by our physical structure and life experience." She created the Venn diagram shown below to demonstrate how much of ourselves is reflected in our voice.

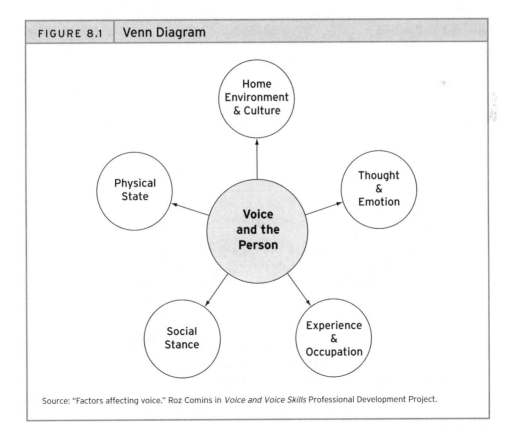

FIGURE 8.1 | **Venn Diagram**

Source: "Factors affecting voice." Roz Comins in *Voice and Voice Skills* Professional Development Project.

We take our voices for granted. Yet voice is such a valuable tool that, when used efficiently, it will make us far more dynamic speakers. You can improve your voice and speech. Ask yourself the following questions right now: How does my voice affect other people physically? Does it make them uncomfortable? Does it soothe them to such an extent that it puts them to sleep? Does it put them off because of poor intonation? Do I use vocal variety?

Here's an experiment you can try easily. All you need is a quiet corner and a portable audiocassette recorder.

1. Place a tape into the recorder and read the following extracts.

    The notion that the writer might be prevented from returning to a favourite spot inspired this passage written in 1992.

The Man Stood Alone

A.R.D. Nesbitt

The man stood alone on the dock in the late afternoon sun. A noise on the far side of the lake had caught his attention and he saw that it was a loon, flapping its wings in the water, preparing for the long and arduous takeoff common to such heavy birds. It was September.

The loon propelled itself the length of the lake, beating the water with its wings most of the way. At the end of the lake it turned around and flew in the opposite direction, just clearing the surface. By the time it reached its original starting point, it was quite high in the air.

The man hoped that the loon could in some way sense his admiration. As if in acknowledgement, the loon flew across the lake and wheeled right over where the man was standing, before it disappeared over the trees on the far side.

In their own ways, the man thought, each of them knew that it was time once again to move on. There was a difference this year, however, that filled the man with sadness. Of the two of them, the man knew that only the loon would return in the spring.

A sermon delivered from Timothy Eaton Memorial Service, September 16, 2001.

In Search of...Healing

Reverend Dr. Andrew Stirling

It was an idyllic New England day. The night before there had been some slight rains and the mist of the early morning was hovering at the foot of the beautiful Green Mountains of Vermont. As the sun began to rise and burn off the mist, the emerald green mountains of Vermont seemed brighter than any jewelry I had ever seen in my life. It was a glorious morning.

Marial and I were driving on Route 30 from Manchester Center to Brattleboro, one of the most serene and peaceful and gorgeous parts of that free and fair land. The air had a chill to it and, as the sun warmed it, we thoroughly enjoyed the freedom of America.

After a while, having driven along that beautiful route, we switched on the radio to find out what the weather would be for the rest of the day and we heard the most ridiculous thing that we had ever heard in our lives: that planes had flown into the World Trade Center; that the Pentagon might have been bombed. It sounded like one of those silly hoaxes the morning shows often air in the United States. There was only one difference: the voice delivering the news was familiar. It was a Canadian voice. It was Peter Jennings, and it was real.

In a state of shock, we continued to drive through the mountains, although their beauty seemed to have lost its hue and its glow. I pulled over into a gas station just outside of the town of Keene. When I got there, the woman who was to take my money was weeping uncontrollably. The mechanics had put down their tools and their greasy hands were grasping their cups of coffee like they had never clasped their cups of coffee before. There was an eerie silence and I realized the world would never be the same.

2. Rewind the tape and analyze your voice and speech by filling in Form 8.1 - Voice and Speech Analysis Chart, below. This sheet is designed to assist you in evaluating your areas for development. You will become aware of the particular areas you need to focus on in your vocal delivery.

3. Once you have evaluated your voice, continue to the next section in the chapter that offers practical exercises for vocal improvement.

Each voice is unique. Cultivate your unique quality and polish the areas that need embellishment.

FORM 8.1	**Voice and Speech Analysis Chart**

Check the appropriate box:

Volume ❏ Very Good ❏ Average ❏ Needs Improvement

  ❏ Too loud

  ❏ Too soft

  ❏ Appropriate

  ❏ Other

Pitch ❏ Very Good ❏ Average ❏ Needs Improvement

  ❏ Too high

  ❏ Too low

  ❏ Lacked variety

  ❏ Contrast too exaggerated

  ❏ Other

FORM 8.1	Voice and Speech Analysis Chart (continued)

Pace   ❏ Very Good   ❏ Average   ❏ Needs Improvement

 ❏ Too quick

 ❏ Too slow

 ❏ Lacked variety

 ❏ Hesitant

 ❏ Appropriate

 ❏ Other

Pause   ❏ Very Good   ❏ Average   ❏ Needs Improvement

 ❏ Used sense pause well

 ❏ Used dramatic pause

 ❏ Used emphatic pause

 ❏ Did not use pause effectively

 ❏ Other

Stress   ❏ Very Good   ❏ Average   ❏ Needs Improvement

(Stress is the weight or force put on a word or phrase to bring out the meaning)

 ❏ Appropriate

 ❏ Inappropriate

 ❏ Other

Vocal   ❏ Very Good   ❏ Average   ❏ Needs Improvement

 ❏ Breathy

 ❏ Nasal

 ❏ Throaty

 ❏ Shrill

 ❏ Shaky

 ❏ Dull

 ❏ Lacks modulation

 ❏ Other

FORM 8.1	**Voice and Speech Analysis Chart** (continued)

Speech   ❏ Very Good   ❏ Average   ❏ Needs Improvement

    ❏ Indistinct

    ❏ Slurring

    ❏ Defective speech sounds

    ❏ Mispronunciation

    ❏ Over-articulated

    ❏ Dialect/Accent

    ❏ Other

Overall Vocal Impression

    ❏ Positive – What aspects conveyed a positive impression?

    ❏ Negative – What aspects conveyed a negative impression?

    ❏ I need to work on the following areas:

        ❏ Volume

        ❏ Pitch

        ❏ Pace

        ❏ Pause

        ❏ Stress

        ❏ Vocal Quality

        ❏ Clarity

Voice

Have you ever asked yourself, "What is voice?" Voice is vibrating breath. To develop a strong, well-modulated, resonant voice, we need to begin with basic breathing. We must make certain we have the following:

1. Sufficient breath capacity
2. Good control of our breath

    To make a sound we need the following three things:

1. An exciter – a force that enables the instrument to move
2. A vibrator – which sends out sound waves
3. A resonator – which amplifies the sound

Our breath is the exciter, the vocal chords are the vibrator, the pharynx, the oral cavity, and the nasal cavity act as resonators.

The following illustrates how sound is made:

1. We inhale and fill our lungs with air.

2. Air is expelled from the lungs.

3. This air passes between our vocal chords and vibrates.

4. The vibrations pass through the resonating chambers where the sound is amplified.

5. The movements of the organs of articulation shape the sounds into vowels and consonants. These are connected into words and subsequently phrases and sentences.

Voice Routine

Our aim is to develop a voice that is full, firm, forward, and flexible. We need to remember that our voice is housed in our bodies and that a tense, restricted body will produce a tense, restricted voice.

Therefore, our voice routine must begin with a few minutes of relaxation, resulting in a greater flow of sound and more efficient sound production. What follows now is a series of exercises for you to work on. Remember theoretical instruction will not substitute for actual practice and application. We'll begin with relaxing the body.

Relaxation

1. Find a quiet place.

2. Wear loose, comfortable clothes and remove your shoes.

3. Lie on your back. Let your arms rest at your sides with your palms facing upwards.

4. Feel that the floor supports your spine.

5. Gently roll your neck from side to side, releasing any tension in the neck.

6. Become aware of your breathing and feel the breath entering, then leaving the body.

7. Take five slow, deep breaths, first filling, then emptying the lungs completely. Feel the ribs expanding forwards, sideways, and along the floor on the back, as they accommodate the expansion of the lungs.

8. Push your heels away, turning your toes in towards you. Relax them.

9. Pull up your kneecaps and tighten your thighs. Relax them.

10. Tighten your buttock and stomach muscles simultaneously, pulling them towards each other. Relax.

11. Arch your back off the floor. Relax.

12. Make a fist of your hands, tighten the muscles of the arms and pull your shoulders up to your ears. Hold the tension. Relax.

13. Roll the head from side to side gently. Check that the neck muscles are relaxed.

14. Screw up your eyes tightly. Now tense all the muscles of the face so that it feels like a shrivelled prune. Relax.

15. Feel a sense of calm and harmony.

16. Close your eyes. Imagine yourself in a serene, beautiful place where you feel totally peaceful and relaxed. Linger there for a few minutes.

17. Slowly open your eyes and take a deep breath. Exhale. Take a few more deep breaths.

18. Breathe in and exhale on a sigh. Relax the jaw while sighing. Repeat this three times.

19. Breathe in and exhale on the sound *AHH*. Again keep the jaw relaxed and feel the sound becoming fuller.

20. Open the mouth wide and yawn. Do this three times.

Now your body, which houses your vocal instrument, is ready to practise the resonance exercises that follow. These exercises will help you utilize the resonating chambers, the chest, head, and nasal cavities, where sound is amplified. Your voice will become fuller and richer as a result of this practice.

RESONANCE EXERCISES

1. Yawn and as you do so, become aware of the position of the tongue. The back of the tongue is depressed while the soft palate rises. Feel a sense of openness in your throat. Yawn between vowels:

   Yawn-AH, Yawn- OH, Yawn-EE, Yawn-OO

2. Take in a deep breath and exhale on the sound *HUM*. Make sure that you start on the *H* consonant. You should feel a tingling sensation behind your lips. This indicates that your voice is now moving forward towards the mask of the face. Allow the *HUM* sound to last for the duration of the exhalation. Repeat this 10 times.

3. Place your hand on your sternum, and repeat Exercise Number Two. A slight vibration should be felt underneath your hand. Repeat this five times. Now you should feel the chest resonance.

4. Now place your hand on your forehead and as you exhale on *HUM*, check whether you feel the vibration underneath the palm of your hand. Here, we are feeling the head resonance. Repeat this five times.

5. To maintain the forward placement of the voice, do the following:

   Say: B...................... m m m m
   P...................... m m m m
   W...................... m m m m
   M M M ah
   M M M ay
   M M M ee
   M M M I
   M M M oo
   M M M oh

6. Breathe in, then intone (for example, make a singing sound)

    AH........................
    OO........................
    OH........................
    OW........................
    EE........................

7. Intone on different pitches while concentrating on lengthening the vowel sounds:

High pitch:	AH	OO	OH	AY	EE
	↓	↓	↓	↓	↓
Medium pitch:	AH	OO	OH	AY	EE
	↓	↓	↓	↓	↓
Low pitch:	AH	OO	OH	AY	EE

8. For nasal resonance intone the sound *NG* (as in the word si*ng*). Hold this sound for ten seconds. Repeat this and then stop for five seconds and produce the sound *NG* again. You will feel the movement of the soft palate if you are doing this correctly.
    Now intone NG – AH, NG – AH, NG – AH. Drop your jaw when making the AH sound.

9. Say:

MAH	MAY	MEE	MI	MOH	MOO
NAH	NAY	NEE	NI	NOH	NOO
NGAH	NGAY	NGEE	NGI	NGOH	NGOO

10. Breathe in and intone 1 to 10.

11. Breathe in and intone the odd numbers and speak the even numbers. Do this on the numbers 1 to 10.

12. Intone 1, 2, 3. Speak 4, 5, 6. Repeat this five times.

13. Intone the following words:

    Ding - Dong
    King - Kong
    Wing - Wong
    Sing - Song
    Ling - Long
    Ning - Nong
    Bing - Bong

14. Test forward resonance by making the continued sounds of:

    vvvvvvvvvvvvvvvvv
    zzzzzzzzzzzzzzzzz
    th th th th th th th th

15. Say the following poem and focus while lengthening the vowel sounds:

Ode

Arthur O'Shaughnessy, 1844-1881

We are the music-makers,
    And we are the dreamers of dreams,
Wandering by the lone sea-breakers,
    And sitting by desolate Streams;
World-losers and world-forsakers,
    On whom the pale moon gleams:
Yet we are the movers and shakers
    Of the world forever, it seems.
With wonderful deathless ditties
    We build up the world's great cities,
And out of a fabulous story
    We fashion an empire's glory:
One man with a dream, at pleasure,
    Shall go forth and conquer a crown;
And three with a new song's measure
    Can trample an empire down.
We, in the ages lying
    In the buried past of the earth,
Built Nineveh with our sighing,
    And Babel itself with our mirth;
And o'erthrew them prophesying
    To the old of the new world's worth;
For each age is a dream that is dying,
    Or one that is coming to birth.

VOLUME AND PROJECTION

You have prepared a detailed, well-researched, well-structured talk. Now you need to deliver it with vitality and enthusiasm.

The audience should never have to work to get your message. Therefore, it is vital to project your voice so that the listener receives your words with ease. A good speaking voice should be full, firm, forward, flowing, and flexible.

Now practise the following exercises:

PROJECTION EXERCISE 1

1. Stand erect. Place your hands on your ribs with the fingertips touching. Inhale, swing the ribs outwards. Exhale while the ribs return to their original position. Repeat each exercise 5 times.

2. Inhale, then exhale and intone 1, 2, 3, 4, 5

3. Inhale, then exhale while intoning 1, 2, 3, then speak 4, 5, 6

4. Inhale then exhale and intone 1, 2, then speak 3, 4, 5, 6

5. Inhale, then exhale and intone 1, then speak 2, 3, 4, 5, 6

6. Inhale then exhale and intone 1, 2, 3, 4, 5, 6

   At this point your voice should be forward and projected.

7. Inhale. Exhale and say, "My name is (fill in your own name)."

PROJECTION EXERCISE II

Read the following aloud in the following ways:

1. In a whisper
2. To a person standing next to you
3. To an audience gathered in a large auditorium
4. To people standing across the street
5. To people standing across a river

Utilize your breathing to be more proficient while projecting. Do not project from your throat. A well-projected voice should emanate from well-filled lungs being used efficiently.

> We have before us an ordeal of the most grievous kind. We have before us many, many long months of struggle and of suffering. You ask, what is our policy? I will say: It is to wage war, by sea, land and air, with all our might and with all the strength that God can give us: to wage war against a monstrous tyranny, never surpassed in the dark, lamentable catalogue of human crime. That is our policy. You ask, What is our aim? I can answer in one word: Victory—victory at all costs, victory in spite of all terror, victory, however long and hard the road may be; for without victory, there is no survival. Let that be realized; no survival for the British Empire; no survival for all that the British Empire has stood for, no survival for the urge and impulse of the ages, that mankind will move forward towards its goal. But I take up my task with buoyancy and hope. I feel sure that our cause will not be suffered to fail among men. At this time I feel entitled to claim the aid of all, and I say, "Come, then, let us go forward together with our united strength."

Sir Winston Churchill

House of Commons, May 13, 1940, in his first address as the newly appointed Prime Minister

PROJECTION EXERCISE III

Say the following words reflecting the onomatopoeic quality of each:

1.

soft	soft
medium	medium
loud	loud

2.

soft	soft	
medium	loud	soft
soft	medium	
loud	soft	
loud	medium	

3.

soft	medium	loud	
medium	loud	medium	loud
loud	medium	loud	
medium	loud	medium	

4.

soft	loud	soft	loud
medium	loud	loud	
loud	loud	loud	

5.

very loud	soft
very loud	medium
very loud	loud

PITCH

Pitch can be defined as the height or depth of the voice.

A high-pitched voice does not convey credibility. Have you ever thought about the fact that voice can have a physical impact on the listener? A high-pitched voice can have a negative, grating impact on the audience.

When Jack Nicklaus won a golf tournament back in the 1970s he spoke with such a high, squeaking voice that it was difficult to take him seriously. Recently, he appeared on television and his pitch had dropped a full octave. Speech coaching or age had lowered the timbre of his voice.

PITCH EXERCISES

Here are some exercises to help you improve your vocal pitch.

Take a look at the following pitch chart. The number (1) represents the lowest pitch. Number (2) represents the middle pitch and (3) the highest pitch. When you reach exercise 3, the range increases with (3) being your middle pitch. For exercise 4, begin speaking from highest pitch (5) down to your lowest pitch (1). For exercise number 5, (6) is your highest pitch. Say the following numbers out loud, using the appropriate pitch,

1. Speak from lowest to highest pitch

```
        3        3        3        3        3
    2        2        2        2        2
  1        1        1        1        1
```

2. Speak from highest to lowest pitch

```
  3        3        3        3        3
    2        2        2        2        2
      1        1        1        1        1
```

3. Speak from lowest to highest pitch

```
            5        5        5        5            5
          4        4        4        4        4
        3        3        3        3        3
      2        2        2        2        2
    1        1        1        1        1
```

4. Speak from highest to lowest pitch

```
  5        5        5        5        5
    4        4        4        4        4
      3        3        3        3        3
        2        2        2        2        2
          1        1        1        1        1
```

5. Start with your lowest pitch and adjust your pitch according to the rise and fall of the numbers

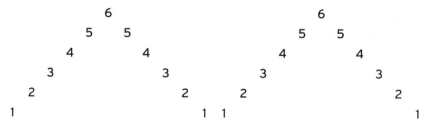

```
              6                            6
          5     5                      5     5
        4           4              4           4
      3               3        3               3
    2                   2    2                   2
  1                       1  1                     1
```

6. Repeat Exercises 1 to 4 on the word "Hello."

7. Repeat Exercise 5 on the word "Go."

8. Do the following exercise beginning with a high pitch and continue practising using descending pitches.

HO	HEE	HI	HA	HOO
↓	↓	↓	↓	↓
HO	HEE	HI	HA	HOO
↓	↓	↓	↓	↓
HO	HEE	HI	HA	HOO

9. Begin this exercise starting at your lowest pitch.

HO	HEE	HI	HA	HOO
↑	↑	↑	↑	↑
HO	HEE	HI	HA	HOO
↑	↑	↑	↑	↑
HO	HEE	HI	HA	HOO

10. Select an extract from a novel or newspaper.

    Read it at a low pitch

    Read it at a medium pitch

    Read it at a high pitch

11. For a little fun, tell the story of *Goldilocks and the Three Bears* into a tape-recorder. Remember to vary your pitch when speaking the words of the baby bear (high-pitched), the mother bear (medium-pitched), and the father bear (low-pitched). Listen back to hear how accurately you altered your voice.

12. Read the following while using variety in pitch:

    a) May the road rise up to meet you,
        May the wind be always at your back,
        May the sunshine warm upon your face
        And the rains fall soft upon your fields,
        And, until we meet again,
        May God hold you in the palm of his hand

        Gaelic Prayer

    b) To everything there is a season, and a time to every purpose under the heaven:
        A time to be born, and a time to die;
        A time to plant, and a time to pluck up that which is planted;
        A time to kill, and a time to heal;
        A time to break down, and a time to build up;

A time to weep, and a time to laugh;
A time to mourn, and a time to dance;
A time to cast away stones, and a time to gather stones together;
A time to embrace, and a time to refrain from embracing;
A time to get, and a time to lose;
A time to keep, and a time to cast away;
A time to rend, and a time to sew;
A time to keep silence, and a time to speak;
A time to love, and a time to hate;
A time of war, and a time of peace.

Ecclesiates 3:1-8

PACE

Pace is the rate at which we speak. We are generally comfortable when a speaker speaks at a rate of between 140-180 words per minute. When listening to a speaker talk at the rate of 120-140 words per minute, we may find it rather slow. If you speak at the rate of 180-200 words per minute, this will not satisfy the audience except if your aim is to convey anxiety, fear, anger, or excitement.

An interesting voice that captures the audience's attention will embrace variety in pace. Naturally, the use of pace is dictated by the meaning that the speaker intends to convey.

If you tend to speak too quickly, the audience may miss many of your thoughts. Learn to slow down and utilize pause. Here are some exercises to help you master the use of pace.

1. Choose an extract to read into a tape-recorder, reading

   a) at a slow pace

   b) at a medium pace

   c) at a quick pace

2. Read one paragraph

      at a slow pace

   Read the next paragraph

      at a medium pace

   Read the next paragraph

      at a quick pace

3. Read alternating sentences

   a) at a slow pace

   b) at a medium pace

   c) at a quick pace

4. Take an extract and read it backwards, start reading from the right-hand side of the line. You cannot read backwards quickly since you cannot anticipate the words that follow. Continue reading a full page in this manner. This practice will slow you down considerably.

PAUSE

He knew the precise psychological moment when to say nothing.

—Oscar Wilde

Pause gives public speaking a conversational quality. How frequently have you heard a speaker race through a speech without giving a thought as to whether the listener is keeping up? Remember the audience needs time to grasp your meaning, and to absorb and digest what has been said. Pause is punctuation for the ear.

When you read a novel, you get a visual cue indicating that the author is changing thoughts. This normally occurs at the end of every paragraph. When we speak, we need to give the audience the cue that we are changing direction or beginning a new topic. We do this by pausing.

Many speakers are afraid of silence. They abhor "dead air." They feel they need to fill the silence with every word. Sometimes they resort to using fillers such as, "you know," "um," "like," and "okay" when they ought to be pausing.

Students will often ask, "Well, what can I do when I feel so self-conscious about silence?" Let silence be your friend, and if you need to fill that silence, take a breath to give you something to focus on.

A skilled, eloquent speaker understands the power of pause and knows the "precise psychological moment when to say nothing."

There are different types of pauses, each serving a different purpose. There is the pause for *emphasis*. You pause before or after the important word. It frames the word that you want emphasized. When you see a forward slash represented by a /, this will represent PAUSE. Here is an example of an *emphatic pause*:

"The winner of the prize is / David."

The word that follows the pause is then given vocal weight. That means the speaker would pause for one or two beats before the word, David, and would vocally stress the word.

Then there is the *sense pause*. Simply put, you pause where it makes sense to pause, at a comma, a colon, a period, or before or after quotation marks. This pause helps the listener digest and process our message. The following is an example of a *sense pause*: "Thinking cannot be clear till it has had expression. / We must write / or speak / or act our thoughts / or they will remain in half torpid form. //" Henry Ward Beecher

The *dramatic pause* is self-explanatory. We create a sense of drama when utilizing it. We can manipulate or create suspense through this. Read the following aloud, observing the pause marks. "As he entered the darkened dungeon / he was enveloped by / silence. Enter this world with me // Stay with me a while as we sink into the depths of this / perilous place. //"

Pause can change the meaning of the sentence. Note the difference in meaning engendered when the same sentence is spoken in two different ways:

"Eat a little Billy./"

"Eat a little / Billy."

Accurate usage of pause helps the audience to understand you. It elucidates, titillates, and adds spice to your delivery.

When preparing your speech, mark up your speech appropriately. Record it and listen back to evaluate your effectiveness.

STRESS

Stress is the force or weight put on a word or phrase to bring out the meaning.

When you are given a piece of written material you have never seen before, stress the verbs and nouns. You will sound as if you are familiar with the material. Give adjectives and nouns equal stress, for example, "She wore a *green suit*." However, if a question is posed, for example, "What colour suit did she wear?" then you stress the adjective. "She wore a *green* suit."

When typing out your speech, you can indicate stress by **bolding** the word or underlining it.

Read this extract from a sermon by the Rev. Dr. Andrew Stirling entitled, "The Child's Kingdom," December 2001, and mark the appropriate stresses.

> I took my mother by the arm and rushed her down the aisles and through the many different floors of what was, certainly when I was a 10-year old boy, the most famous toy store in England. It was called Selfridges, and every child wanted to go there and play with their trains and their other toys.
>
> This was the first time that my mother had ever taken me on a pre-Christmas shopping tour. So we had taken the train into London and I eagerly headed down the aisles, wanting to introduce my mother to what I thought was the most spectacular gift that had ever been made in the history of toys. So, via many forms of manipulation, I finally got my mother to see the toy that every boy dreamed of in 1968: The Secret Sam Spy Case.

EXERCISES FOR VOCAL VARIETY

Now let's put it all together and see how well-modulated your voice is. Read the following, accurately reflecting the intention of the sentences:

1. What terrific news!
2. Get away from me!
3. Can you believe it?
4. How sad!
5. How exciting!

6. Don't tell him.

7. Hold tight!

8. What do you want?

9. It's dark in here.

10. I'm in a hurry.

11. Slow down, take your time.

12. What a waste of time!

13. He's so aggressive.

14. Don't be late.

15. Relax in front of the fire.

16. She has a big black rottweiller.

17. Get a move on.

18. I'm sick and tired.

19. Speak up, I can't hear you.

20. Oh, what a pity.

21. I'm scared, don't leave me.

22. I love you!

23. Let me go right now.

24. I'm very curious.

If you feel that your voice lacks clarity, you need to work on your organs of articulation—the tongue, lips, jaw, and soft palate.

Chapter 9 focuses on Clear Speech and Articulation and provides a detailed guide to assist you in achieving clear, audible speech.

SUMMARY

A well-modulated, clear voice plays an important role in conveying the spoken message effectively. The student is encouraged to make a tape recording of her or his own voice and then to use the Voice and Speech Analysis Chart to assess it. A voice routine is offered to help the student develop a voice that is full, firm, well-projected, and vital. The characteristics of a good voice are explained, and specific exercises to develop a resonant voice are given. In addition, exercises for volume, pitch, pace, pause, and stress are presented. By engaging in the correct practice and application of these exercises, all students can improve their vocal variety and learn to use their voice with impact.

SUGGESTED READING

Berry, Cicely. *Voice and the Actor*. London: George G. Harrap and Co. Ltd., 1973.

Burniston, Christabel and Jocelyn Bell. *Into the Life of Things*. Lancashire, England: The English Speaking Board, 1977.

Burniston, Christabel and John Parry. *Direct Speech*. London: Hodder and Stoughton, 1987.

Cole, Wilton. *Sound and Sense*. Great Britain: John Dickens and Co. Ltd., 1973.

Colson, Greta. *Voice Production and Speech*. London, England: Museum Press Limited, 1967.

Marash, J. G. *Effective Speaking*. London: George G. Harrap and Co. Ltd., 1967.

Thurburn, Gwenyth L. *Voice and Speech, An Introduction*. Herts, England: James Nisbet and Company Ltd., 1963.

REFERENCES

Comins, Roz. "Factors affecting voice." *Voice and Voice Skills*. Professional Development Project.

The Canuck Uptalk Epidemic

By Hank Davis

Uptalk was barely present 10 years ago. Now it's threatening to infect all of us like some sort of conversational anthrax.

I attended an international conference this past summer and one of the British hosts sidled up to me during a Canadian presentation. He leaned over and whispered, asking about the presenter: "What's wrong with her? Do all Canadians talk like that? It sounds like all she's doing is asking questions."

I felt both saddened and vindicated. For years, I've been getting on my students for this needless vocal tic that devalues what they have to say. I want them to sound professional, not only in content but in style. Most of them are batting .500. They do their homework, but when it comes time to speak out loud, they revert to uptalk.

It's become an epidemic.

Talk to a teenager and you're almost guaranteed to hear it although the problem is more prevalent among young women. And now it's spreading from the kids to their parents. It's getting so we don't even notice uptalk anymore.

I hear it from other university professors (especially the young ones), high school teachers, students, secretaries, receptionists, telephone operators—adults who never talked that way before have become prime agents of the virus.

Uptalk is the inability to utter a declarative sentence without curling up your voice at the end to signify a question. Do you understand me? Are you still listening to me? Can I go on?

Declarative sentences have gone through some kind of politically correct meat grinder and have been turned into questions. I can easily remember when

Canadians, even young ones, just stated their business—including simple things like their names—without curling their voices into a desperate plea for approval and understanding.

When I tell my students about this vocal habit, they often react as if they are hearing about it for the first time. Within days they tell me, "I see what you mean. It's everywhere. I can't believe how much my friends and I do it."

Granted, uptalk is a lot harder to take when it's used continually and indiscriminately. Like any verbal tic, it becomes all the more grating when every sentence (even individual phrases within a sentence), is turned into a question. You might think uptalk would be reserved for difficult concepts, but it isn't.

What has happened to simply stating your piece? Has it become impolite to speak assertively in Canadian society? Every day I hear the simplest statements turned into interrogatives. My name is Jennifer? I live in Guelph? I'm here to fix your washer?

They've all become questions. But what is at issue here? One's name? The location of one's home? One's job? Why can't those things be stated politely but firmly? Has tentativeness become the hallmark of polite discourse in Canada? Is it rude to sound confident? Must we seek consensus at every syllable with vocal inflections that say: I'm not sure about any of this. I can take it back at a moment's notice if it displeases you.

Not all of my colleagues agree with me. Mind you, there is little debate about the spread of uptalk, or—as is the case with cigarette smoking—that young women are its biggest practitioners. The debate surrounds why people uptalk, or whether they uptalk for a single reason. Perhaps they don't, but I think there's enough of a pattern to offer a working theory.

It's been suggested to me that uptalk is a direct descendent of Valley Girl Talk. The thing is, Valley Girl Talk never really caught on in the States. Its tentative, unsure nature never really fit the American psyche. So it moved north in search of different values. And what did it find? It found a culture known for politeness. A place where "If you have nothing nice to say, say nothing" is printed on restaurant placemats and embroidered on our souls. Here, in Canada, uptalk found a home.

Let me tell you about an unusually honest conversation I recently had with a student. I asked her about the use of uptalk and other interrogatives she strategically placed at the end of her statements. She paused reflectively and said: "I'll tell you exactly why I do it. I do it to tone down what I say. I don't want to come across too assertively. I'm afraid people won't like me or some of the things I say. I don't want to alienate my friends or the kids in class. This way, I can take the stuff I say back if people around me seem uncomfortable."

And there you have it. An admittedly small sample, but an insight from the lips of an actual practitioner.

So now we have at least one working theory on the table. Uptalk suspends a statement in some kind of social limbo until you get approval. No feathers ruffled. No friends lost. No opinions. No harm done.

When my British host wondered aloud about this non-assertive Canadian style of speech, should I have replied that we Canadians are so consumed with politeness and consensus-seeking that we can no longer state anything without checking in several times a sentence to make sure we haven't offended anyone?

I think we need to take a step back and listen to ourselves. Let's at least call attention to how we sound. Uptalk was barely present 10 years ago. Now it's threatening to infect all of us like some sort of conversational anthrax.

Understandably, Canada wants a distinctive cultural identity but please, not this! There are many things that make me proud to be a Canadian. Uptalk is not one of them.

Hank Davis is a professor of psychology at the University of Guelph. Used by permission of the author.

Clear Speech
and Articulation

Speech is a mirror of the soul; As a man speaks, so is he.
—Publilius Syrus, 1st Century B.C.

LEARNING OBJECTIVES

- To understand the importance of speaking with clarity

- To identify the organs of articulation

- To improve your speech through the practice of speech exercises and tongue twisters

Clear speech. The student running for class president needs it. The coach of the hockey team needs it. Managers, executives, leaders, teachers, doctors, lawyers, architects, researchers, pilots, businesspeople, travel guides, marketing and salespeople, chairpersons, and bankers need it. You need it if you are defending a thesis. You need it for everyday social, educational, and business interaction.

The ability to convey your thoughts and ideas through the medium of clear speech is a vital, lifelong asset.

Many students today are adept at mastering the skill of communicating via the Internet. They possess excellent academic and technical skills. Yet when asked to stand up in front of an audience to present a project or their research findings, they lack clarity of speech. An earth-shattering new concept will go unnoticed if it is not clearly articulated. The latest innovative product will go nowhere if you cannot express how well it is designed, what functions it serves, and how the buyer will benefit. You will not receive an extension for a deadline if you cannot clearly articulate why you need it.

CLEAR SPEECH

What do we mean by clear speech? Clear speech is spoken language that is intelligible, audible, and easily understood. This means that the words we hear should make sense; we should be able to hear them easily, and we should to have no difficulty interpreting them.

In an earlier era, the word "elocution" was used to describe a very precise, standardized way of speaking English. In Canada, we embrace our differences and do not subscribe to a standard that requires everyone to speak with the same accent and manner. An accent defines who you are, so it is not necessary to eliminate it. However, when the accent interferes with the reception of the message, then it may be wise to alter particular sounds to achieve clarity. For example, if what you are saying sounds like "It is very ko here," the listener will not understand you. Yet, what you intended to say was: "It is very cold here." In this situation, the speaker has not pronounced the final "d" consonant in the word "cold" and therefore the sentence becomes unintelligible. This example shows why clear pronunciation is so important.

Speech is a physical process and it requires effective use of the organs of articulation to produce clear speech sounds. The organs of articulation are the lips, the tongue, the jaw, the teeth, the teeth ridge (which is the ridge between the upper teeth and the hard palate), the hard palate (the roof of the mouth), and the soft palate (which hangs down from the back part of the hard palate, is arched, and can move freely) as shown in Figure 9.1 below.

FIGURE 9.1	**Cross Section of the Head**

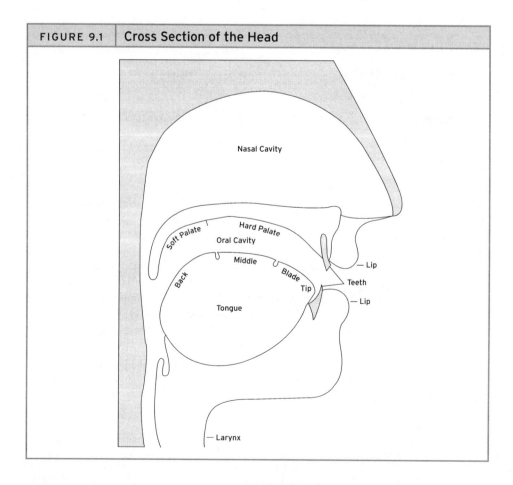

This chapter will offer you concrete exercises for the organs of articulation. Think of these exercises as "speech aerobics." Well-exercised organs of articulation will increase your awareness of the physical nature of the speech process. They will also help to improve the clarity of your speech.

If you experience more serious speech problems, such as stuttering or stammering, you might consider seeking professional guidance from a qualified speech pathologist.

There are two kinds of speech sounds. They are **vowel sounds** and **consonant sounds**. A vowel gives purity to speech, while a consonant gives speech a sense of clarity. A **vowel** sound is made when vibrating breath passes through the mouth. The tongue and lips are used to shape the vowel sounds. In English, we have five letters—A-E-I-O-U—to represent all of the vowel sounds. As you know, the letter "a" can represent different sounds. Say these words aloud: bat, rate, ball, many, arm. Here you will notice that each vowel sound is different, although they are all represented in written form by the letter "a."

Phonetics is the science of speech sounds. The International Phonetic Alphabet, which appears at the front of most dictionaries, will show you how specific symbols represent each individual sound. When in doubt as to the pronunciation of a specific vowel sound, refer to this phonetic table that will show you how to pronounce the sound.

Enunciation is the shaping of vowel sounds.

A **consonant** is made when the breath is impeded as it passes through the mouth. Yet, for the sounds "m," "n," and "ng," the breath is emitted through the nose. There is either a partial or complete contact of the organs of speech. To produce clear consonants, the tongue and lips need to be firm and flexible. For example, to produce the "t" sound the tongue tip contacts the teeth ridge behind the upper teeth; when the tongue is released, the "t" sound results. The shaping of consonant sounds is called **articulation**.

Clear speech depends upon the following five factors:

1. Well-formed vowel sounds

2. Clearly articulated consonants

3. Acceptable pronunciation

4. Clarity of thought

5. A well-projected voice

It will help greatly to practise the following exercises for the tongue, lips, jaw, and soft palate. Appropriate use of the phonetic guidelines in the dictionary, reference to previous chapters on formulating and structuring your message, and vocal projection will complete your preparation for clear speech.

TONGUE EXERCISES

Clear speech requires an agile tongue that is capable of moving with precision to produce correct sounds. The tongue is a muscle and therefore needs toning, or a "tune-up," on a regular basis. Here are some tongue exercises for you to practise.
Repeat each one 10 times.

1. Stretch the tongue forward. Retract it.

2. Stretch the tongue up towards your nose. Retract it.

3. Stretch the tongue down towards your chin. Retract it.

4. Stretch the tongue out and then move it from side to side.

5. Circle your tongue in a clockwise direction around the outside of your lips. Do this ten times and then circle your tongue ten times in a counter-clockwise direction.

6. Press the tongue against the inside of the left cheek and move it up and down. Repeat this inside the right cheek.

7. Stretch the tongue out and then curl it inward.

8. Imagine that your tongue is a broom and it is going to sweep the roof of your mouth from behind the upper teeth ridge backwards. Perform this action.

9. Circle the inside of your lips, first in a clockwise direction, then in a counter-clockwise direction.

10. Place the tongue behind the top teeth and then move the tip of the tongue down to behind the lower teeth. Keep the jaw open while you move the tongue up and down.
    For Exercises 11 to 15, we are using the [AH] sound. For [AH] the tongue is relaxed and the jaw is lowered.

11. Hold the tongue tip behind the teeth ridge and feel the sides of the tongue against the top gums. Feel the energy in the tip of the tongue.
    Say:
    (a) tah tah tah tah

       (Note the explosion of air as you release the sound)

    (b) tah-tah, tah-tah, tah-tah, tah-tah

    (c) tah-tah-tah, tah-tah-tah, tah-tah-tah, tah-tah-tah

    (d) tah-tahtahtah, tah-tahtahtah, tah-tahtahtah, tah-tahtahtah

12. Repeat 11 but with the sound "dah"
    Say:
    (a) dah dah dah dah

    (b) dah-dah, dah-dah, dah-dah, dah-dah

    (c) dah-dah-dah, dah-dah-dah, dah-dah-dah, dah-dah-dah

    (d) dah-dahdahdah, dah-dahdahdah, dah-dahdahdah, dah-dahdahdah

13. Repeat with:
    (a) lah lah lah lah

    (b) lah-lah, lah-lah, lah-lah, lah-lah

    (c) lah-lah-lah, lah-lah-lah, lah-lah-lah, lah-lah-lah

    (d) lah-lahlahlah, lah-lahlahlah, lah-lahlahlah, lah-lahlahlah

14. Repeat with:
    (a) nah nah nah nah

    (b) nah-nah, nah-nah, nah-nah, nah-nah

    (c) nah-nah-nah, nah-nah-nah, nah-nah-nah, nah-nah-nah

    (d) nah-nahnahnah, nah-nahnahnah, nah-nahnahnah, nah-nahnahnah

15. Repeat with:

    (a) rah rah rah rah

    (b) rah-rah, rah-rah, rah-rah, rah-rah

    (c) rah-rah-rah, rah-rah-rah, rah-rah-rah, rah-rah-rah

    (d) rah-rahrahrah, rah-rahrahrah, rah-rahrahrah, rah-rahrahrah

16. Say:

    (a) t-d t-d t-d t-d

    (b) t-d-l, t-d-l, t-d-l, t-d-l

    (c) t-d-l-n, t-d-l-n, t-d-l-n, t-d-l-n

    (d) t-d-l-n-r, t-d-l-n-r, t-d-l-n-r, t-d-l-n-r

During this exercise you will notice that when you speak, your tongue is positioned at the teeth ridge when it produces the "t" sound and it gradually curls backwards until it produces the "r" sound.

The following two exercises offer practice for the back of the tongue.

17. Press the back of the tongue up against the soft palate and make a firm contact and say:

ke-ke-ke-ke	ke-ke-ke-ke	ke-ke-ke-ke	ke-ke-ke-ke
ge-ge-ge-ge	ge-ge-ge-ge	ge-ge-ge-ge	ge-ge-ge-ge

18. Say the following as fast and as clearly as possible while using the front and back of the tongue efficiently:

t-k	t-k	t-k	t-k	t-k	t-k
d-g	d-g	d-g	d-g	d-g	d-g
k-t	k-t	k-t	k-t	k-t	k-t
g-d	g-d	g-d	g-d	g-d	g-d

Notice how the organs of articulation first connect and then explode apart for these sounds.

19. Now we'll go through the consonants and repeat each one seven times. Say these sounds in an exaggerated manner.

b	b	b	b	b	b	b
d	d	d	d	d	d	d
f	f	f	f	f	f	f
g	g	g	g	g	g	g
h	h	h	h	h	h	h
j	j	j	j	j	j	j
k	k	k	k	k	k	k
l	l	l	l	l	l	l
m	m	m	m	m	m	m
n	n	n	n	n	n	n

p	p	p	p	p	p	p
r	r	r	r	r	r	r
s	s	s	s	s	s	s
t	t	t	t	t	t	t
v	v	v	v	v	v	v
w	w	w	w	w	w	w
y	y	y	y	y	y	y
z	z	z	z	z	z	z

voiceless

th	th	th	th	th	th	th

(as in the word *think*)

voiced

th	th	th	th	th	th	th

(as in the word *then*)

sh	sh	sh	sh	sh	sh	sh

(as in the word *shout*)

zh	zh	zh	zh	zh	zh	zh

(as in the word *pleasure*)

20. Practise the following. Start by saying the vowel sound and end with the consonant, for example, OO<u>B</u>.

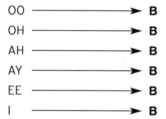

Then substitute the next consonant listed under Exercise 19 and say aloud– for example: ood, ohd, ahd, ayd, eed, id.

LIP EXERCISES

Clear articulation requires efficient movement of the lips. The lips need to be flexible to form vowel sounds and consonants. Consonant sounds that are made with the lips are p, b, m and w.

Let's begin with lip drills. Repeat each one 10 times.

1. Round the lips in the shape of a circle. Relax.
2. Press your lips together and smile. Relax.

3. Purse your lips by pushing them forward. Relax.

4. Alternate smiling and pouting.

5. Now open your mouth and smile.

6. Purse your lips, and move them like a goldfish.

7. Turn the lower lip down in a pouting position. Relax.

8. Raise the left side of your upper lip. Relax.

9. Raise the right side of your upper lip. Relax.

10. Close the lips and blow between them.

11. Say: oo-ee, oo-ee, oo-ee, without sound.

12. Say: oo-ee-ah repeatedly. Remember to round your lips on "oo," spread them on "ee," and drop the jaw on "ah."

13. Say:

    me-me-me-me-me-me-me-me

    we-we-we-we-we-we-we-we

    pe-pe-pe-pe-pe-pe-pe-pe

    be-be-be-be-be-be-be-be

Make sure that the consonant sounds are firm and clear.

14. Say:

    mo-mo-mo-mo-mo-mo-mo-mo

    wo-wo-wo-wo-wo-wo-wo-wo

    po-po-po-po-po-po-po-po

    bo-bo-bo-bo-bo-bo-bo-bo

15. Say:

    ma-ma-ma-ma-ma-ma-ma-ma

    wa-wa-wa-wa-wa-wa-wa-wa

    pa-pa-pa-pa-pa-pa-pa-pa

    ba-ba-ba-ba-ba-ba-ba-ba

16. Press the lips together. Feel the pressure and let the breath explode like a cork popping, as you say:

poo	poh	pah	pay	pi
boo	boh	bah	bay	bi
poo-boo	poo-boo	poo-boo		
poh-boh	poh-boh	poh-boh		
pah-bah	pah-bah	pah-bah		
pay-bay	pay-bay	pay-bay		
pi-bi	pi-bi	pi-bi		

17. Say the following, clearly pronouncing the initial and final consonant:

pop	pop	pop	pop	pop	pop	pop	pop
pip	pip	pip	pip	pip	pip	pip	pip
pep	pep	pep	pep	pep	pep	pep	pep
pap	pap	pap	pap	pap	pap	pap	pap
pup	pup	pup	pup	pup	pup	pup	pup
pipe	pipe	pipe	pipe	pipe	pipe	pipe	pipe
payp	payp	payp	payp	payp	payp	payp	payp
poop	poop	poop	poop	poop	poop	poop	poop
poppety	poppety	poppety	pop				
pippety	pippety	pippety	pip				
peppety	peppety	peppety	pep				
pappety	pappety	pappety	pap				
pipety	pipety	pipety	pipe				
paypety	paypety	paypety	payp				
poopety	poopety	poopety	poop				

18.   Repeat Exercise 17, substituting the consonant "b" for "p."

19. Repeat Exercise 17, substituting the consonant "m" for "p."

20. Round the lips for the sound "w."

Say:

woo	woo	woo	woo	woo
woh	woh	woh	woh	woh
wah	wah	wah	wah	wah
way	way	way	way	way
wi	wi	wi	wi	wi
woo	woh	wah	way	wi
we were	we were	we were	we were	

21. Now place the lip consonant at the end of the vowel.

Say:

oop	ohp	ahp	ayp	eep
oob	ohb	ahp	ayb	eeb
oom	ohm	ahm	aym	eem

22. Say the following rhythmically:

p-p-p-poo	p-p-p-poh	p-p-p-pah
p-p-p-pay	p-p-p-pee	p-p-p-pi
b-b-b-boo	b-b-b-boh	b-b-b-bah
b-b-b-bay	b-b-b-bee	b-b-b-bi
m-m-m-moo	m-m-m-moh	m-m-m-mah
m-m-m-may	m-m-m-mee	m-m-m-mi

23. Imagine that you have toffee stuck inside your mouth. Keep the lips closed and move them around in all directions.

JAW EXERCISES

It is important that the lower jaw is flexible. Mumbling is often the by-product of a tight jaw. So, too, is nasality or a flat tone. Therefore, we need to exercise the jaw so it can perform its speech work effectively.

Practise each of the following 10 times:

1. Yawning. Stretch your mouth into a wide-open position.
2. Drop the jaw slowly until the mouth "lands" in a wide-open position (never force this).
3. Let the jaw drop quickly.
4. Let the jaw drop and then protrude it forward. Return it to its natural position.
5. Circle the jaw in a clockwise direction. Then repeat the circling in a counter-clockwise direction.
6. Move the jaw to the left and right.
7. Place your fingertips above the cheekbone. Slowly move your hands down the sides of your face, relaxing all the muscles beneath your fingertips, and finally relax the jaw.
8. Say ah-ah-ah, dropping the jaw loosely.
9. Say each of the following lines five times:

OO-AH	OO-AH	OO-AH	OO-AH	OO-AH
EE-AH	EE-AH	EE-AH	EE-AH	EE-AH
OO-AH-EE	OO-AH-EE	OO-AH-EE	OO-AH-EE	OO-AH-EE
AH-EE-OO	AH-EE-OO	AH-EE-OO	AH-EE-OO	AH-EE-OO

10. Say the following words keeping the jaw loose and relaxed:

wobble	wobble	wobble	wobble	wobble
gobble	gobble	gobble	gobble	gobble
hobble	hobble	hobble	hobble	hobble

11. Let the jaw remain loose and flexible and say:

ya	ya	ya	ya	ya	ya	ya
yoo	yoo	yoo	yoo	yoo	yoo	yoo
yo	yo	yo	yo	yo	yo	yo
yay	yay	yay	yay	yay	yay	yay
yi	yi	yi	yi	yi	yi	yi
ha	ha	ha	ha	ha	ha	ha
hoo	hoo	hoo	hoo	hoo	hoo	hoo
ho	ho	ho	ho	ho	ho	ho
hay	hay	hay	hay	hay	hay	hay
hi	hi	hi	hi	hi	hi	hi
ya	yoo	yo	yay	yi		
ha	hoo	ho	hay	hi		

SOFT PALATE EXERCISES

1. Stand in front of a mirror. Drop your jaw and notice your soft palate that hangs down at the back of your throat. Say "ng" as in the word "ring," and then say "ah" as you drop your jaw. Repeat NG-AH, NG-AH, NG-AH, NG-AH, NG-AH.

2. Yawn five times.

3. Practise making a panting sound.

It is important to practise exercising the soft palate if you have a problem with nasality. When the soft palate does not work efficiently, the voice often takes on nasal overtones.

PROBLEM CONSONANTS

Voiceless and Voiced "TH," "S," "F," "V," "W," and "B"

There are a few sounds that present more of a challenge for some Canadian speakers, especially if an individual's first language is, among others, Chinese, Indian, Spanish, French, German, or Japanese. For instance, the Chinese language does not have the "th" sound; neither does German. Italian speakers will find "th" to be a new sound; so, too, will Japanese and French speakers. But regardless of your first language, the exercises below will help you improve pronunciation of these "problem" consonants."

"TH" There are two forms of the "th" sound: the voiceless sound "th," as in the word "think," and the voiced sound "th" as in the word "then." We will represent the former by the symbol "th" and the latter by symbol "th".

To produce these sounds you will need to educate the tongue to move into a new position.

EXERCISES FOR "th" AND "th"

1. Place the tip of your tongue between the upper front teeth. Feel as if the tongue is poking out slightly between your teeth. Retract it. Repeat this action 20 times.

2. Place your tongue between your teeth. Try and make a hissing sound as you feel the air passing between your teeth. The voiceless "th" sound as in "think" will result.

3. To produce the voiced sound "th" as in "then," make a buzzing or voiced sound as you push the air through.

4. Practise saying the following for the voiceless "th" sound as in the word "think."

    (i) th-th, th-th, th-th, th-th

    Say these words:

think	thank	thread	throw
three	thunder	thief	threw
thirteen	thrill	thistle	threat
thirty	thick	Thursday	throat
thief	throne	thought	through
thud	throb	thrust	threshold

(ii) Now practise saying the following where "th" appears at the end of the words:

north	moth	teeth
south	cloth	wreath
Ruth	truth	mouth
fourth	fifth	Keith

(iii) Now say these words where "th" appears in the middle of the words.

author	lethal	ether	cathedral	enthusiasm
ethics	athletics	sympathy	pathetic	mathematics

(iv) Say these sentences:

- There is a thunderstorm in the north.
- As a youth, Keith always told the truth.
- Both are made from the same cloth.
- Thirty-three thrushes flew through the bush.
- Ethel, Ruth, and Thelma are good friends.
- Cathy is thrifty and thoughtful.
- The thief was apprehended as he threw the brick through the window.

(v) Practise saying the following for the voiced "<u>th</u>" sound:

<u>th</u>-<u>th</u>, <u>th</u>-<u>th</u>, <u>th</u>-<u>th</u>, <u>th</u>-<u>th</u>, <u>th</u>-<u>th</u>

(vi) Say these words:

this	them	theirs	these
that	then	those	they
their	the	there	themselves

(vii) Say these words and notice that "<u>th</u>" appears in the middle of the words:

gather	mother	bother	leather	another
either	father	Heather	teething	seething
northern	brother	breathing	wither	slither

(viii) Say these words and notice that "<u>th</u>" appears at the end of the words:

seethe	loathe	clothe
writhe	smooth	bathe
breathe	lathe	scathe

(ix) Say these sentences aloud:

- My mother was seething when my brother came home late.
- These clothes belong to my father.
- I would rather choose another leather belt.
- The leaves have withered on the vine.
- Heather was breathing heavily when she entered the hospital.

"S" For the "s" sound, open the mouth slightly, and keep the teeth closed. Raise the tip of the tongue and curl it upward toward the teeth ridge. The sides of the tongue are pressed against the upper side teeth. When the "s" is produced, the breath passes down the groove in the middle of the tongue and emerges between the tongue and upper front teeth.

When an individual lisps, the tongue is mistakenly placed in the position for "th" as opposed to the "s" sound.

EXERCISES FOR "S"

1. Place your tongue in the correct position for "s" and say:

    s s s s s s s s s s

    Repeat this ten times.

2. Say the following words with the "s" sound appearing at the beginning of the word:

sit	see	silly	sad	sing	Sally
say	save	Sam	sip	slip	silk
saw	side	stick	song	said	Simon

3. Now read the words below aloud. The "s" sound appears at the end of the words.

miss	mass	nice	guess	this	glass
bliss	press	rice	face	price	fuss
ice	place	price	bus	lace	grace

4. Speak the following where "s" appears in a middle position:

misses	noticed	pressed	hostile	dressed
missile	escape	greased	harassed	fleeced

5. Speak the following sentences aloud:

    *   Sally sang a sad song on Sunday.
    *   Sam served his country until the ceasefire was declared.
    *   The sisters sat in the sun and observed the snake.
    *   Pass the salt to Sarah.
    *   Her dress was a blend of silk and satin.
    *   Stop, stand still, and salute.

"V" and "W" The "v" sound is called a labio-dental consonant. Labio means lips and, as you know, dental concerns the teeth. So what does this mean with regards to the production of the sound? It means that when you say "v," the edges of the upper front teeth touch the lower lip. The breath emerges through the small space between the teeth and lips.

To develop the habit of pronouncing these sounds clearly, practise the following "v" and "w" exercises:

EXERCISES FOR "V"

1. Say:

v-v	v-v	v-v	v-v	v-v

2. Say:

voo	voo	voo	voo	voo
voh	voh	voh	voh	voh
vah	vah	vah	vah	vah
vay	vay	vay	vay	vay
vee	vee	vee	vee	vee
vi	vi	vi	vi	vi

3. Say the following words:

velvet	vein	vinegar	very	Veronica
violet	violent	van	village	visit
even	every	leverage	lives	driving
cave	wave	pave	save	gave
weave	live	glove	sieve	leave

4. Say these sentences aloud:
   - Vera wore a vivid red gown.
   - The violent knave hid in a cave.
   - Every visitor saves to go on a vacation.
   - There are beautiful vineyards and vegetables in the valley.
   - Wave goodbye when you leave by van.
   - Invite Victor along for the drive.

The "w" sound is a labial sound. It is made by pushing the lips slightly forward and rounding the lips.

Now practise the following, keeping your lips in the correct position:

EXERCISES FOR "W"

1. Say:

w-w	w-w	w-w	w-w	w-w

2. Say:

woo	woo	woo	woo	woo
woh	woh	woh	woh	woh
wah	wah	wah	wah	wah
way	way	way	way	way
wee	wee	wee	wee	wee
wi	wi	wi	wi	wi

3. Say the following words:

wine	waiter	waste	wool	well
wonder	worry	weep	weed	wood
win	winter	warning	wall	web
one	once	Wendy	Willy	walk
wolf	weather	weasel	wave	water

4. Say the following sentences aloud:

- We communicated via the World Wide Web.
- Wendy walked along a winding pathway.
- William wore a warm winter overcoat.
- The waiter poured the wine willingly.
- Will Walter win the award?
- Winnie won the prize and wept with joy.
- He was warned not to approach the weasel.

"B" and "V" For some individuals, particularly those whose first language is Spanish, the "b" sound is often confused with the "v" sound. The "b" sound is a **plosive lip consonant,** which means the lips initially make contact and then they "explode" apart to produce the "b" sound.

To correct this substitution, you can refer to the exercises for "v" and practise placing your top teeth over the bottom lip to produce the "v" sound.

TONGUE TWISTERS

Now let's indulge in a little fun as you twist your tongue while speaking the following tongue twisters. Using your tongue, lips, and jaw efficiently, aim for crisp, clear speech. As you become more proficient in speaking these tongue twisters, you can challenge yourself by increasing your pace while still pronouncing the sounds clearly.

1. A proper copper pot and a proper coffee cup.
2. Pam's plain plum pies are perfect.
3. She threw three fresh fish.
4. Quizzical Kate, kiss me quick.
5. Three thrushes flew through three thick thorn hedges.
6. How many cuckoos could a good cook cook
    If a good cook could cook cuckoos?
    If a good cook could cook cuckoos so fine
    And a good cook could cook cuckoos all the time
    How many cuckoos could a good cook cook
    If a good cook could cook cuckoos.
7. Rubber baby buggy bumpers.
    Rubber baby buggy bumpers.
    Rubber baby buggy bumpers.

8. Truly rural, purely plural, truly rurally, purely plurally.

9. Red leather, yellow leather.
   Red leather, yellow leather.

10. A big black bucket of blue blueberries.

11. A skunk sat on a stump and thunk the stump stunk.
    But the stump thunk the skunk stunk.

12. You can have:

    Fried fresh fish
    Fish fried fresh
    Fresh fried fish
    Fresh fish fried
    Or fish fresh fried.

13. Six slippery seals slinking silently ashore.

14. Whether the weather be fine, or whether the weather be not
    Whether the weather be cold or whether the weather be hot
    We'll weather the weather, whatever the weather, whether we like it or not.

15. Can you imagine an imaginary menagerie manager managing an imaginary menagerie?

16. Ned Nott was shot and Sam Shott was not.
    So it's better to be Shott than Nott.
    Some say Nott was not shot, but Shott swears he shot Nott.
    Either the shot Shott shot at Nott was not shot or Nott was not shot.

    If the shot Shott shot shot Nott, Nott was shot,
    But if the shot Shott shot shot Shott himself, then
    Shott would be shot and Nott would not.
    However, the shot Shott shot shot not Shott but Nott.
    It's not easy to say who was shot and who was not,
    But we know who was Shott and who was Nott.

17. A tutor who tooted a flute
    Tried to tutor two tooters to toot.
    Said the two to the tutor,
    "Is it harder to toot or
    To tutor two tooters to toot?"

18. I thought I thought a thought. But the thought I thought I thought wasn't the thought I thought I thought. If the thought I thought I thought had been the thought I thought, I wouldn't have thought so much.

19. Wipe Wright's wife's white knife.

20. lick-lick-lick
    lickety-lickety-lickety
    lickety-lickety-split
    lickety-lickety-split-pop
    lickety-lickety-split-pop-shop

21. bush-bush-bush
    ~~bushy-bushy-bushy~~
    bushy-bushy-blush
    bushy-bushy-blush-bus
    bushy-bushy-blush-bus-push

22. Stop at the top shop for fish and chips in a deep dish.

23. Daniel Duncan dashed into a doctor's dispensary.

24. Three thousandths of an inch is the width of the line.

25. It is estimated that three-fifths of the earth's surface is covered by seas.

26. She sells seashells, sherry, sandshoes, and shaving soap on the seashore, and the seashells that she sells are seashore shells, I'm sure.

27. Pop bottles, pop bottles in pop shops
    The pop bottles Pop bottles poor Pop drops
    When Pop drops pop bottles, pop bottles plop
    When pop bottles topple, Pop mops slop.

28. Violet offered Fred three free throws.

29. Vera required a visa for her vacation to Venezuela.

30. If Timothy Theophylliss Thicklewade Thackham thrust his two thick thumbs through three hundred and thirty-three thousand three hundred and thirty-three thick and thin thistles, where are the three hundred and thirty-three thousand three hundred and thirty-three thick and thin thistles that Timothy Theophylliss Thicklewade Thackham thrust his two thick thumbs through?

31. Six skyscrapers stood snugly side by side shimmering by the seashore.

We can all benefit from surrounding ourselves with well-spoken words. Listen to the CBC radio, pay attention to the pronunciation of well-spoken university and college professors, or visit a store that rents out audiotapes of classical books, and devote the time to listen to them. Exposure to clear speech and correct pronunciation will seep into your consciousness so that when you need to reproduce those words you will do so with ease.

We can all list words that cause us some degree of uncertainty. You may simply avoid using these words because you feel unsure of their pronunciation. In this case, refer to the dictionary. You will notice how frequently American and English pronunciations may differ. For example, Americans pronounce "herb" as "erb" while the British pronounce the initial "h" sound and say "herb." A dictionary such as *Webster's Collegiate Dictionary* will provide you with a guide to correct North American pronunciation. So embrace new words instead of avoiding them and you will enrich your vocabulary.

To speak clearly in support of an idea, a proposal, a paper, or a project is a commendable skill in terms of academic, career, and social development. You will discover long-lasting rewards when you master the art of articulating your thoughts with clarity.

SUMMARY

The ability to speak with clarity is a vital prerequisite for a presenter. The audience needs to receive the speaker's message effortlessly. This means that the spoken words should be clearly articulated and intelligible. Clarity of expression will promote understanding. If a speaker mumbles or does not project his or her voice, the listener will have to work hard to receive the message.

To speak clearly, we need to form our vowel sounds correctly and articulate consonants crisply. By exercising your organs of articulation—the tongue, the lips, the jaw, and the soft palate—you will develop clear speech. To keep your lips and tongue working with precision have fun speaking the tongue twisters.

There are particular sounds that often present a challenge for many speakers: "th," "th," "s," "v," "w," and "b." Pronunciation will improve with the help of specific practical exercises.

A speaker who prepares a presentation, practises it, and develops the visual support to accompany it, is well on the way to a successful delivery. But if the same speaker does not pay attention to the clarity of speech, she will shortchange herself and the listener.

SUGGESTED READING

Burniston, Christabel. *Sounding Out Your Voice and Speech*. Southport, Lancashire: English Speaking Board, 1989.

Cole, Wilton. *Sound and Sense*. London: George Allen and Unwin Ltd., 1964.

Colson, Greta. *Voice Production and Speech*. London: Museum Press, 1967.

Morrison, Malcolm. *Clear Speech*. London: A+C Clack Publishers, 1991.

Skinner, Edith. *Speak With Distinction*. New York: Applause Theater Book Publishers, 1990.

Interview   Richard Bradshaw

Richard Bradshaw is the voice of the Canadian Opera Company. He is a passionate advocate for opera and the arts in Canada, and has conducted a wide-ranging selection of both operatic and orchestral music with leading international opera companies, symphony orchestras, and music festivals.

Q **Who do you consider to be a strong Canadian speaker?**

A A lot of people have tremendous information to impart but they aren't necessarily very good at doing it. Eddie Greenspan—he's my idea of natural charisma and the ability to really take the floor and immediately engage an audience.

Q **What do you admire about his style of speaking?**

A I think he's direct, he's intelligent, and he's charming, and he manages to communicate all three....When I speak, what matters to me is that I am actually interested in what I've got to say. That sounds absurd, but sometimes if you're repeating the same pitch, if you're having to sell the fact that there should be an opera house—in a way, you're going through your mantra and that's boring and doesn't grab you. What's interesting is if you're actually thinking on your feet.

Q   How do you feel your public speaking skills have contributed to your ability to have the Opera House built?

A   I think we've broken a lot of barriers surrounding the arts. There are a lot of preconceptions that I think are wrong. I also think that we usually have a good turnout—I say this, I hope not arrogantly—but, we have a good turnout for our press conferences because they don't think I'm really going to stand up and say predictable things.

Q   What are the attributes and qualities of a good speaker? You mentioned charisma.

A   I think it's the ability to engage an audience. I mean, sometimes you see people who are not particularly eloquent, whose voices are not particularly attractive and, yet, they have the ability to immediately draw an audience to them….To engage an audience usually means that you've got something to say and you have to do so with confidence. Do not underestimate your audience— if you give them credit that they're possibly more intelligent than they even know themselves, they tend to come out feeling a good deal better for the experience because they have realized that actually, they have a more exciting vision of life than they realized.

Q   What are the vital elements of a good speech presentation?

A   Well, I think it should have a beginning, a middle, and an end—the obvious things. I think humour is important. There is almost no subject that doesn't benefit from certain amusement.

Q   How do you plan a talk?

A   There has to be structure. You need something arresting in itself and in terms of whether you're speaking for an hour, half an hour, or fifteen minutes. There has to be a structure whereby you come to the big climax at the right moment in a great speech.

Q   How can a speaker connect with the audience?

A   I once had to make a convocation speech. Bob Rae was the chairman and to open he said, "As I was leaving home just now to come to this event, my daughter said to me, 'Remember, Dad, this afternoon's not about you.'" And you know, immediately he made the connection with the audience. The point of this illustration is that, too often when we speak, we're thinking about ourselves. We're thinking about me, myself, and I. Whereas actually, if you want to really be successful you should be thinking about the people that are listening to you, what they need, and how you're going to take them into your confidence.

Q   How do you prepare for a speech?

A   Depends how much time I have. I'm not on the professional speakers' circuit; I usually do it for a charity. So if it's a big event, then I jot down notes. I decide what I want to say and I might look up a quotation to include. I write notes and sometimes I don't even take them out of my pocket. If I'm nervous I take them out and I've got them there, but I find it's much better if you leave them in your pocket. A public speech is different than writing an article to be read, where you write your thoughts in a very coherent way. I think a speech is much more a means of communication to get people thinking and talking and excited…. The more one is able to take the mood of the moment and play that moment, the better.

Q   Can you tell me about the very first speaking experience you had?

A   I don't really remember. I only remember embarrassments! I do remember when I was invited to San Francisco to talk to what I was told was a very informed, high-level group about a very specific subject, and I prepared something very carefully. I became absolutely aware within five minutes into the speech that the audience was not at all what I had been led to believe. I had fifty-five minutes and already they were lost. I remember trying to recover from that, realizing that they hadn't got a clue what I was talking about. So I remember things like that and I try to find out who is in the audience.

Q   Are there any speaking habits that annoy you?

A   Yes. I'm guilty of it. Particularly when I'm thinking on my feet. A lot of "um's" and a lot of clearings of the throat. I don't mind unusual mannerisms—they quite entertain me—and I think that someone who has a nervous tic can be very charming. But it's the continual clearing of throats or continual "um's" and "ah's" that are boring.

Q   Tell me about the importance of voice.

A   I think what you want is a "naturalness;" you want to hear the person behind the voice. Of course, if you have a voice like Churchill, it's great, and you can command just by the range. I think if you really want to be a public speaker—and I'm not talking about amateurs like me—if you really want to

be good, then you should perhaps pay some attention to the range of the voice. If you watch a director like Robin Phillips work with an actress like Fiona Reed, he's already working with an extraordinary actress, but the range he gets from bottom to top is very exciting, and that can be mesmeric.

Q   Do you take steps to ensure that the audience understands you?

A   You can't ensure it—you can only be sensitive to who is your audience. On the other hand, I would never speak down or go for the lowest common denominator. I would rather feel that if one pitches things a little above, the audience will be elevated.

Q   Can you comment on audience reaction and involvement?

A   Audience reaction is like a drug. Every summer I have to perform at Harbourfront in Toronto. We do three open-air concerts and there are literally thousands and thousands of people there. I have to entertain like Johnny Carson. I mean, I conduct but I keep them happy. You have to be very careful that the "drug" of audience laughter doesn't take over from the content because it's so easy to make them laugh and lose the thread.

Q   What advice would you give to novice speakers? This is my last question.

A   Be yourself. If you've got anything to offer—and probably if you've been asked to speak you may very well have something to offer—if you have the guts to be yourself, people will respect you. That's all.

chapter ten

Delivery Methods

It's always a shame when a guy with great talent can't tell the board or a committee what's in his head. The most important thing I learned in school was how to communicate.

—Lee Iacocca

LEARNING OBJECTIVES

- To explain the four different methods of delivering a speech

- To describe the advantages and disadvantages of using each method

- To learn how to mark a manuscript speech

Many students experience a certain degree of fear when faced with the task of delivering their first speech. They ask themselves, "How can I possibly remember all the information I want to impart?" "What happens if I forget a segment of the speech?" "How can I use my notes effectively?"

Depending on your speaking purpose, the occasion, and the audience, you can choose one of the following delivery methods:

1. The extemporaneous method
2. The manuscript method
3. The memorized method
4. The impromptu method

THE EXTEMPORANEOUS METHOD

The extemporaneous method involves careful, detailed preparation of the speech, which is then ultimately reduced to note form or a keyword outline. The speech is not written out word for word, nor is it memorized. The speaker outlines the key ideas and refers to the brief notes as he or she speaks. Most speakers prefer this type of delivery as they sound more spontaneous and sincere.

The advantages of using the extemporaneous method are as follows:

1. You have the opportunity to prepare thoroughly and develop a framework for your speech.

2. You are able to deliver in a conversational manner and therefore appear more natural.

3. You will be able to refer to your notes quickly and then look up and make good eye contact with your audience.

4. You will feel more confident and secure having your notes with you.

5. You have more flexibility when using this method and can change examples and anecdotes to suit your audience, the occasion, and the prevailing mood in the room.

6. You will not sound as if you have memorized your speech and the audience will feel as if your speech is being formulated on the spot.

7. You also do not need to be concerned about delivering the precise wording you originally planned. You can adjust your vocabulary and language accordingly.

8. You will sound more authentic and genuine.

The disadvantages of the extemporaneous method are as follows:

1. Without proper preparation and practice, you could compromise the fluent delivery of your speech.

2. You might forget what it was that you wanted/planned to say and consequently sound slightly hesitant.

As the advantages outweigh the disadvantages, this method is strongly advocated. In order to overcome the disadvantages, memorize the opening and closing of your speech. Commit to memory the quotations, anecdotes, or memorable phases you wish to deliver accurately. Practise frequently to become familiar with your material and less dependent on your notes. Simply refer to your notes and then resume contact with your audience.

THE MANUSCRIPT METHOD

A manuscript speech is delivered from a prepared word-for-word text and the entire speech is read to the audience from the manuscript. This method is used when precision of wording is required and is favoured by presidents and premiers, political candidates, government officials, television and radio announcers, business executives delivering a corporate message, boards of education, and those in the medical and scientific fields. When an individual knows that he or she will be quoted in the media this frequently becomes the delivery method of choice. When a policy statement is issued, it is safer to deliver from a prepared text. You will notice that this method is usually chosen for a very structured speaking situation.

Again, there are advantages and disadvantages of this method.

The advantages are as follows:

1. You will not forget what you want to say, as you will be totally scripted.

2. You will deliver the precise message using the exact wording upon which you have decided.

3. You might feel more comfortable and secure knowing that you will not need to improvise or "fill in the blanks," which you need to do for extemporaneous speaking.

4. You can hand out copies of your speech in advance to the press or the audience. Alternatively, you may wish to hand them out at the end of your speech.

5. You can predict accurately the duration of the speech.

The following are the disadvantages:

1. The speech may be delivered in a monotonous, wooden manner and the speaker consequently sounds dull and artificial.

2. It curtails your freedom of movement since you cannot move away from the lectern where the script resides.

3. Some speakers find it difficult to read from the script while making effective eye contact at regular intervals.

4. If the speech requires last minute "tweaking" or changes, it might be difficult to do.

5. There are speakers who do not read well and the delivery will sound stilted and hesitant.

Tips for Delivering from a Manuscript Speech

1. Type the speech in 18-point font size for easy reading, double-spacing each line.

2. Number the pages on the top right-hand corner of each page.

3. Leave a margin on the left-hand side of the page for making notes for yourself.

4. Practise the speech sufficiently so that you develop a sense of where the words are placed on each page. Continue doing so until it is embedded in your memory. When you become familiar with your script, you can train you eye to move ahead, scoop up the phrase you are about to deliver, then look up and speak directly to the audience.

5. The biggest problem that speakers make when delivering from a written word-for-word speech, is that they speak with no vocal modulation, they use little animation, limited eye contact, and no gestures.

Marking your Script

You can mark a script so that when you deliver your message you will sound energetic as you use vocal variety and appropriate gestures. The following symbols will assist you in the marking of your speech, making it more dynamic and convincing.

FIGURE 10.1	Speech symbols

↓	=	Lower the pitch
↑	=	Raise the pitch
LOUDER	=	Volume increase
SOFTER	=	Volume decreases
G	=	Gesture
◉	=	Eye contact
∿∿∿	=	Stress the phrase
____	=	Stress the word
/	=	Pause
//	=	Longer pause
FASTER	=	Faster pace
SLOWER	=	Slower pace
N.T.	=	New tone

Now let us take an excerpt from an acceptance speech given by Albert Schultz when he accepted a $50 000 prize for Soul Pepper Theatre at the Lieutenant Governor's Awards.

Your Honour, ladies and gentlemen,

We are all now in a more precarious position than we were a year ago. Our spirit has been shaken and our economy is under attack. However, it is precisely in such circumstances that we *most* need to come together and share our stories in the dark. I am reminded of a wonderful story about Winston Churchill during the bombing blitz of London. During this catastrophe Churchill was criticized in Parliament for awarding a grant to the Old Vic Theatre for the performance of Shakespeare's plays. That money—said the opposition—must be used to help the war effort.

Churchill's response was (and I paraphrase): "If we are unable to hear the plays of Shakespeare, for what are we fighting?"

What Churchill intrinsically understood—as the architects of *this award* so clearly do—is that one of the brightest candles we have to light our darkest nights is our ability to share these stories. The stories that are told in the theatre, at the opera, the symphony, the ballet—in our galleries, concert halls and our museums, help us to collectively celebrate our accomplishments; to laugh at our frailties; to rail at our cruelties; to better comprehend our tragedies; and to find our way into the light.

Knowing how much grinding work they have done over the last year, I would like to congratulate all of today's recipients. And on behalf of all past, present, and future recipients, applaud the founders for the vision and generosity of this award which will go a long way towards helping each of us tell our stories.

Now, this is how the speech would appear on the page with markings to indicate how it should be delivered.

FIGURE 10.2	Marked Speech

👁 Your Honour, / ladies and gentlemen, /

We are all now in a more <u>precarious position</u> than we were a <u>year</u> ago. /

Our <u>spirit</u> has been shaken and our <u>economy</u> is under attack. / However,

FASTER   G

it is precisely in such circumstances that we *most* need to come together

and <u>share</u> our <u>stories</u> in the dark. // I am reminded of a wonderful story

about Winston Churchill during the <u>bombing blitz</u> of London. / During

this <u>catastrophe</u> Churchill was <u>criticized</u> in Parliament for <u>awarding</u> a

<u>grant</u> to the Old Vic Theatre for the <u>performance</u> of <u>Shakespeare's plays</u>. /

That money / − said the opposition / −must be used to help the <u>war effort</u>. /

Churchill's response was / (and I paraphrase): / "If we are unable to

<u>hear</u> the <u>plays of Shakespeare</u>, / for <u>what are we fighting</u>?" /

What Churchill intrinsically <u>understood</u> − / as the architects of

this award so clearly do − / is that one of the <u>brightest candles</u> we have

to <u>light</u> our darkest nights is our ability to <u>share</u> these <u>stories</u>. / The

FASTER

stories that are <u>told</u> in the theatre, / at the <u>opera</u>, / the <u>symphony</u>, / the

<u>ballet</u> − in our <u>galleries</u>, <u>concert halls</u> and our <u>museums</u>, / help us to

collectively <u>celebrate</u> our <u>accomplishments</u>; / to <u>laugh</u> at our <u>frailties</u>;

to <u>rail</u> at our <u>cruelties</u>; / to <u>better comprehend</u> our <u>tragedies</u>; / and to

find our way into the <u>light</u>. /

FIGURE 10.2	**Marked Speech** (continued)

N.T.
Knowing how much <u>grinding</u> work they have done over the last year,

I would like to <u>congratulate</u> all of today's <u>recipients</u>. / And on behalf of

all past, / present / and future recipients, / <u>applaud</u> the <u>founders</u> for the

<u>vision</u> and <u>generosity</u> of this award which will go a long way towards

helping <u>each</u> of us tell <u>our stories</u>. //

EXERCISES

1. Read this acceptance speech aloud and notice how interesting it sounds once it has been marked up and delivered following those suggested indications.

2. You have been asked to represent Canada at an international conference for youth. Prepare a five-minute speech, which will share information about Canada's culture, its industries, the population, agriculture, and geography. Write out your speech using the manuscript method. Mark up the speech according to how you plan on delivering it. Record the speech on a tape-recorder and listen back to evaluate yourself. Make the necessary changes, based on your evaluation, and re-record the speech. Finally, deliver the speech to the class.

3. Visit one of the following Web sites:

   www.historychannel.com/speeches.index.html
   www.stanfordplus.com/education/inspirationals/speeches.php#abc

   Download a speech that has special appeal to you. Mark the script and then deliver in class.

4. Prepare a three-minute emotional speech of your own choice. Write it down word for word. Mark the speech. Deliver it using good vocal variety, appropriate gestures, and body language.

5. Prepare a scripted speech to be delivered at your local Rotary Club. Your purpose during the speech is to encourage local business owners to hire more college students during the summer school break.

THE MEMORIZED METHOD

This method is only advocated for those who have a superb memory. Students who have a photographic memory will excel here. For the rest of us, the fear of forgetting some of the words will always prevail. When speaking from memory, write out the exact wording of your speech, learn it by heart, and then speak it. This is not a method that is encouraged in public speaking classes because of the obvious risk of forgetting, sounding artificial, or hesitant. You may also sound insincere if the delivery appears to be mechanical.

There are some advantages to committing the speech to memory. You can devote a lot of time to preparation beforehand and decide on the style you wish to embrace. You will also be able to move freely while delivering your message as you will not be restricted to a podium or your notes. You can plan the timing of your speech with precision. It is more effective to use this method when introducing a speaker, thanking a speaker, or when giving or accepting an award. Provided you speak with sincerity and fluency in these situations, the memorized method will work for you.

Even though you might choose to memorize the entire speech, have a back-up plan in case you encounter a memory lapse. Take an extra copy of your speech with you. Leave it close by, on a lectern or table, just in case you need it. This precaution will give you an added sense of comfort even though you may never refer to it at all.

THE IMPROMPTU METHOD

We speak using the impromptu method on a daily basis. We do not always have time to frame our thoughts prior to an ordinary interaction with a friend, a colleague, a family member, or someone with whom we have a chance encounter. We do not always have time to prepare a response to a question, make a comment on a controversial topic, or offer an opinion on a particular subject. Yet we can acquit ourselves adequately. We frequently speak "off the cuff," as impromptu speaking is sometimes referred to. When you use the impromptu method, there is little or no time for preparation. So, if you think about it, impromptu speaking should not be such an intimidating experience for you.

The more public-speaking techniques you know, the easier it will be for you to embrace this method. It will help when you take a moment to organize your thoughts. Always plan your opening comment and your conclusion. A safe structure for the body of the impromptu talk would be to divide it into three sections. You can also memorize the structures for an informative speech and a persuasive speech, discussed in Chapter 3. Use these as roadmaps for your talk.

The following are advantages of impromptu speaking:

1. You will appear natural and spontaneous.
2. Eye contact will be more sincere.
3. Gestures will emanate with greater ease.
4. You will speak authentically as the speech will be based on personal knowledge, opinion, and experience.
5. If you do well, the audience will be suitably impressed.

The following are the disadvantages:

1. There is no advance preparation.
2. You have no time to do research.
3. There is no time to practise.
4. There is the chance that you could begin to ramble on and lose your focus.
5. You need to think quickly and decide on the content and format almost immediately.
6. The speaker fills the silences with "um," "you know," "okay," and unnecessary fillers.
7. No notes are used.

Tips for Impromptu Speaking

1. Follow the rules of structure for preparing a speech.
2. The content of the speech can be confined to three key points.
3. Have a point of view.
4. Support your viewpoint with a reason, logic, and data of which you have knowledge.
5. Stay focused on the subject.
6. Do not ramble on unnecessarily.
7. Organize the body of your speech using one of these methods:

   a) The PREW method
   b) Chronological structure
   c) A topical structure
   d) A problem/solution structure
   e) A spatial structure
   f) A cause and effect structure

8. Conclude by using one of the ways of closing a speech, suggested in Chapter 3. End with a memorable statement.
9. Use good verbal variety and body language.
10. Deliver your message with clarity and confidence.

Here are two reminders of the structures for the PREW Method and the Basic Impromptu Structure.

a) The PREW method
   1. Give your **point of view**
   2. Offer your **reason** to support your point of view
   3. Support your viewpoint by giving a concrete, vivid **example**
   4. **Wrap up** the impromptu talk with a strong conclusion

b) The Basic Impromptu Structure
   1. **Open** with an attention getter
   2. Divide the **body** of your talk into **three main sections**
   3. **Close** on a strong note

EXERCISES

1. Each class member writes down a topic on a piece of paper. Place the topics in a hat. Each student takes a topic and immediately speaks for one minute on the topic. Repeat the exercise, choose a different topic and this time increase the time frame for speaking to two minutes.

2. You are stranded on a desert island. You have been able to bring three books with you. Which books have you chosen? In a short impromptu speech tell us the names of the books, the reasons why you chose each book, and suggest why we should agree with your choices.

3. Choose a topic from the following list and talk for two minutes on one of the following:
   - A great invention
   - A famous discoverer or explorer
   - Mythology
   - The Ten Commandments
   - The Seven Wonders of the Ancient World
   - The five senses
   - The government
   - Theatre
   - Archaeology
   - Sports
   - Leisure
   - Diet
   - The responsibilities of a citizen
   - The art of living
   - My favourite vacation spot

4. Choose a subject that you are an expert in. Speak for two minutes on your expertise. The audience should be left with a good understanding of your expertise.

5. Choose one of the following quotations. Begin your talk by reading the quotation. Then explain what the quotation means to you. Follow the explanation by illustrating the meaning of the quotation with a concrete example. Close the talk by reading the quotation again.

   "Men and nations behave wisely once they have exhausted all the other alternatives."

   —Abba Eban

   "Imagination is the highest kite one can fly."

   —Lauren Bacall

   "We are generally more convinced by the reasons we discover on our own than by those given to us by others."

   —Marcel Proust

"Integrity simply means a willingness not to violate one's identity."

—Erich Fromm

"Try not to become a man of success but rather a man of value."

—Albert Einstein

"You can't push a wave onto the shore any faster than the ocean brings it in."

—Susan Strasberg

"A great many people think they are thinking when they are merely rearranging prejudices."

—William James

"Everything is funny as long as it happens to someone else."

—Will Rogers

"Every exit is an entrance somewhere else."

—Tom Stoppard

"Opportunity is missed by most people because it is dressed in overalls and looks like work."

—Thomas Edison

"If you give a man a fish he is fed for a day; if you teach him how to fish, he is fed for life."

—Confucius

"An eye for an eye makes the whole world blind."

—Mohandas K. Gandhi

"Success is never final, failure is never fatal, it is courage that counts."

—Winston Churchill

"There is no education like adversity."

—Benjamin Disraeli

"Nothing in life is to be feared. It is only to be understood."

—Madame Curie

"Good people do not need laws to tell them to act responsibly, while bad people will find a way around laws."

—Plato (427-347 B.C.)

"Masterpieces are no more than the shipwrecked flotsam of great minds."

—Marcel Proust

"Criticism comes easier that craftsmanship."

—Zeuxis (c 400 B.C.)

"A critic is a man who knows the way but can't drive the car."

—Kenneth Tynan

"Nothing is particularly hard if you divide it into small jobs."

—Henry Ford

"I don't want to pull through life like a thread that has no knot. I want to leave something behind when I go; some small legacy of truth, some work that will shine in a dark place."

—Nellie McClung

6. Choose one of these proverbs and speak for one minute about the proverb and the meaning of it. Again, you can use a colourful example or anecdote to support your understanding of the proverb.

- Knowledge is power.
- Empty vessels make the most noise.
- Flattery brings friends, truth enemies.
- Nature abhors a vacuum.
- Necessity is the mother of invention.
- No gains without pains.
- Put not your trust in money; put your money in trust.
- The end justifies the means.
- The last straw breaks the camel's back.
- The strength of a chain is its weakest link.
- Rumour is a great traveller.
- Second thoughts are best.
- See a pin and let it lie, you're sure to want before you die.
- Set a thief to catch a thief.
- Study the past if you would divine the future.
- Cut your coat according to your cloth.
- Discretion is the better part of valour.
- Distance lends enchantment to the view.
- Union is strength.
- What can't be cured must be endured.
- When poverty comes in at the door love flies out of the window.
- There is no venom like that of the tongue.
- Time and tide wait for no man.
- To forget a wrong is the best revenge.
- To stir up a hornet's nest.
- If a man deceive me once, shame on him; if twice, shame on me.
- If you wish for peace, prepare for war.
- Flies are easier caught with honey than with vinegar.
- Hasty climbers have sudden falls.
- A guilty conscience needs no accuser.
- Where there is nothing to lose there is nothing to fear.

- Where there is smoke there is fire.
- Who judges others condemns himself.
- You cannot get blood out of a stone.
- You cannot make a silk purse out of a sow's ear.
- You cannot shoe a running horse.
- Youth lives on hope, old age on remembrance.
- Zeal without knowledge is a runaway horse.

SUMMARY

This chapter examined the four different methods of delivering a speech: the extemporaneous method, the manuscript method, the memorized method, and the impromptu method. The extemporaneous method involves the detailed preparation of the subject matter and then the speaker develops brief notes or a keyword outline from which to deliver the speech. For the manuscript method of delivery, the entire speech is written out word for word and the speaker delivers from these notes. For the memorized mode, the speaker writes out the entire speech and then commits it to memory. You have little or no time to prepare for the impromptu method. The pros and cons of each method are presented. In addition, the student is offered a method for marking a script, which will help him or her to deliver the speech with good vocal variety and body language.

SUGGESTED READING

DeVito, Joseph A. *The Elements of Public Speaking*. New York: Longman, 2000.

Fletcher, Leon. *How to Design and Deliver Speeches*. New York: Longman, 2001.

Peterson, Brent D., Eric G. Stephan, and Noel D. White. *The Complete Speaker, An Introduction to Public Speaking*. St. Paul, MN: West Publishing Company, 1992.

Interview | **Buzz Hargrove**

Buzz Hargrove has been National President of the Canadian Auto Workers Union since 1992. He is one of Canada's most prominent labour leaders and is an advocate of social unionism and human rights.

***Q* Buzz, which public speakers have made an indelible impression on you?**

A From my younger days, the president of my local union was Charles Brooks. He was a wonderful speaker. Then there was Walter Ruther, who was the international president of the UAW. One was killed in a plane wreck and one was shot. Tommy Douglas of the NDP impressed me. Those would be the three people from my early days who were really impressive.

***Q* Can you list some of the attributes of a good speaker?**

A First you have to have a clear and concise message that you want to deliver; you have to be knowledgeable on the subject matter. Know your audience, and be able to control the time frame in which you deliver. I talk for about 25 minutes if I'm speaking to a business audience to an hour when I'm speaking in universities. When I give my speeches to my councils, it could last for 2 to 2.5 hours. I do not have a written speech. I always work from notes.

Q   Do you have a keyword outline for your main points?

A   Yes, I just put the main points down and, if you look at the way I do it, you would never believe that I could do it. That is just something I developed over the years.

Q   Do you think the ability to speak is a gift?

A   It was not for me. It's something I worked very hard to master. I always kid young people when I go to a conference in our union and somebody gets up and says, "I'm nervous because this is the first time I've ever spoken in front of a large audience." I always respond by saying that my knees are still sore from cracking together from the first time I spoke, so I can appreciate what you are going through.

Q   Now that you've spoken about the attributes of a good speech, what do you consider to be the elements of a good speech.

A   The elements of a good speech? It is always the subject matter—introducing the subject matter and then focusing in on my perspective. I then try to convince people that this particular view of the topic offers the right perspective.

Q   How do you prepare for a speech?

A   I focus on the audience I want to speak to and then I assess whether my knowledge on the subject matter is sufficient to make a difference and to have

a real input. And then I just sit down and go about preparing it. Usually, I work on the fly; I do it on the plane or, if I am driving, I will have a pad besides me in the car. If something comes to mind, I just make a rough note, scribble it, and when I get to where I am going, I sit down and put those notes in some kind of order. I then go ahead and give the speech.

Q   Do you think that the ability to give a speech and presentation is a vital skill for students?

A   Yes. I think in today's environment it is a real plus for anyone. No matter what you are doing, to be able to have the confidence to speak publicly, not just about the issues you are working on, but about broader issues, is a tremendous advantage. I do a lot of reading, which is one of my strengths. I read three newspapers every morning when I'm at home and when I am on the road, I read the national paper and a couple of local papers. So I think reading and research add richness to your talk.

Q   Sometimes you watch someone and they have habits that are annoying. What kind of speaking habits do you find distracting?

A   I suppose someone who just delivers a monologue and reads a speech.... I think you have to have some feeling, some emotion about your subject. So, lack of emotion, I suppose. If you don't care why should they care?

Q   How do you ensure that your audience understands your message?

A   One of my skills is to be able to speak to a diverse audience, to demonstrate knowledge beyond the subject that I'm speaking about and then be able to deliver it.

Q   **Who do you think is a masterful speaker?**

A   The most masterful speaker I know today is a guy who turned 90 years old in January—his name is Victor Ruther. He is the brother of Walter Ruther. And he has been retired for many, many years, but he spoke to our convention in Quebec last August. It was a dinner, attended by 1800 people. The attendees were delegates to our convention, their spouses, and their children. It was a huge audience, and Victor spoke for 40 minutes, without a note, and you could hear a pin drop. And this was after cocktail hour, dinner, and a lot of wine. Yet, he had that audience spellbound. And he has done this time after time after time—just a masterful speaker. He spoke about the history of the union, the work that he and his brother had done in building the union, and the time he spent working on the Marshall Plan after the war to help rebuild Europe. You would have thought that the subject matter would not have been very interesting, but his delivery was just masterful.

Q   **How do you tailor your message to your audience?**

A   Know your audience. Know your audience, and know your subject matter. This is key to me. I am not sophisticated, in any sense of the word; my vocabulary does not come from a university degree. So yes, for me it's simple. I never, ever get carried away by who is in the audience; I don't care who they are—university professors, or a business group, or a group of shop stewards. I never, ever worry about not being able to get my message across. That gives you confidence.

Q   **Some people fear the question and answer period, while others love it. How do you feel about it?**

A   I love the exchange. First of all I like to know what is on people's minds. I like to know what people get out of what I am saying. It is quite interesting because sometimes, different audience members get completely different messages from what I say. I love to be challenged about the issues. If do not know the answer, I always say, "Look, that is a good question. I've made a note of it, and I'll get back to you personally, or somebody will get back to you with the answer." I learned that as a young shop steward on the shop floor. I always carried a notebook with me, and if somebody had a question and I didn't know the answer, I never tried to convince him or her that I knew it. I just said, "Look, I have no idea, but I will get back to you," and I did. This is a habit I still have today.

Q   **What advice would you offer to beginning speakers, to novice speakers?**

A   Work hard at knowing what the issues are; do your research to get there, and then structure the message you want to deliver to your audience. Know your audience and deliver with confidence. Put some emotion into it. You have to show emotion or else people will not buy into it, no matter what else you are doing.

   Speaking is a skill that you have got to keep up. So, never say no when invited to speak, no matter how small the audience. If I can fit it into my schedule I always do it and I enjoy it.

chapter eleven

The Question
and Answer Period

The important thing is not to stop questioning.

—Albert Einstein

LEARNING OBJECTIVES

- To recognize the important role of the Question and Answer period

- To learn the key factors that contribute towards mastery of this segment

- To understand the skills that are required to conduct an effective question and answer period

- To learn how to respond to the various types of questions that could be posed

You have prepared thoroughly for your presentation and you feel that you have done a rather good job of practising too. Now you are faced with the segment that either causes you fear and trepidation or anticipation and excitement: the question and answer period.

No matter how brilliantly you execute your presentation, if you fail to conduct the question and answer period with confidence and competence, the audience will walk away unimpressed.

Many years ago I attended a lecture at the University of Toronto given by an internationally renowned professor. This influential, contemporary thinker delivered a provocative 20-minute talk that excited and stimulated the audience. At the end of the speech, he informed us that he would take our questions. A middle-aged gentleman then approached a standing microphone that had been placed at the rear of Convocation Hall. This questioner proceeded to pose his first question; a second question followed, and a third, all posed by the same man. The questioner continued to monopolize the microphone for a full forty minutes. No one else was offered the opportunity to pose a question. The audience became restless and clearly dissatisfied with how poorly the speaker had controlled and directed the question and answer period. I remember leaving the hall feeling disappointed and frustrated. The questioner had dominated the evening and the speaker's message quickly faded into oblivion. What is the lesson to be learned here?

When your presentation incorporates a question and answer period, bear in mind that these two segments, the presentation and the question and answer period, are part of the whole. Preparation for the question and answer period is essential. French inventor Louis Pasteur's words echo this thought. He said, "Chance favours the prepared mind." In other words, don't leave things to chance. The question and answer period is a time when you want to convey credibility, candour, and competence. It is a time to respond with confidence and clarity; it is an opportunity to genuinely connect with your listeners, to convey your understanding of their concerns, and to deliver your response using language they understand. It is also the time to exhibit control over the situation, the questioners, and the allotted timeframe.

The ability to master the question and answer period will stand you in good stead if you have to respond to questions in class, if you have to defend your thesis, if you enter a business, if you practise law or medicine, if you become a financial advisor or teacher, or if you enter sales, politics, or public service. This is a partial list of potential areas in which you could employ this skill.

As the speaker, your purpose during the question and answer session should be clear in your mind. You want to maintain control, furnish the audience with any additional information, and clarify or, if necessary, expand upon certain points to counter any criticism. Respect your audience, even if hostility is evident, and reinforce your message so that the audience leaves remembering your message and not the questioners'. Throughout this process always maintain your integrity by giving honest answers.

One of the biggest fears that both students and adults alike express is the fear of not knowing the answer. This is where preparation and honesty come into play. Don't fake and don't feign knowledge.

AUDIENCE CONTROL

Let's look at an approach to assist you during the question and answer period. The key to conducting an effective question and answer period is to maintain control. How do you do this? The answer lies in your planning. During the opening of your presentation, inform the audience that you will be having a question and answer period at the end of your presentation. State the duration of the period by saying, "I will leave ten minutes at the end of the presentation for questions." This will give your audience the opportunity to formulate their questions in either written or oral form.

Another alternative you may offer would be to say, "I will be speaking for the next 20 minutes. Please feel free to pose your questions as we go along." This method presupposes that you are comfortable enough with your material that you can deal with interruptions. Only use this method if you feel that you can maintain your focus and not be led away from your designated message. This method works well with an audience that is learning new material and enjoys interaction with the speaker. It also gives you the opportunity to assess your audience's level of understanding. By listening to the questions they pose, you will be able to check whether they have grasped your key message. You will then be able to fill in the knowledge gaps with appropriate responses to their questions.

Question cards are also a useful device; they may be placed on participants' chairs prior to the presentation. Let the audience know why you have placed the cards there—tell them to use them to write down their questions and that you will collect them at the conclusion of the talk. You, the speaker, can then review the questions and answer the pressing concerns first. This is also a way of selecting the questions you prefer to answer.

At most presentations your audience will want to ask questions. This is an important time period for you and it can be regarded as another opportunity to communicate or reinforce your message. The following key factors for this portion of your presentation are:

- Anticipate the questions
- Prepare your answers
- Observe the timeframe

Anticipate the type of questions you think the audience will ask you. To build a sense of comfort for yourself, write down a list of 20 questions you might receive. Include in this list questions of a controversial or hostile nature.

Next, plan your answers to these questions by writing out the questions and the answers. Plan how you will deliver the answers by stating your responses aloud. By going through this preparation step, you will feel increasingly confident and discover answers that will enhance your credibility. Please see the sample Question and Answer Preparation Sheet, Form 11.1, below to help you in your planning.

FORM 11.1	Question and Answer Preparation Sheet

Topic of Presentation: _____

Key Message: _____

Audience: _____

Question 1: _____

Answer: _____

_____

Question 2: _____

Answer: _____

_____

Question 3: _____

Answer: _____

_____

FORM 11.1	**Question and Answer Preparation Sheet** (continued)

Question 4: _____

Answer: _____

_____

Question 5: _____

Answer: _____

_____

Question 6: _____

Answer: _____

_____

Question 7: _____

Answer: _____

_____

Question 8: _____

Answer: _____

_____

Question 9: _____

Answer: _____

_____

Question 10: _____

Answer: _____

_____

You can add an additional ten questions to this sheet for your practice.

Once you have concluded your presentation, the time to entertain questions from your audience will follow. Deliver the closing line of your speech and stand firmly for two to three seconds. This gives time for your final words to be absorbed by your listeners. You might then transition to the next stage with statements such as, "I'll now take your questions," "Are there any questions?", or "I'd be happy to entertain any questions you may have."

On some occasions you may find that there are no questions. What can you do? There are a few options. One method to stimulate a response is to use a hand signal. As you call for questions, raise your left upper arm level with your shoulder, so that the forearm and palm are facing outward towards the audience. The position will resemble that of a traffic cop at a busy intersection, but do not appear too rigid. The forearm should be extended towards the audience. When the questioner poses his or her question, you can then use the same raised arm to point towards him or her. Here's a pointer to bear in mind: never point your forefinger at any one. It can be perceived as an intimidating or threatening gesture. Instead, turn your palm upward and gesture in the direction of the questioner.

Should the raised hand fail to elicit a response—and that does happen—you can pose the first question and bridge the gap by saying, "One question I am frequently asked is..." and then pose it. So plan a question or two in advance in case you need them.

Now you have entered the throes of the question and answer period. The following are further pointers to help you maintain contact with and control over your audience.

Pointers to Remember:

1. Remain in control.

2. Identify the questioner by his or her clothing, or by his or her location in the room. You might say, while gesturing towards the questioner, "The man in the blue tie" or "The woman sitting beside the pillar." This offers a more accurate identification of the individual to whom you are pointing.

3. Listen to the question. If you sense that the entire audience has not heard the question, repeat it aloud. Sometimes it may be necessary to rephrase or paraphrase the question.

4. Remain calm at all times. Avoid revealing any impatience or anger that you may feel. Check to see that your body language is not revealing any discomfort or defensiveness.

5. Answer the question concisely and clearly, and back up your claims with evidence. Do not over-answer. Many speakers fall into this trap.

6. Remember it is fine to pause and think before responding. It shows the listener that you are thoughtful and measured.

7. Answer the question while looking at the audience. As you finish your answer, immediately make eye contact with the next questioner.

8. Respect the person asking the question, but don't allow this individual to "hog" the floor.

9. Maintain credibility. When you don't have an answer, be candid and say, "I'm sorry, that is not my area of expertise," or "I do not have the information at present, but I will be happy to do some research on it and get back to you." If you don't know the answer, always follow up your statement by volunteering to obtain an answer for the questioner.

10. Avoid negativity and pedantic language.

Handling the Questions

As the leader of the question and answer period, it is important to look upon this time period as another opportunity to share information. There are, as you will discover, an infinite variety of questioners and the majority of them will be upfront and straightforward. The questions you receive will illustrate your audience's level of understanding of your message. They will also unveil the audience's interest level in your topic. If you feel that you may not have all the answers at your fingertips, be mindful of the fact that you will not be asked all the questions you anticipate. You probably don't know anyone who knows everything; so don't put that burden upon yourself.

Your aim during this period is to listen actively to the question, formulate a specific response, and articulate it with clarity and confidence. Remain composed and gracious. Tailor your response based on your audience analysis. For example, a group of environmentalists will want to know how legislation will affect the environment, whereas a group of legislators will want to know how the law will be tabled. Frame your answers in accordance with the needs of your particular audience.

Tips on how to word your response

1. Be clear. Use language that the audience understands. Do not use jargon or highly sophisticated phrases with which your audience is unfamiliar. Pronounce your words clearly and project your voice so that those in the last row can hear you with ease. Don't make the listener work to receive your message.

2. Be concise, but also be concrete. If someone poses a 50-cent question, don't offer a $100 answer.

3. Offer supporting evidence, anecdotes, statistics, and examples to elucidate and assist understanding.

4. Structure your response appropriately. You can use the PREW method (see impromptu speaking in Chapter 10), or a topical, spatial, chronological, cause and effect, or problem-solution structure.

5. Identify the "type" of question being posed. You may say, for example, "That question calls for an interpretation of the findings..." or, "Here is my professional opinion on that issue..." or, "Here is my personal opinion..." or, "Based on the facts we have examined, we can conclude that..." In this way you are identifying the type of question—factual, interpretative, or opinion-based.

6. Avoid words that diminish your authority. For example, "I think this will be the most efficient way of executing the plan." Replace the word "think" with "believe" or "know," or simply eliminate the two words "I think" and say, instead, "This will be the most efficient way of executing the plan." Eliminate the word "try"; for example, "We will try" does not convey conviction. Say rather, "Our plan is to reduce debt and improve the bottom line." Another wishy-washy word is "hopefully." Do not say, "Hopefully, I have answered your question." You will not exude confidence by using this word.

Types of Questions

Let's look at some types of questions that demand the need to listen, stay focused, and remain in control when under pressure.

The Emotional or Political Question   This type of question is designed to provoke you or put you "on the defensive." The issue could be a sensitive one. There was an amusing line I came across which said that many politicians refuse to answer questions on the grounds that it might eliminate them. Some of you may choose to enter politics where a different set of responses may be required for particular issues. For political questions, you must prepare yourself for the issues and concerns of the audience. You need to reach the listener by being tactful, diplomatic, and sincere. A political response may be preceded by these sentences, "You've asked an interesting question about our policy. Have you looked at it this way...?" You then proceed to deliver your message. In this textbook, we are dealing with questions that might emerge after you deliver a presentation in a college, university, or business setting.

When an emotional or political question is asked, always restate the question, omitting the emotionally laden words or language. The question might be "What on earth are you incompetent bureaucrats doing by feathering your own nests when you promised to build homes for the elderly?" You can begin by saying, "The question is, 'What are we doing to build homes for the elderly?'" Do not repeat the bait words "incompetent bureaucrats" and "feathering your own nests" in your response. Then proceed to provide evidence, proof, and statistics as you answer: "In fiscal year 2002, we allocated a budget of $40 million to develop three senior housing complexes in the province of Nova Scotia. We are on target with regard to our completion date, and housing for 400 seniors will be provided through this undertaking."

The key to remember with this type of question is to control your emotions and your body language, and to rephrase the question using neutral language before responding with the details.

The Anticipatory Question   In this case someone will interrupt your presentation with a question that you plan to address later on. Do not let the questioner pre-empt you. Do not jump ahead in your talk merely to satisfy her or him. Answer briefly by telling the questioner that you will be addressing this issue later on and continue your presentation.

The Technical Question   It is not necessary to answer a technical question with a technical answer if the audience is a non-technical one. Imagine that you are speaking to a group of stay-at-home parents who are attending a presentation titled, "The Use of the Computer in the Home." They are attending because they want to learn some practical tips on how to schedule car pools, keep a record of birth dates and anniversaries, and comfortably search the Internet. A more advanced member of the audience poses a question related to the inner components of the computer hard drive. If you have done your audience analysis, you will know that this audience has little or no desire for this type of technical information. You may be capable of answering this question in great detail but you will do so at the expense of boring the rest of the audience. Instead, you may do the following: label the question and offer the questioner a solution by saying, "That is a technical question. I'd be happy to meet you after the presentation and give you a detailed explanation." Don't forget to deliver on this promise once the session is over. Refer to Chapter 2 on audience analysis. See the segment on *Prior Knowledge of the Audience*.

The Several Part Question   Sometimes, an audience member might ask you a three-part question. You commence the answer and, while you are answering the first part of the question, your mind is already formulating the answer to the second part. At this point, you might begin fretting since you cannot remember the nature of Part Three. You can solve this dilemma by labelling the question and saying, "That is a three-part question; may I have Part One?" Now answer Part One. Then say, "And may I have Part Two?" Answer that segment next. When you say, "And finally, I'll take Part Three of your question," the questioner has frequently forgotten Part Three. Obviously, if the original question is a logical three-part question that does not tax your memory, you can simply respond by saying, "You have asked a three-part question. I'll begin by answering Part One." Once you have completed your response to the first part, restate the question and answer Part Two. Repeat the same technique for Part Three. With an easy three-part question you will not have the pressure of remembering three questions simultaneously.

The Argumentative Question   Allow the questioner the dignity of his or her opinion but do not get into an argument. Stay out of emotional territory and don't resort to becoming critical or defensive. This is a time when you need to veer away from arguing and stick with the facts. One response could be, "I appreciate you believe that...however, our findings suggest that..."

Always be prepared to prove your points with examples, data, testimony, or perhaps a slide that you have prepared in advance to back up your point. Using a visual aid or object to reinforce your message can have great impact. Let's return to the earlier example of housing for the elderly. Someone tries to disparage you during the question and answer session by saying, "You have spoken about all these grandiose plans and the budget allocation for building senior citizen housing, but so far all we have is your word and empty promises." How do you negate this? This is a case where you can respond by presenting a slide showing the architectural plans for development, photos of the housing under construction, and documents demonstrating your financial budget. You will be more convincing when you present your audience with this proof.

If the questioner is antagonistic, but correct, you need to acknowledge his or her point and describe how you plan to redress or rectify the situation. If you have promised that your corporation would grab an increased market share for your product and you have failed to meet those projections, you could be confronted at a shareholders' meeting with an angry shareholder who might say, "Your sales for the year have not met your projections. How do you account for this dismal failure?" You need to agree that sales have not met your target, explain why not, and then offer detailed plans of how your company will increase its market share and position itself to beat the competition next year.

A framing statement could also be useful with this type of question. You begin your response in this way: "There are two reasons why market share has declined..." and give the reasons. Continue to say, "We have a two-pronged plan to overcome this and drive market share to new heights." Describe your plan. Close your answer with a positive comment such as, "We are confident that we will meet and exceed expectations." Don't forget to respect each member of the audience, even while you are being confronted. The audience may not side with this hostile questioner. Yet, if you respond by attacking your antagonist, the audience will more likely side with him or her. Using a non-confrontational response will promote understanding and diminish antagonism.

Clarification Needed   On occasion, a questioner may offer a rambling statement that has an underlying, unstated question or pose a question that is obtuse or unclear. Don't hesitate to ask for clarification: "I'm not sure I understand. Could you clarify your concern and give me the question once again?" Alternatively, you can choose to use the clarifying technique suggested under "Listening Skills" in Chapter 15 of this text. You can then state, "Let me understand your question, what you are asking is..." and restate the question as you understand it.

If the question posed revolves around an issue you have already discussed, you might conclude that the listener did not grasp your message. In your answer, therefore, cloak your message in different terms. Your message remains the same, but you must simply word it differently.

The Unclear Question   The question may be unclear due to accent, deficient language skills, or plain fuzzy thinking. Instead of responding in a way that makes the questioner feel inept, make the problem yours by saying, "I am having difficulty understanding your question. Could you please repeat it or rephrase it?" This will make the audience member cognizant of the fact that it is necessary to project his or her voice and speak clearly.

The Loaded or Falsely Based Question   When a question is loaded or based on faulty logic or assumption, it is important to acknowledge its falsity and follow up with the relevant and correct information. Begin by saying, "This is not true or correct. The truth is..." You can then supply the accurate information.

Again in this situation, do not repeat back the loaded words. If the question says, "Isn't it true that you are a crook?" and you reply with, "No, I am not a crook," the audience has heard the word "crook" twice. Instead you may respond with a phrase such as, "My actions were always honourable and you will discover that when the facts are revealed in court, I will be vindicated."

Do not let false information hang in the air. Always provide proof and evidence to counter the falsely based or loaded question. Use a vocal tone that is firm and authoritative when negating a false statement.

The Irrelevant Question   What do you do when a questioner has missed the point and asks a question that has nothing to do with the topic you have spoken about? Such a question is off base or irrelevant. First, avoid becoming impatient or annoyed. Some individuals have a poor attention span, don't listen well and allow their minds to stray. The temptation may be to say, "Didn't you listen to a word I said?" Well, try not to take this inattention personally. Instead, remind the questioner of the topic under discussion: "The topic under discussion today is 'The Effects of Pollution on the Environment.'" Proceed to ask, "Do you have a question related to the topic at hand?" In this way you gently guide the listener back to the focus of the presentation.

The Hypothetical Question This type of question begins with a supposition. The questioner makes an assumption and uses it as a basis for an argument. The purpose of the hypothetical question is to invite speculation. Resist the impulse; decline to speculate. If you choose to speculate, preface your response with: "Your question is hypothetical, however…"

A donor to a particular charity might ask, "If our foundation donated $1 million to your cause, how would you allocate the funds?" If you answer this hypothetical question and lay out a plan for expenditure, you may be laying the foundation for future criticism. Let me show you why: Five years down the road, the donor asks for your financial records and your original business plan. She or he then compares your initial promise to the actual execution of your promise. Your plans might not have unfolded as you originally intended and now you are held accountable. So be careful when answering hypothetical questions. Do your homework first and offer answers based on facts, not on hypotheticals.

The Blanket Statement When you designate this section of your presentation as a question and answer session, it should remain just so. It is not a discussion period. A blanket statement is a statement rather than a question. For example, at the end of a talk on "Global Warming," a member of the audience states, "The Canadian government has not done enough to address the issue of global warming, which presents a danger to humankind." This is a blanket statement. When someone in the audience makes such a comment, he or she is not adhering to the expectations of the question and answer period. Remind the questioner that he or she has made a blanket statement and ask instead for a question: "Thank you for your opinion or observation. May I have your question, please?"

The Rambling Question In this case, the questioner shows the promise of delivering a question but ultimately does not. There is typically a degree of negativity behind the words. Avoid confrontation yet subtly interrupt at the earliest moment. At this point, you can do one of two things. You can say, "If I understand correctly, what you are saying is…" and echo a few key words. Continue to say, "May I have your question please?" Alternatively, you can say the same opening phrase, echo a few key words, and then bridge to another question. It is an assertive technique and one that your audience will appreciate. Furthermore, this technique allows you to regain control.

Often the rambler will try to dominate. Do not let this happen. On other occasions, an individual will try to dominate by posing numerous questions. One solution to the multiple-question audience-member is the following: When the first question is asked, look at the questioner and look at the rest of the audience to include them. As you end the answer, look back at the questioner. Now, when she poses another question, answer using the same technique. As you return to her, you see that she has a third question. Now, the light bulb should go on in your head. Recognize this sign and realize that this questioner wants to dominate the question and answer session. This time, begin by looking at her and turn your head away to make eye contact with the rest of the audience as you answer the question. Do not renew eye contact with this person; in fact, you can angle your body language away from her, and toward the conclusion of your answer, say, "Can we take a question from someone else now?" If the questioner is persistent and says that she has more questions, invite the questioner to meet with you afterwards in order to address any outstanding concerns.

The Bait Question   Bait questions put words in your mouth. Do not take the bait or you will become the bait. These questions may start with any of the following: "Would you say…?" "Are you satisfied?" "Given the fact… would you agree/disagree…?" The "Would you say…?" question essentially aims to put words into your mouth. You will, with experience, learn to give a flat "No" response or you will offer your own point of view. If the president of a large chemical company was asked, "Are you satisfied that your company has done enough to clean up the atmosphere after that disastrous toxic spill?" and he responded, "Yes," can you picture the headlines in tomorrow's newspaper? They could likely read, "President of ABC Chemical said he's done enough," offering a slightly misleading tone. If, however, the president of ABC Chemical responded to the same question with a well-thought out response such as, "ABC Chemical has allocated $38 million to clean up the atmosphere," the newspaper headlines would have been different. Respond to an "Are you satisfied?" question with a pre-planned, clearly defined message. You keep control when you respond in this way.

When you are asked a question beginning with "Given the fact…" be cautious of being set up. Again, state your point of view and turn the question around so that you impart useful and relevant information.

Closing the Question and Answer Period   Once you come to the end of the time period you have designated for questions and answers, let the audience know by saying, "We'll have time for one or two more questions." Conclude by stating, "Thank you." Avoid the expression, "Thank you for listening to me." This will diminish you. You are worthy of being listened to.

You may choose to end this session in a different way if the last question is a hostile or antagonistic one. You do not want your listeners to leave the room remembering a final negative interaction; rather, you want them to leave keeping *your* message in mind. In this case, provide a mini summary of your presentation that will leave your message imprinted on the minds of the audience. Say your final words. Stand still for three or four seconds, leave the platform with your head held high, and exit with upright posture.

You have now created a final impression of a speaker who is in control; equally important, you have ended the question and answer session on a positive note.

EXERCISES

1. Using your own Question and Answer Preparation Sheet, prepare a list of questions that you have found hard to answer in the past when you delivered a presentation. Now write down the answers to these questions incorporating the techniques you have learned in this chapter.

2. Select a topic on which you will be giving a presentation.

   a) Prepare the following types of questions and relate them to your material:

   - an emotional or political question
   - a technical question
   - a several part question
   - an argumentative question

- a question which needs clarification
- a loaded question
- an irrelevant question
- a hypothetical question
- a rambling question
- a bait question
- a straightforward genuine question

b) Now choose a partner and give your partner a list of your prepared questions. Your partner will now pose the questions one at a time and you will respond appropriately. Once you have gone through this exercise, your partner will offer you constructive feedback by pointing out what you did well and offer suggestions for improvement.

3. a) Read the following speech, "The Need for Critical Thinking," delivered by Scott MacMillan, a student at the University of Toronto.

   b) Divide into groups of four. Discuss the content of the speech and draw up a list of questions that you would pose if you were an audience member listening to that speech.

The Need for Critical Thinking

Can you give an "informed" opinion on the Kosovo crisis? Can you give an "informed" opinion on how to solve Toronto's homeless problem?

I have a difficult time with these questions because I don't know that much about the real issues involved. Most people have a problem answering questions such as these, when you ask for an "informed" opinion.

Our topic tonight is critical thinking. It's a subject I find fascinating because how we think determines how we live. The definition comes from the Greek word "critic" which means to question and evaluate. Unfortunately, in our society we tend to use it to tear down someone else's thinking, to criticize. Critical thinking is not a bad thing. It's a good thing. It means that when you say, "I believe . . .", it is followed by, ". . . because of these reasons." That's what critical thinking is.

In a recent survey in the United States, it was found that most Americans feel their government is spending far too much on foreign aid and that it should be reduced. But the same survey also found out that most Americans don't know how much is being spent on foreign aid. It's actually one percent of the total budget. Most Americans thought it was twenty percent or higher. In reality it's one percent, yet still most Americans said we spend far too much.

Critical thinking is about looking at all the information and then coming to an "informed" conclusion. Critical thinking is analyzing, organizing, evaluating, and applying information. It's "I think, because...."

John Chaffee, the Director of the New York Center for Critical Thinking, in his book *The Thinkers Way*, defines critical thinking as "an active, purposeful, organized cognitive process we use to carefully examine our thinking and the thinking of others, in order to clarify and improve our understanding."

There are three basic types of thinking. The first is what can be called "Garden of Eden" thinking. It's when everything is clear-cut, yes or no, right or wrong. I have friends who believe that something is either right or it's wrong. You ask them a question and boom, "This is the answer," no matter how complex the issue. Issues that I'm not that clear on. Right or wrong, that's Garden of Eden thinking. The second type of thinking is "anything goes" thinking. It's when everything is right. That view is right, that view is right, and that view is right. Nothing is wrong. Your opinion is correct but so is *your* opinion. It's very wishy-washy thinking. And the third type is "critical thinking." It's when we analyze information, when we organize it, evaluate it, and we bring it together, as an informed opinion.

Let's use a circle to illustrate an issue. What we tend to do, unfortunately, is to make a decision about the total circle, when we only know a small piece of the total pie. We may either ignore some of the other information in the circle or we don't know it. Critical thinking is making a decision based on the total circle of information.

Here are some basic perceptions. Politicians are corrupt. Teenagers are irresponsible. Police are violent people. Men are thoughtless and insensitive. Women are very emotional. Many people believe these stereotypes. The reality though, if we apply the principles of "critical thinking," is that we know that they may be true for some people but not for all. And yet our society tends to make these judgements every day.

Generally, we're not great at critical thinking. There are three reasons for this.

First, it's hard work. It means we have to question ourselves. We have to recognize that our beliefs could be wrong. And that's difficult work. We don't like to do that. We're not naturally good at saying, "Maybe I'm wrong and I have to question myself and rethink that."

Second, our school system tends to give information, but we don't teach people how to think that well. We focus on content, not thinking skills. We're probably getting better, but we still don't teach people how to think clearly.

And the third reason we're not great critical thinkers is the fact that we live in such an age of information. We're suffering from information overload, information smog as some call it. We get so much information coming at us all the time, from new technology, that we're in a haze. My boss e-mailed me a couple of months with the message, "Hallelujah, I can now email you from my phone." We're in the information age.

So how do we think critically? To think critically we need to do four things. One, we need to recognize different perspectives. Two, we need to look for evidence and reasons. Three, we need to recognize our personal lenses through which we view the world. We each see the world through our own eyes. I see something like this. You might see it very differently.

But my personal lenses are also biased. They're based on my experiences. And four, we have to synthesize all the information to come to a conclusion. We put these things together, different perspectives, look for reasons and evidence, and recognize our personal lenses, and we bring it all together to analyze information and come to an informed opinion.

I'll give you two examples.

I moved to Toronto last August from Halifax. When I told my friends I was moving to Toronto, many of them were critical. They said, you'll hate Toronto. They said, it's too big, too dirty, too stuck-up. Halifax is a beautiful city on the ocean. You'll hate Toronto. And if I had just listened to my friends I would have thought, maybe I shouldn't move to Toronto. Maybe I should stay right here. But when I looked at other parts of the circle my conclusion was different. I realized that my past experiences visiting Toronto were all good. I had met a lot of nice people from Toronto. There are a lot more restaurants, sports teams, good universities, and I've read a lot of good things about Toronto. Some not so good things too. But when I put it all together with a critical eye, it looked like it was worth a shot. And I'm glad I did my critical analysis.

My second example is discrimination. I'm a white male. My experiences with discrimination are negligible. I have not had any personal experiences. And if I view the extent of discrimination in the world based on my personal experiences, I'd say there probably wasn't much. But, if I look at the research, and I talk to my friends and other individuals, if I look at different perspectives, if I really looked at what's going on in the world, I'm going to obviously come to the conclusion that there is a tremendous problem with discrimination, both racial and gender, in this country and in the world.

So it's very important to look at the entire circle. Now, if I just looked at Toronto through my friends' eyes, I would never have come here. And if I looked at discrimination through only my personal experiences, I'd think that there was very little of it. These are but two examples of thousands of other issues and decisions we make.

The issue is to learn to think critically. Recognize that you may be wrong. Question yourself. Always remember the total circle of information. And if you only know a small piece of it, then try to find out the rest, or make your decision based on just that piece, but keep in mind that you don't have the full circle.

Thank you.

SUMMARY

In this chapter you have learned the importance of preparing efficiently and conducting the question and answer period with competence. Control this segment by establishing a fixed time span allocated for questions. Alternatively, when the situation calls for interaction or active participation, ask the listeners to pose questions at any point during the presentation. Elicit questions by raising your arm and asking, "Are there any questions?" If one is not forthcoming, suggest a question that you are frequently asked in order to get the ball rolling. Clearly identify the questioner while listening actively and remaining calm. Answer the questions concisely and back up your claims with supporting evidence. The different types of questions you may encounter include emotional, political, anticipatory, technical, several part, argumentative, clarifying, unclear, loaded, false, hypothetical, rambling, or bait. When closing the question and answer session, inform the audience that you will have time for one or two more questions. If this period ends with a negative or antagonistic question, deliver a mini summary of your presentation in order to ensure that your key speech statements become the "take home" message and you complete the presentation on a positive note.

SUGGESTED READING

Berg, Karen and Andrew Gilman with Edward P. Stevenson. *Get to the Point – How to Say What you Mean and Get What You Want*. New York: Bantam Books, 1989.

Martel, Myles. *Mastering the Art of Q&A. A Survival Guide for Tough, Trick and Hostile Questions*. Illinois: Dow Jones-Irwin, 1989.

Snyder, Elayne with Jane Field. *Speak for Yourself with Confidence*. New York: New American Library, 1983.

Interview   **Josey Vogels**

Josey Vogels, author of *Dating: A Survival Guide from the Frontlines* and *The Secret Language of Girls*, is a nationally syndicated columnist on sex, dating, and relationships. She does regular speaking engagements at universities.

Q   Is there a big difference between writing and public speaking?

A   I think we [writers] have a much more intimate experience with the page, the written word. When you're addressing the public there's much more of a performance aspect involved that isn't involved with writing. You have many writers who are introverted, very quiet and soft spoken, yet their writing can be very gregarious. So, I think it's sometimes hard to bridge that gap if you're not a very outgoing gregarious person as a writer.

Q   Is it easy to be funny and irreverent while delivering a speech?

A   Definitely. I rely on humour a lot whenever I do any public speaking. For me, the best public speaker is somebody who can combine a sense of humour and a little bit of irreverence, just to put people at ease, but is also respectful and not cynical and negative. I like to stay very positive.

Q   Which public speaker has left an indelible impression upon you?

A   In my field, the person who stands out the most is sex educator Sue Johanson because she has a really wonderful way of being funny, direct, honest, and practical with her information. She is very quick and able to handle a delicate subject in a way that is fun, informative, and useful. Those are always the things I am striving for.

Q **Who do you consider to be a great Canadian speaker?**

A Rex Murphy and Stewart McLean, who is just a great storyteller. That is something that really appeals to me in a public speaker, someone who can bring their message to me through story. Broadcaster Brent Banbury is someone else I've followed in broadcasting, and Vicky Gabereau—people who really know how to engage their audience in conversation and really keep things moving along as well.

Q **Describe the attributes and qualities of a good speaker.**

A Being able to engage your audience. The thing that I'm always most affected by when I see a good public speaker is that I leave feeling like my mind's been stimulated and massaged, and I'm thinking about things that I hadn't thought about, in a way that I hadn't thought about before. It's not necessarily that they had been talking about anything brand new that I've never heard before, it's just a way of presenting it that shakes up my thinking about it. Being very visually engaging is important. Someone who knows how to use the space, and through body language and facial expressions is able to make me excited about what they're talking about.

Q **How do you prepare for a speech?**

A I'll get a good idea and I'll work at writing it really well because that's what I'm good at, and that's what I'm comfortable with. But then I'm always surprised when I go to present it that I haven't gauged the difference between the words on the page and the public experience of delivering it.

Q **Do you use notes?**

A Yes, I do. Ideally, I will write the speech out, then I'll write it in point form and then, even from the point form, I'll reduce that down to simple words so that I'll stay on the path I've written. Finally, I practise it several times.

Q **Are there any speaking habits that annoy you?**

A I'm the worst culprit. I come in as one of the worst offenders of saying, "you know." It's always annoying when someone has a repeated behavior. Also, self-deprecation is good, but I don't like people to be too self-deprecating. I think it's good to show confidence, but at the same time you don't want to be too cocky.

Q **What detracts from a good speech?**

A I think negativity. Also, bad habits: looking down, not making eye contact, and having a false genius. I have problems with a lot of motivational speakers because I just feel like it's salesmanship. That's not to say that there isn't a certain amount of salesmanship in public speaking, but I think you need to keep that in check if you are interested in being taken seriously as a genuine speaker.

Q **What kind of voice do you like to listen to?**

A A voice of authority in our culture is a very strong, solid voice that is well-projected and has confidence and dynamism in it that makes you want to listen.

Q **Ralph Waldo Emerson said "It is a luxury to be understood." How do you ensure that a diverse audience understands your message?**

A I think you need to check in with your audience and make sure that they understand. I would like to think that if someone didn't understand, they would feel comfortable asking. Again, I think it's preparation and knowing who you're speaking to.

Q   **There is a Chinese proverb that says, "Square words won't fit into a round ear." How do you tailor your message to your audience?**

A   I use a lot of humour. When I'm speaking to students I speak very much in their language because they're going to be bored if I don't. It's knowing your audience.

Q   **Irving Layton, the famous Canadian poet and writer said "An aphorism should be like a burr: sting, stick and leave a little soreness afterwards." How important is it to use aphorisms, quotations, and anecdotes in a speech?**

A   I think anecdotes are the Number One for me because, again, it comes back to storytelling. I think you can have statistics and factual information, but the thing that is going to drive the message home is the story. Girlspeak is that telecommunication that women have that comes very easily where we can engage on a very personal, anecdotal, warm way—that is what I try to do when I'm public speaking.

Q   **What advice would you offer to novice speakers?**

A I'm a novice speaker myself. I think leaving your self-consciousness, and that things always seem worse to you than they do outwardly. Also, prepare and practise more; make sure that you don't surprise yourself on stage.

chapter twelve

Special Occasion Speeches

A word is not a crystal, transparent and unchanged; it is a skin of living thought, and may vary greatly in colour and content according to the circumstances and time in which it is used.

—Oliver Wendell Holmes, Jr.

LEARNING OBJECTIVES

- To structure speeches that are delivered on special occasions
- To explain the speech of introduction
- To know how to deliver a thank you speech
- To understand the elements required for an acceptance speech
- To develop a speech of tribute
- To plan a eulogy
- To plan, organize, and deliver a team presentation

INTRODUCING A SPEAKER

When you introduce a speaker to the audience, it is your job to prepare the audience for the upcoming speaker and the speech. Your aim is to create a friendly environment and relationship between the speaker and the audience. The person giving the introduction should arouse the interest of the audience in the speaker and the subject matter of the speech. He or she should create a comfort level for the speaker and encourage the audience to listen further. The introducer should not attempt to capture the limelight since he or she is simply the link between the speaker, the audience, the speech, and the occasion.

A speech of introduction should be brief and last between 1 to 1.5 minutes. The focus of your introduction is on the speaker. Below is a structure you can follow when designing this introduction:

Structure for a Speech of Introduction

1. Discuss the nature of the occasion.
2. Acknowledge the reason for the meeting.
3. State the reason why the audience is getting together.
4. Present the purpose of the speech.
5. Thank the speaker for making this appearance.
6. Share the information about the speaker. Offer biographical information that is pertinent, important, and interesting.
7. Highlight any unique quality the speaker possesses. Know about any important positions he or she has held or mention any notable achievements that are relevant.
8. Conclude by mentioning the name of the speaker and the topic of the speech.

Make certain that you pronounce the speaker's name and title correctly. When in doubt call him or her prior to the occasion and pose the question. You can also use this opportunity to find out how the speaker wishes to be addressed. For example, the premier of a province would need to be addressed in the following way: "Ladies and gentlemen, it is with great pleasure that I present to you today the Honourable John P. Harris, Premier of … who will address us on 'Tax Cuts in the Healthcare Industry'." Here's another example closer to home. For a class speech, ask Jim, your classmate, if he wishes to be called by his birth name, James, or by the shortened form of his name. Then address him with the form he chooses.

If you were going to be the speaker, it would be very helpful for you to provide the introducer with your biography or profile, written in a business-like style. It should be no longer than one typed page and written in the third person singular, that is, use "he" or "she." In this biography, highlight your education, experience, affiliations, important work, and achievements. To provide an extra safety net for the person who is introducing you, take an extra copy of your biography to the speech or event in case this person has mislaid your information.

EXERCISE

Choose a famous person that you would like to meet. Imagine that he or she is coming to address your public speaking class. Decide upon a speech topic and prepare the introduction you would give. Follow the suggestions given and prepare an introduction for the person you select. Introduce:

    a) The mayor of your town

    b) A famous astronaut visiting your college

    c) A survivor of an earthquake

    d) A Hollywood celebrity

    e) A speaker who will spark a controversy

f) The valedictorian

g) A war hero

h) A wrongly convicted convict

i) A reformed drug-addict

j) A government official

k) Mother Theresa

l) A politician

THANKING A SPEAKER

When it is your task to thank a speaker, it is vital that you give the speaker your undivided attention and listen attentively. A thank you speech should not be too long. It should last for about 1 to 1.5 minutes.

Your role is to offer thanks on behalf of the audience and it should be a heartfelt and genuine expression of thanks.

The following are some guidelines:

1. Thank the speaker for all that she has given in terms of inspiration, value, ideas, information, or entertainment.

2. Make a note of a few salient points that were mentioned during the speech and reiterate them. In this way, the speaker will be flattered that you have itemized the points that were noteworthy in her address.

3. Refrain from repeating the entire speech, though. Rephrase only the important segments.

4. Remember you are not offering your personal thanks, you are offering thanks on behalf of your class or group.

5. Thank the speaker for having made the sacrifice of time and energy to be with you.

6. At all times be courteous, be generous, and be kind.

EXERCISES

1. A career counsellor has addressed your class on the topic of "Choosing a Career." Prepare and deliver a thank you speech to the counsellor.

2. A large donation has been offered to a charity of which you are the chairperson. Give a thank you speech to your benefactor.

3. Your hockey team has just won the Stanley Cup. Give the thank you speech after the awards dinner.

4. You have won the lottery. You have been asked to deliver a thank you speech at a celebratory luncheon.

ACCEPTING AN AWARD

Awards are given so often in the course of a lifetime—at school, in business, for sporting and academic achievements, in clubs, for community affairs, in government, from religious organizations, for acts of bravery, at the point of retirement, and when accepting donations.

When an individual is honoured by an award or gift, an acceptance speech is frequently required. Depending on the occasion or the event, sometimes a simple "thank you" will suffice. However, it is always safer to prepare a few words of thanks, in advance, should you be required to speak. The recipient of an award also might not know ahead of time that he or she will be honoured in this way. Knowing what the expectations are of you, the honouree, will help you plan a speech should it be necessary for you to speak.

An acceptance speech will reveal you as a worthwhile recipient of the award and should demonstrate your sincerity and modesty.

Convey a friendly attitude and show deep appreciation for the honour being bestowed upon you. Express your gratitude and appreciation during your speech.

Every good acceptance speech should contain the following elements:

1. A thank you to the presenter and the organization or person donating the award.

2. An acknowledgement of the significance of the award.

3. An expression of gratitude. If the award is a surprise to you, you can also mention your surprise at receiving the award.

4. If others have assisted you in any way in attaining this award, give them credit and thank them for their valuable contribution.

5. If relevant, discuss how this award holds meaning for you with regard to your future.

6. Close by reiterating your thanks.

Here is an example of an acceptance speech delivered by Jim Van Horne, the sports broadcaster, when he received the Honourary Andy Award from Mohawk College at its 2001 MediaFest.

I want to thank the broadcasting class, here at Mohawk College, for bestowing this honour upon me. I can honestly say that I never entered this business to win awards. I got into the media because it was something I wanted to do. My work is something I look forward to doing every day.

I listened to the radio every day as a child, and dreamed about being on the radio one day. When I reached that goal, I wanted to try television. So far everything has worked out well. But there is no secret to my limited success. It all comes with hard work. If you are willing to put in the hours, you can be successful at anything you try to do. Believe me, if I can make it, so can you.

You are at the crossroads of your lives. In the very near future, you will be thrust into the world to make your way. Some of you will be successful. Some will not. That's life. Sometimes it can be fulfilling, sometimes disappointing.

As I stand before you and see your faces, eager and ready to embrace the challenges awaiting you, I remember the day when I first started working in my chosen profession. I have never regretted a single minute. I love what I do and I love the people I work with. I have said many times over that I have never worked a day in my life. I hope you will find the same satisfaction in your professional and personal lives that I have found in mine.

Thank you once again for this award. It truly is an honour to be here tonight.

EXERCISE

Choose one of the following suggestions and prepare an acceptance speech relating to the topic.

1. Accept a medal for saving someone's life.
2. Accept an award for community service.
3. Accept a school prize for winning a math contest.
4. You team has won the hockey championship. Accept the award.
5. Your team has won the debating contest. Accept the cup awarded to your team.
6. Accept a scholarship to a university of your choice.
7. Accept the trophy for winning a golf tournament.
8. Accept a donation for your favorite charity.
9. You have won a certificate of achievement. Decide upon the achievement and prepare an acceptance speech.
10. A donation of a prominent building to house the homeless has been made by a rich philanthropist. Deliver an acceptance speech.
11. You have won a musical award. Decide upon the name of the award and the criteria for winning the award. Prepare an acceptance speech.
12. Watch an awards show on television such as the Geminis, the Emmys, the Oscars, or the Grammys. Listen closely to the acceptance speeches and note the strengths and weaknesses of each address.

COMMEMORATIVE SPEECHES

When we recognize and honour a person, an organization, or an event in a speech, we call this a commemorative speech. We will discuss two types of speeches here, the tribute and the eulogy.

The Tribute

The purpose of a tribute speech is to recognize and pay tribute to a living person, an accomplishment, or an occasion. We inform the audience about the importance of this individual, group of individuals, or the event, and convey our admiration and appreciation during the tribute. The tribute should relate to and involve the audience. A tribute is given to the living and when offering one, a closer bond develops between the speaker and the audience members. For example, after the attacks on the World Trade Center, many tributes were paid to the New York firefighters and police officers who risked their lives so courageously, and survived. A tribute to them would be meaningful to the audience composed of these valiant people and their families, who lived through a common experience and shared history together. When composing a tribute:

1. Relate the tribute to the audience.
2. Present the reason for the tribute.

3. Mention the significance of the occasion.

4. Offer genuine not effusive praise.

5. Reflect the feelings that the person or event engenders.

EXERCISE

1. Prepare a tribute to a close friend who has made a remarkable impact on the lives of his neighbours by alerting the fire department to a fire that was about to engulf the neighbourhood.

2. You are the master of ceremonies at a rock show. Choose a famous star of your choice and pay tribute to this individual.

3. Pay tribute to Canadian soldiers who have returned from a war overseas.

4. Prepare a tribute to a doctor who has saved the life of a critically ill child.

5. Prepare a tribute to a group of volunteers who have generously donated their time to answer the Kids Help Phone line. (If you would prefer to do so, you can select your own charity for which the volunteers work.)

The Eulogy

A eulogy is a tribute we pay to someone who has died. Sometimes a eulogy is delivered for animals. If you have a deep emotional attachment to the person or animal, it can be a challenging task to deliver the eulogy. With preparation and practice, though, you will be able to accomplish the task. Be as natural and sincere as you can be and tailor your remarks to honour the deceased and meet the needs of the audience that has gathered to honour him or her.

In a eulogy, the deceased is praised and the speaker speaks about the character, the personality, the achievements, and positive qualities of the person or animal who has passed away. The speaker can also discuss the contribution this individual has made to society, and mention how so many people have been impacted by having had the privilege of knowing the deceased. By the end of the eulogy, the audience should feel favourably inclined towards the deceased and be inspired. The eulogy should also provide the audience with a sense that life continues and that our memories will survive despite the physical loss of a loved one.

A eulogy can be structured chronologically. You can talk about the different stages or periods in the individual's life, his significant accomplishments, when they were made and how they impacted his family, friends, and society. In addition, you may want to delineate how you view the deceased's potential place in history. A strong opening and closing will provide two solid bookends for the eulogy. Let your message convey the essence of the person, the solemnity of the occasion, and a sense of nobility.

EXERCISE

Here is a list of famous people. Choose one and prepare a tribute or a eulogy to deliver.

1.	John Diefenbaker	16.	Frederick Banting
2.	Marilyn Monroe	17.	John Polanyi
3.	Stephen Leacock	18.	Billy Bishop
4.	Marie Curie	19.	Oscar Peterson
5.	Pierre Elliot Trudeau	20.	Norman Jewison
6.	Leonard Cohen	21.	Robertson Davies
7.	Peter Gzowski	22.	Norman Bethune
8.	Northrop Frye	23.	Pierre Berton
9.	Madonna	24.	Marshall McLuhan
10.	Winston Churchill	25.	Farley Mowat
11.	Bobby Orr	26.	Mordecai Richler
12.	John Lennon	27.	Pamela Anderson
13.	Robert Bateman	28.	A.Y. Jackson
14.	William Lyon Mackenzie King	29.	Jim Carrey
15.	Jacques Villeneuve	30.	Wayne Gretzky

TEAM PRESENTATIONS

A team presentation is a collaboration. At school and later on in the workforce, you will probably be required to work as part of a team. A well-functioning team has a common goal and during a public speaking course you might be called upon to deliver a team presentation. Your common goal, as members of the team, would be to work together amicably and efficiently to develop a first-class presentation that will earn you an excellent grade.

Any team that works well together has a goal and a strategy to achieve that goal. The goal needs to be clearly defined and focused. Each team member will have a specific role and responsibility. Team members collaborate and orchestrate their actions to achieve a common goal. A good team presentation will result from a mutual need and constructive independence.

To deliver an effective team presentation you need the following:

1. A team leader.
2. Team presenters.
3. A topic that can be broken down into different aspects.
4. A clearly defined time frame for each speaker.
5. Solid content that is well-organized and includes good support, evidence, and examples.
6. Confident and polished delivery of the material.
7. Professional-looking presentation aids.

8. Energy and enthusiasm.

9. Vocal variety.

10. Fluid transfer from speaker to speaker.

The role of the team leader is to do the following:

- Introduce and clarify the topic
- Introduce each team member
- Present a segment of the presentation
- Provide the transitions between speakers
- Give internal summaries when necessary
- Conclude the presentation
- Conduct the question and answer period

The role of each team member is to do the following:

- Do thorough research for his or her particular segment
- Prepare an effective presentation
- Practice the presentation alone
- Observe the time limit
- Rehearse as part of the team presentation
- Offer answers to questions posed on his or her specific topic

To work effectively as a team it is important to do the following:

- Define your roles clearly
- Discuss group expectations
- Establish a clear purpose for the overall presentation
- Define the purpose for individual presentations
- Select a leader who is strong and articulate
- Set firm deadlines for initial drafts of the presentations
- Create a rehearsal timetable
- Give honest constructive feedback to each other
- Plan a list of potential questions that might be posed
- Plan the answers to those questions
- Practise the full-team presentation, plus a mock question and answer period, in the room in which you will be presenting.

The initial team presentation preparation sheet is shown below.

FORM 12.1	Team Presentation Worksheet

Topic of Presentation: _____

Specific Purpose of Team Presentation: _____

Key Message: _____

Name of Team Leader: _____

Topic for Team Leader: _____

_____

Team Member Name: _____

Topic for Team Member: _____

_____

Team Member Name: _____

Topic for Team Member: _____

_____

Team Member Name: _____

Topic for Team Member: _____

_____

Date for first draft of individual presentations to be distributed to group members:

_____

Date for First Rehearsal: _____

Date for Second Rehearsal: _____

Final Rehearsal: _____

FORM 12.2	Structure for the Team Presentation	

	Order	Visual Aids
1. Introduction by Team Leader	_____	
Transition by Leader	_____	
2. First Speaker's Topic	_____	
Transition by Leader	_____	
3. Second Speaker's Topic	_____	
Transition by Leader	_____	
4. Third Speaker's Topic	_____	
Transition by Leader	_____	
5. Fourth Speaker's Topic	_____	
Transition by Leader	_____	
6. Conclusion by Team Leader	_____	
7. Question and Answer Period	_____	

It works smoothly when the leader transitions from speaker to speaker, yet there is another alternative. For example, you can let Speaker Number One offer the transition to Speaker Number Two, and so forth. Try out both methods and discover which one serves you better.

You have, by this stage, given a few speeches. For a team presentation you can use the same suggestions given in Chapter 3 for preparing a speech. The structure of an informative speech and persuasive speech are presented in Chapter 4. Refer to Chapter 5 for more information on how to organize a speech.

Planning and delivering a team presentation can be a creative, challenging, and rewarding endeavour. It also provides you with preparation for the real working world where one day you may present as part of a team. You may work on a committee, you may become an educator, an executive, a lawyer, a doctor, a technology expert, an accountant, an architect, a salesperson, a businessperson, or a healthcare worker. Some of you may have to present in court, at therapy sessions, at problem-solving meetings, to clients or customers, or at conferences.

The skills you now possess, having practised for and learned how to deliver a team presentation, will stand you in good stead for your future.

EXERCISES

1.   Select a team composed of four or five members. Choose one of the Informative or Persuasive Topics in Chapter 4. Break the topic down into sub-sections. Allocate a section to each team member. Choose a team leader. Prepare and practise for the presentation. Each participant will speak for five minutes and the question and answer period will last five minutes.

2.   Give a team presentation on one of the following:

    a)   Famous educators

    b)   Famous reformers

    c)   Famous philanthropists

    d)   Famous navigators

    e)   Famous scientists

    f)   Famous leaders

    g)   Famous musicians

SUMMARY

There are certain occasions that call for a specific type of speech to be delivered. In this chapter we examined how to structure and deliver a speech of introduction, a thank you speech, and an acceptance speech. We also discussed commemorative speeches in which we recognize and honour a person, an organization, or an event. The two types of commemorative speeches we looked at were the tribute and the eulogy. When a group of individuals work together to deliver a presentation, it is called a team presentation. Each team member has a specific role and contributes toward the aim of achieving a common goal. The role of the team leader and each team member is outlined and a worksheet to assist in the initial preparation stage is included. A worksheet that will help the student to structure the overall presentation is also given.

SUGGESTED READING

Detz, Joan. *Can You Say A Few Words?* New York: St. Martin's Press, 1991.

Detz, Joan. *How to Write and Give a Speech.* New York: St. Martin's Press, 1992.

McManus, Ed and Bill Nicholas. *We're Roasting Harry Tuesday Night.* Englewood Cliffs, NJ: Prentice Hall, 1998.

Pasta, Elmer. *Complete Book of Roasts, Boasts and Toasts.* West Nyack, New York: Parker Publishing, 1982.

Rogers, Natalie H. *The New Talk Power.* Virginia: Capital Books Inc., 2002.

Wolvin, Andrew, Roy Berko, and Darlyn Wolvin. *The Public Speaker / The Public Listener.* Boston: Houghton Mifflin Company, 1993.

Interview	Jim Van Horne

Jim Van Horne, a well-known Canadian sports-broadcaster, has 25 years of experience in television, radio, and public speaking.

Q   Which public speakers have left an indelible impression upon you?

A   There have been many, John F. Kennedy with his clarity, Pierre Elliott Trudeau with his passion, Bill Clinton with his arrogance and confidence.

Q   Who do you consider to be a great Canadian speaker, and why?

A   I heard a speech by Stephen Lewis, who was the former leader of the New Democratic Party. And while I don't agree with his politics, I found him to be very intelligent. He delivered a message that was clear, concise, and thought provoking. I also admired former Prime Minister Pierre Trudeau whenever he spoke. He was very much in tune with the times and what was happening in Canada. He always spoke with a great deal of confidence.

Q   Describe the attributes and qualities of a good speaker.

A   Confidence, good preparation, and sense of humour. A good speaker does not talk down to his or her audience—he or she relates to them on an individual basis. A speaker who makes eye contact with as many people in the room as possible will always be successful.

Q   What are the vital elements of a good speech or presentation?

A   Simplicity in the message. A speaker should never assume he or she knows more than the audience. I always approach every speech I make with the knowledge that there is someone in the audience who knows more than I do. It keeps me honest. It's critical to be prepared. Speakers who don't know their topic are like fish out of water; they will drown very quickly.

Q   How do you prepare for a speech?

A   It depends on the topic. If the speech relates to my career, I make notes about anecdotes that the audience may find interesting. I'll usually offer a question and answer period at the end of the talk. If it's more technical, I will gather any pertinent information I need from books and the Internet. I find the Internet invaluable when it comes to doing research.

Q   How much time do you spend preparing for a speech?

A   Again, it depends on the topic. If it's about me, not very much—maybe an hour or so. If it's related to a specific topic, it may take a few days or a week before my idea is completely formulated.

Q   Do you use notes? If so, what form do they take?

A   I may have a complete script if it's a subject I have had to research. If it's a personal talk, I'll just have "cheat sheets" about specific ideas, just to remind me.

Q   Do you experience nervousness before or during your speech?

A   I am usually very nervous before a speech, but I settle down when I start. Often I'll get nervous again during the course of the talk. Once I get to the question and answer session I am usually okay.

Q   Is the ability to give an effective speech or presentation a crucial skill in the business and professional world? Do you feel that students

should spend more time practising this skill?

A If an individual is in the public eye with a company, whatever that company may be, it is critical to present a polished image. It not only serves the individual well in his or her career, but may also help him or her land a better position with the company or another organization. I think it is an important part of students' curriculum to practise public speaking whenever possible. It teaches them poise, and gives them confidence in their professional lives.

Q **Are there any speaking habits that annoy you?**

A Individuals who mumble, speak too quickly, or speak in a condescending manner. Constantly using "um" or "ah" or "like" during the course of a speech shows a lack of preparation and consideration for the listener.

Q **What detracts from a good speech?**

A Lack of preparation. A speaker who is not prepared will not deliver a clear and concise message. A speaker who underestimates the audience will leave them frustrated and ill-informed.

I prefer a speaker who changes tone, pitch, and the quality of his or her voice—a person who adjusts to the mood he or she is trying to create. I like a speaker who can be dramatic when necessary, loud when necessary, and quiet when necessary. I like speakers who can smile, sound conversational, and generally connect with their audience.

Q **Tell me about your most successful speech?**

A It was at a going-away party for the golf pro at my club. He was retiring after 25 years. I was the master of ceremonies. I knew all of the speakers, so I tailored a joke for each one. Because it was an adult setting, and everybody knew everyone else, I was quite liberal with the stories I was telling. As I introduced each speaker, I told a joke using each one as the central figure. The audience loved it—they were rolling in the aisles. When I was finished everyone came up and congratulated me and thanked me for my contribution. It was extremely gratifying.

Q **Ralph Waldo Emerson said, "It is a luxury to be understood." How do you ensure that a diverse audience understands your message?**

A Know your audience, know your message and what you are trying to say. Understand what they want to hear, and give it to them.

Q **Can you describe someone who you feel is a masterful speaker?**

A René Lévesque, when the PQ lost the referendum and he gave his farewell speech. You could feel his emotion. Bill Clinton and the state of the union address when he was in the middle of the Monica Lewinsky scandal. He was defiant to the end. George Bush at Ground Zero when he was consoling the workers after the 9/11 attack at the World Trade center. His concern and determination were clearly evident.

Q **Irving Layton, the famous Canadian poet and writer, said, "An aphorism should be like a burr: sting, stick and leave a little soreness afterwards." How important is it to use aphorisms, quotations, and anecdotes in a speech?**

A They can add life to what may be a very boring speech. The goal of a speaker should not only be to enlighten, but to entertain as well, and aphorisms, quotations, and anecdotes can add that much more life to a presentation.

Q **What prepared you for your role as a public speaker?**

A My work. As a broadcaster, I speak to the public every day. I guess you could say I am a public speaker in everything I do on a daily basis.

Q **What advice would you offer to novice speakers?**

A Make sure you know your topic. Always be prepared. If you're prepared for any eventuality, your speech will be a success. A lack of preparation is a formula for failure.

chapter thirteen

Practising
the Speech

I am the most spontaneous speaker in the world because every word, every gesture, and every retort has been carefully rehearsed.
—George Bernard Shaw

LEARNING OBJECTIVES

- To polish your speaking skills through self-evaluation

- To use the video camera to assess your strengths and make improvements

- To use a tape-recorder to judge the vocal impact you are making

- To discuss the dos and don'ts of public speaking

By this stage of your development, you have learned numerous public speaking skills. You are armed with the knowledge of how to prepare for and organize your presentation. You also know how important it is to articulate your thoughts with clarity while using vocal variety. You understand how the nonverbal message contributes to the overall impression the audience forms. Now the time has arrived to practise aloud.

You can practise by making use of:

- a video camera or a mirror
- the audiocassette recorder
- a self-evaluation sheet

Always allow sufficient time to practise. It is not good enough to merely compose your speech, you now need to hear it spoken aloud. This is the time when you can assess the impact of the spoken word. Speeches should be written for the ear. Your delivery will be judged by the ear, the eye, and the attitudes and emotions of the listener.

PRACTISING WITH THE VIDEOCAMERA

If you have a videocamera at your disposal you are really fortunate. If you can locate or borrow one, this method of practising will serve you well. Videotaping will give you the opportunity to assess your speech and delivery objectively. Place the camera on a tripod in the centre at the back of the room. Aim to get as wide a shot as possible of the front section of the room. You should also be able to include a head-to-toe shot of yourself. Ensure that the microphone on the camera is in good working order, and check that it can pick up the sound of your voice as you project from the front of the room.

If you plan to speak from behind a lectern, angle the camera towards the lectern. If you have control over the lighting, make certain that you, the speaker, are well lit.

Test the setup initially. Record the first minute of your speech, then place it in the VCR to check that everything is working seamlessly. If you have a friend who can do the videotaping for you, it will make it much easier. Now you are ready to go. Do a full run-through of your speech while imagining that the room is peopled with an audience. Do not let the camera intimidate you. In fact, think of the camera as a friend in the crowd.

Once you have recorded the entire speech, rewind the tape and sit yourself down comfortably in front of the VCR and monitor to assess yourself. It is always easiest to see our flaws first. Aim for a balanced self-assessment.

Giving Feedback

We grow and develop as speakers when feedback is offered. Here are a few tips to take into account when giving and receiving feedback.

1. Feedback is valuable when you offer the speaker an objective viewpoint and a different perspective. When we give feedback or criticism, we are judging the work of another individual. Ideally, judgements ought to be fair and objective, but this is not always the case. Each audience member judges according to his or her own personal perceptions, attitudes, values, knowledge, and experience. When offering feedback make sure that it is always ethical, positive, and constructive. Refrain from using negative, emotionally laden words.

2. Cultures differ when giving criticism. Some cultures are concerned with saving face and are disinclined to express a negative evaluation. To overcome these barriers, we can establish these guidelines:

    i) Offer a positive comment first.

    ii) State an example of what worked effectively.

    iii) Do not attack the speaker personally.

    iv) Keep your comments focused on the speaker's message and the delivery of the message.

Accepting Feedback

1. Most people are armchair critics, but when you are criticized in a public speaking class the aim is to help you become a better, more articulate speaker.

2. Listen to the feedback with an open mind.

3. If the criticism is unclear, ask for clarification so that the critic can be more concrete and specific.

4. Do not take the criticism personally. We are criticizing the specific speech, the content, the organization, and the delivery of it.

5. Feedback will show you what you do well and what you could do better.

6. If you adopt the worthwhile suggestions you are given, the criticism will add enormous value to your speech.

Write down the following after an initial viewing of your speech:

1. Three things that you did well.

2. Three things that you would do to improve your speech.

3. Fill in the following Speech Evaluation Sheet:

FORM 13.1	**Speech Evaluation Sheet**

Name: _____

Date: _____

Type of Speech: _____

Speech Topic: _____

Audience: _____

Evaluate the speech using the following scale:

1 = Excellent   2 = Very Good   3 = Average

4 = Fair   5 = Needs Improvement

Enter a number on the blank line and then offer your comment. Identify the strengths of the speaker and offer positive, constructive suggestions for improvement.

MAJOR PURPOSE

The purpose was clear   _____

The purpose was worthwhile   _____

The purpose was achieved   _____

TOPIC

Choice of topic   _____

Speaker's knowledge of topic   _____

Development of the topic   _____

Adhered to the time limit   _____

FORM 13.1	Speech Evaluation Sheet (continued)

SPEECH STRUCTURE
Introduction

The introduction captured my attention   _____
The introduction had a clear focus   _____
It established the speaker's credibility   _____
It motivated me to listen further   _____

The Body

The body was well-structured   _____
Used signposts, transitions, and connectives to clarify   _____
Main ideas were clear and easy to follow   _____
Choice of language and vocabulary appropriate   _____
Supporting material provided credibility and interest   _____

The Conclusion

It was clear   _____
It was impressive and memorable   _____
It offered a sense of finality   _____
It ended on a strong note   _____

Delivery

Facial expression and eye contact   _____
Posture and poise   _____
Movement and gestures   _____
Use of notes   _____
Vocal projection, clarity, and variety   _____
Speaker was audience-centred   _____

Visual Aids

Clearly visible   _____
Attractively designed   _____
Easy to understand   _____
Handled smoothly   _____
Introduced at the appropriate times   _____

FORM 13.1	**Speech Evaluation Sheet** (continued)

Overall Impression

The approach to the topic   _____

The speaker   _____

The nonverbal impact   _____

The vocal impact   _____

The content   _____

Rapport with the audience   _____

Comments and Suggestions

I would like to offer the following comments and suggestions:

_____

_____

_____

_____

_____

_____

_____

_____

If you have a friend who is with you during this practice session, you could ask him or her to fill in an evaluation form independently. Then ask for your friend's objective feedback. Remind your friend that feedback should be positive and constructive. It won't be helpful if an evaluator says, "You spoke so quickly, I couldn't understand a word you said." It would be more beneficial to offer this type of comment: " If you spoke a little slower and used more pauses, it would be easier to understand your message." By framing feedback in this way you will not put the speaker on the defensive. In fact, you will have offered a suggestion that the speaker can adopt; he or she is now receptive to your comments as it has been presented in a positive vein.

Keep a record of your initial videorecording. Now practise your speech once more, having made the changes you deemed necessary. Now record the speech a second time. Review it again and notice how and where you have improved. Continue polishing the speech until you are satisfied. As a general rule, you should hear the speech spoken aloud at least six times. Professional speakers will go over their speech at least a dozen or more times before presenting to the public.

Not everyone has the luxury of being able to videotape themselves. Here is another idea for practising. Stand in front of a *mirror*, preferably a tall one, and practise speaking your speech while facing the mirror. This is a slightly more difficult task, as we tend to make judgements along the way such as, "Oh, I shouldn't wear this pair of jeans for my presentation," or, "I hadn't noticed that blemish on my chin before." Try and ignore these extraneous thoughts which serve merely to detract from the task at hand, which is to practise your speech. You don't have the same degree of objectivity with the mirror, but it will certainly help with your practice.

PRACTISING WITH THE AUDIOCASSETTE RECORDER

If you make the purchase of an audiocassette recorder, it will become an invaluable aid to you. Not only can you use it to record lectures or conduct interviews, it will help you tremendously for speechmaking. You can pick up the recorder and record random ideas as they occur to you. You can record the initial draft of your speech to hear how it sounds. You can assess the vocal variety in your voice as you listen to the recording. One big plus is that once you have finalized your speech draft, you can record it and then play it back, over and over, until you have virtually memorized your speech.

The tiny microcassette recorders will not give you an accurate reproduction of your voice. It would be a better idea to purchase a minicassette recorder into which you can insert the 10-centimetre by 6-centimetre audiotape. When selecting a recorder, look for the one that has a built-in microphone and a counter.

The following are a few pointers to observe when using the audiocassette recorder:

1. Use fresh batteries.
2. Use a good quality tape for your recordings.
3. Make sure that the microphone on the tape recorder is at the appropriate distance from your mouth so that the sound of your voice can be picked up with ease.
4. Set the counter at 0 before you begin so that you are able to rewind your recordings to the precise spot where you began.
5. Use the Voice and Speech Analysis Chart on the facing page to assess your vocal impact.

DOS AND DON'TS OF PUBLIC SPEAKING

The Dos

1. Be prepared. Fill in the Preparation Checklist that follows the dos and don'ts.
2. Practise alone. Practise in front of a friend, a peer, or family member. Practise in front of a video camera, a mirror, or with a tape recorder.
3. If possible, practise in the room or on the stage where you will be presenting.

FORM 13.2	**Voice and Speech Analysis Chart**

Check the appropriate box:

1. **Volume:**

	Very Good	Average	Needs Improvement
Too loud	❑	❑	❑
Too soft	❑	❑	❑
Appropriate	❑	❑	❑
Other	❑	❑	❑

2. **Pitch:**

	Very Good	Average	Needs Improvement
Too high	❑	❑	❑
Too low	❑	❑	❑
Lacked variety	❑	❑	❑
Contrast too exaggerated	❑	❑	❑
Other	❑	❑	❑

3. **Pace:**

	Very Good	Average	Needs Improvement
Too quick	❑	❑	❑
Too slow	❑	❑	❑
Lacked variety	❑	❑	❑
Hesitant	❑	❑	❑
Appropriate	❑	❑	❑
Other	❑	❑	❑

4. **Pause:**

	Very Good	Average	Needs Improvement
Used sense pause well	❑	❑	❑
Used dramatic pause	❑	❑	❑
Used emphatic pause	❑	❑	❑
Did not use pause effectively	❑	❑	❑
Other	❑	❑	❑

5. **Stress:**
   (Stress is the weight or force put on a word or phrase to bring out the meaning.)

	Very Good	Average	Needs Improvement
Appropriate	❑	❑	❑
Inappropriate	❑	❑	❑
Other	❑	❑	❑

| FORM 13.2 | Voice and Speech Analysis Chart (continued) |

6. **Vocal Quality**:

	Very Good	Average	Needs Improvement
Breathy	❑	❑	❑
Nasal	❑	❑	❑
Throaty	❑	❑	❑
Shrill	❑	❑	❑
Shaky	❑	❑	❑
Dull	❑	❑	❑
Lacks modulation	❑	❑	❑
Other	❑	❑	❑

7. **Speech Clarity**:

	Very Good	Average	Needs Improvement
Indistinct	❑	❑	❑
Slurring	❑	❑	❑
Defective speech sounds	❑	❑	❑
Mispronunciation	❑	❑	❑
Over-articulated	❑	❑	❑
Dialect/Accent	❑	❑	❑
Other	❑	❑	❑

8. **Overall Vocal Impression:**

Positive—What aspects conveyed a positive impression? _____

_____

_____

Negative—What aspects conveyed a negative impression? _____

_____

_____

Did you sound:
- ❑ dull   ❑ monotonous
- ❑ confused   ❑ boring
- ❑ ended on a flat note

Did you sound:
- ❑ knowledgeable   ❑ informed
- ❑ sincere   ❑ vital
- ❑ self-confident   ❑ energetic

FORM 13.2	Voice and Speech Analysis Chart (continued)

9. I need to work on the following areas:

- ❏ Volume
- ❏ Pitch
- ❏ Pace
- ❏ Pause
- ❏ Stress
- ❏ Vocal Quality
- ❏ Clarity

4. When approaching the podium:
   a) Walk with a sense of purpose and erect posture
   b) Say the following words to yourself:
      I am prepared.
      I am confident.
      I want to give you my message.
   c) Place your notes down and anchor your feet firmly
   d) Look at your audience in a friendly manner
   e) Take a slow, deep breath before beginning and relax
   f) Find a welcoming face in the audience to give you encouragement
   g) Begin

5. Deliver your speech as planned by talking **to** the audience, not **at** them.

6. Maintain eye contact with each listener until you have finished a thought and then move on to make eye contact with the next member of the audience.

7. Do not race through your speech. Make effective use of pace, pitch, volume, stress.

8. Use clear speech and vivid, precise language.

9. Avoid filler words such as, "like," "um," "eh," "you know," "okay," and "sort of."

10. Use good body language and gestures to add impact.

11. Your verbal and nonverbal messages should be congruent.

12. Be authentic, energetic, enthusiastic, and committed to your message.

13. Dress appropriately for the occasion.

14. Your smile and sense of humour are definite plusses.

15. Take ownership of the speaking space.

16. Create visuals that are relevant and well-designed.

17. Know how to operate the technical aids efficiently.

18. Check your equipment, supplies, and handouts: use the Visual Checklist, which follows the Preparation Checklist.

19. Have a good night's sleep prior to giving your speech.

20. Visualize yourself giving a successful presentation.

The Don'ts

1. Do not display a lack of respect for your audience by not preparing adequately.

2. Do not arrive late.

3. Do not apologize for not preparing, for not knowing enough about your subject, or for creating poor presentation aids.

4. Do not exceed the allocated time frame.

5. Do not wear clothing that detracts from your message.

6. Do not focus on the individual in the audience who exhibits closed body language, a stern demeanour, or a negative attitude.

7. Do not avoid making and holding eye contact with individuals in the audience.

8. Avoid fidgeting, touching your face unnecessarily, jiggling coins or keys in your pocket, and swaying.

9. Do not assume another "persona" when you stand before an audience. Be yourself.

10. Do not mumble or clear your throat needlessly.

11. Do not fabricate answers to questions that are posed.

12. Do not procrastinate planning your talk.

13. Do not focus on any negative thought.

14. You have prepared. You have practised. Do not anticipate failure, rather, anticipate success.

SUMMARY

This chapter stressed the importance of practising prior to the presentation. Practising in front of a video camera and then reviewing the performance will provide the student with an objective viewpoint. The student is advised to make use of the Speech Evaluation Sheet when self-assessing the speech on videotape. Once you have critiqued the talk, then you should run through the speech again incorporating the improvements that are necessary. When you review the videotape a second time, the positive changes will be noticeable. If you can practise with a classmate present, you can get additional feedback. If you cannot rehearse in front of a video camera, try doing so before a mirror. Another way in which you can practise and commit the speech to memory is by using a tape recorder. You can also fill in the Voice and Speech Analysis Chart to help clarify which areas of the vocal delivery need polishing. Suggestions are given on how to give feedback and how to accept feedback. Finally, the dos and don'ts of public speaking are addressed. Two checklists are given to assist the student—one is a preparation checklist and the other is a visual checklist.

FORM 13.3	**Preparation Checklist**

1. Topic of the Presentation _____

2. Specific Purpose of the Presentation _____

3. My message is _____

    _____

    _____

    _____

    (What do I want my audience to see, think, feel, and believe once I have
    completed my presentation?)

4. Who is my audience?

    What do they want to know?

    What is the size of the audience?

    Is it a formal or informal occasion?

    What is the dress code?

5. Check the following

    *   What is your position on the agenda?
    *   When will you speak?
    *   How much time are you allotted for your speech?
    *   Will someone introduce you?
    *   Will there be a question and answer period?
    *   Have you visited the room in which you will be presenting?
    *   The arrangement of seats, exits, and backdrop
    *   The positioning of podium, table, chair, props
    *   Audio-visual equipment including microphone working efficiently
    *   Make a note to ask the audience to turn off cell phones
    *   Placement of handouts
    *   Do you need a technician or assistant?
    *   Location of acoustics/light switches
    *   Where is the temperature dial?
    *   Water for the speaker

6. Will I hand out evaluation forms?

FORM 13.4	**Visual Checklist**

THE PRESENTATION

❏ Hard copy of the presentation
❏ Computer disk containing presentation slides
❏ Overhead transparencies in correct order
❏ Flipchart
❏ Markers and masking tape
❏ Video
❏ Handouts
❏ Objects and props
❏ Pointer

EQUIPMENT

❏ Computer
❏ Remote mouse
❏ Data projector
❏ Overhead projector
❏ Screen
❏ Extension cards
❏ Electrical outlets
❏ Microphone—standing, wireless, lavaliere, or handheld
❏ Lights—for dimming and for the lectern
❏ Spare bulbs for the overhead projector
❏ Lectern
❏ Table
❏ Chairs

YOU

❏ Dress is appropriate
❏ Hair is neat and not shielding the face
❏ Comfortable footwear
❏ Jewelry kept to a minimum

chapter fourteen

The Interview

*Talking and eloquence are not the same: to speak, and to speak well,
are two things.*

—Ben Jonson

LEARNING OBJECTIVES

- To define the interview
- To understand the difference between the screening interview and the in-depth interview
- To learn how to prepare for the interview
- To discover ways in which to do research
- To realize the importance of visual presentation
- To develop a list of interview questions
- To present yourself effectively
- To conduct the follow-up
- To learn how to conduct a research interview

If we break down the components of the word "inter" and "view," something interesting emerges. We discover that "inter" means between and "view" is the act of seeing or surveying mentally in order to form an impression.

The interview is a two-way interaction between individuals. An interview is designed to achieve a specific goal through gathering and exchanging information.

In this chapter we will look at two types of interviews that will help to prepare you for school assignments and entrance or re-entrance into the workforce. In each case, you will need to know how to better prepare yourself for the job interview and the research interview.

THE JOB INTERVIEW

You have spent years at school preparing yourself academically for the field you are about to enter. Have you given much thought to the process of landing a job in your chosen line of work? Perhaps you have. You have written your résumé, you have submitted it to potential employers, and now the big day of the interview arrives. How strong are your oral skills? Will you be able to articulate your work objectives with clarity? Will you be able to present yourself with confidence and competence? Can you frame your responses to interview questions with intelligence and appropriateness? Are your interpersonal skills in need of polish? Can you establish rapport with the interviewer? This interview can land you the job of a lifetime—are you prepared for it? Your résumé has helped you to knock on the door and gain entry. To secure the position, the following information will be helpful to you.

Type of Job Interview

There are different types of interviews that you could encounter.

The Screening Interview   If you are applying for a position where numerous applicants have also sent résumés, someone will meet you for an initial interview but this may not necessarily be the person for whom you will ultimately work. The interviewer will pose questions that may or may not have been answered on the résumé. Once you pass this level you will move onto the in-depth interview.

The In-Depth Interview   This interview will be designed to see if you are an appropriate "fit" with the corporation, to assess your credentials, your competence, and your potential. This interview will be structured, focused, and goal-driven. To be a successful candidate, you need to prepare thoroughly, practise for the interview, plan the answers to a variety of questions, and present yourself positively and confidently. We will look at the following:

Preparing for the interview

Interview questions

Presenting yourself effectively

The follow-up

Preparing for the Interview

Research   There's an old saying: "If you fail to prepare, you prepare to fail." With thorough preparation you should anticipate success. You have received notification to tell you that you have been granted an interview and now your preparation for the interview begins.

- Find out as much as you can about the company, the firm, the organization, the association, and the individual for whom you will be working. The first step is to go on the Internet and search the Web. Also pay a visit to the library to learn about your potential employer. Read the company brochure, trade journals, newsletters, business magazines, and annual reports and search through industry records. If you want the position of a chartered accountant with a professional firm, become well acquainted with relevant data and figures on the firm. Know who their clients are. To indicate that you have done your homework, you may also want to check comparative information about the employer's competitors.

- Learn about who the top executives are and find out about their background. Find out about the management style and corporate vision. Get a copy of their Mission Statement. Investigate what the major trends are in this field. Who is the competition? Uncover the needs and goals of the organization and see how you can fill those needs and embrace its goals. Are there any changes occurring within the organization or within the industry?

- Search through newspaper archives for pertinent corporate information.

- Locate someone who has been a past employee of the organization you want to work for and ask him or her to offer you some insights or background information on the company. You may gain some valuable tidbits that you can use in your favour during the interview. For example, if John tells you that the chief financial officer is a stickler for detail and that she loves to play tennis, you may casually bring up the fact that you are drawn to the profession of accountancy since you enjoy paying great attention to detail and that you always adhere to strict deadlines. Then, when you can slip it in appropriately during the conversational stage of the interview, you may bring up the fact that you enjoy tennis and recently attended the Canadian Tennis Open.

- Take cues from your surroundings when you are in the interviewer's office. If the interviewer has a framed picture of a sailboat on his wall, chances are he enjoys sailing. Here's your cue to mention that an interest of yours has always been sailing (provided, of course, that it truly is).

- Visit the Career Centre at your campus.

- Visit the Chamber of Commerce for information about smaller firms.

- Research the actual position for which you are applying. Talk to contacts in the organization and professionals in the field. Get as much detail as you can about the job requirements and duties. What will your career path be? Is there room to grow and develop? Is it a challenging position? What kind of salary can you expect? What is the work environment like? Will you have to travel? If so, how much travel is involved? Do other employees enjoy working for the organization? What can you contribute to this position?

- Make use of your personal contacts. Speak to friends, fellow students, colleagues, and family members who may possess knowledge of your potential employer.

- Find out who will be conducting your interview. This may not always be possible, but do some investigating and find out as much as you can about his or her interviewing style. Is this an interviewer who speaks in concepts, is encouraging, likes details, has no time for small talk, or is technically inclined? For example, when you deal with someone from the human resources department, the interview questions will be less technical than when you are interviewed directly by the head of information technology. Will there be more than one person at the interview? What type of interview will this be: a screening or in-depth interview?

- Visit the facility before the interview. Note how long it will take you to get there. Is the business close to the transit system? Plan to arrive early for the interview. Arrive at least 15 minutes before the interview so that you can enter the interview free of stress.

By now, you should be familiar with details on the position you wish to hold, your employer, and the field you are entering. The time spent on this aspect of your research will arm you with the necessary knowledge and facts and, as a result, you will feel more confident entering the interview.

Appearance and Grooming

How we present ourselves visually at the interview speaks volumes. Judgements are made within the first 30 seconds of meeting someone. So pay close attention to how you appear for the interview. Appearance incorporates posture, dress, body language, facial expression, and eye contact.

The way you dress sends a message, so use dress as a business tool. Dress should be appropriate. Dress to suit the job you are seeking to acquire. If, for example, you are working in a technology field, the clothes you wear might fall into the category of "business casual." Yet if you are entering the banking field at a managerial level, for a man, a dark suit, a crisp clean shirt, and tie would be appropriate. For a woman, a good suit or tailored dress would work. Also, make certain that your shoes are clean and polished. At the beginning of the year 2001, attire became increasingly casual, eliciting this comment from the business pages of *The New York Times*, "The boardroom is not the beach." A swing back to a more professional style of dress has returned. When in doubt consult your local men's or women's clothing store for guidance, or refer to John Malloy's book, *New Dress for Success*. The principles he discusses are timeless. Classic, conservative dress always works. However, if you are in advertising, the media or a leading-edge career, add a modern touch to your dress. This could be in the form of a scarf, watch, or pin. You don't want to look out of date when you are predicting trends for the future or creating a new, exciting advertising campaign to deliver to a potential client. If you are an architect, dress with the quality that you wish to convey in your work.

It is always a good idea to look for quality when purchasing new items of clothing or accessories. A quality item will last longer. Divide the cost of the item by the number of occasions upon which you will be wearing it and you will note that, in the long run, you will get better value for your money.

Jewelry and fragrance should be used with subtlety. They should not shout, "Look at me" or "Don't I smell good?" They should not detract or distract. They should enhance the impression we convey.

Express your individuality through the accessories you choose. Collect high-quality basics: a high-quality watch, leather belt, pen, portfolio, briefcase, and wallet. Treat yourself to a silk tie or scarf, and classic earrings. This is investment dressing.

Make-up for women should be used with care. If necessary, consult an expert for guidance. Hair should be clean, well groomed, and in keeping with the current length and style. Look at those around you for clues in terms of dress and make-up expectations. Note whether a beard is acceptable in your particular position. Investigate how individuals in your field present themselves; for example, what are the vice-presidents wearing? Dress for the job you want.

Here's a hint for the future. Once you have landed the position for which you have applied, be consistent in your manner of dress for work and project a positive, professional image at all times.

In the interview you will be conveying an image. The following will assess your image:

- You
- Your mode of dress
- Neatness
- Eye contact
- Handshake

- Posture
- Manners
- Smile
- Sincerity
- Interest

Now that we have discussed dress, refer to Chapter 7 on Visual Aids and your Environment to brush up on your knowledge of body language, eye contact, facial expression, appearance, and proxemics.

Make certain that when you offer your handshake while greeting the interviewer, it is firm. Don't be a bone-crusher and, above all, don't offer a jellyfish handshake. In order to get a sense of the degree of firmness that you need to use when shaking hands, go to the doorknob of a door, and turn it. That is precisely the amount of firmness you need to use when shaking hands. Remember, when you enter the interview room, extend your hand to offer a firm handshake, look the interviewer directly in the eye, and smile. Introduce yourself in a confident, warm, and well-projected voice. You could say, "Good morning, Mr. Walter, I am Denise Rose. Pleased to meet you."

You have now set the stage for a successful interview through thorough research and preparation. You have paid attention to your nonverbal presentation and your opening introduction.

Now is the time to gather your research and start to frame the type of questions you anticipate will be asked of you. Also prepare three to five questions that you will ask the employer. Avoid such obvious questions as, "What type of products does this company produce?" Choose more challenging questions instead. This will convey your knowledge about the company.

Preparing your Interview Questions

Here is a list of questions that are frequently asked in an interview. Prepare answers to these questions in a way that will demonstrate your ability, qualifications, professionalism, and "fit" with the organization. Know what you have to offer the employer in terms of skills, knowledge, and experience and know the needs of the company.

1. Tell me about yourself.
2. What are your strengths?
3. What are your weaknesses?
4. Why are you interested in this industry?
5. Tell me about previous jobs you have held? What would your boss say about you?
6. What kinds of work have you done that would prepare you for the duties of this position?

7. Describe a project you have undertaken and what you learned from it. How would you do it differently if you had the chance to do so?

8. Describe your most significant accomplishments to date. These could be personal, work, or educational accomplishments.

9. What did you like best about your last job? What did you like least?

10. What are your long-term career goals?

11. When you encounter a task in which you have numerous obstacles to overcome, how do you stay motivated?" Explain by describing an actual situation when this happened.

12. What are your professional five-year goals?

13. Do you have any objections to a psychological interview and tests?

14. How technologically adept are you?

15. When faced with many tasks simultaneously, how do you proceed?

16. Do you work well under pressure? Give an example.

17. Describe a situation in which your work was criticized and how you responded.

18. Describe the most relevant and specific things in your background that demonstrate that you are perfectly qualified for this position.

19. How competitive are you?

20. How do you cope with change?

21. Do you prefer to work alone or to be part of a team?

22. How do you view our competitors in the marketplace?

23. Describe a situation in which you showed flexibility and an open mind.

24. What new goals and objectives have you established lately?

25. What qualities does a professional possess?

26. How do you see our industry in five years?

27. What can you do for our company?

28. If we offer this position to you, what are your salary expectations?

29. Tell me why we should hire you.

Further questions may be posed relating to your education. Be prepared with answers to the following:

1. What is the value of a college or university education?

2. What were your favourite subjects?

3. Did you belong to any clubs or associations at school?

4. What subjects created difficulty for you?

5. What would your classmates say about you?

6. What books have you read lately?

7. How did attending university or college equip you for life?

8. Who are your role models?

EXERCISE

Prepare a list of questions that you would like to ask the interviewer. Your questions might cover the following topics:

(a) Career Path

- Where will I be in five years from now in the company?
- Will there be regular meetings with my boss when I will be given feedback on my work?

(b) Company Organization

- Who will I report to?
- Will travel be part of my job?
- Will I be part of a team?
- Are you increasing your sales target for the next fiscal quarter?
- Do you anticipate opening a new branch in the near future?

(c) Work Environment

- Can you describe the working environment at this company?
- How has technology impacted this organization?

(d) Personal Qualities or Experience

- What qualities are you looking for in an ideal candidate?
- What job challenges can I expect to encounter?
- What work experience will match the requirements for this position?

Answering Interview Questions

You have submitted your résumé, so anticipate that questions will be posed relating to your application. Always remember that a positive, confident response to these questions will go a long way.

For candidates who are in a visual field, bring along samples of your art, graphics, architectural designs, or storyboards. If you are a writer, bring along samples of your writing.

Here are a few formulas you can use when answering questions. When responding to a question such as Question 23: "Describe a situation in which you showed flexibility and an open mind," you may use the SAR formula:

Situation

Action

Result

You may answer in the following way:

Situation: One of my camera technicians came to me and asked whether he could have the afternoon off as he needed to attend a wedding.

Action: Since I could rearrange the schedule and find a replacement for him, I asked him if he could make up the time by working a weekend shift.

Result: The employee was willing to demonstrate flexibility, just as I did, by agreeing to work on the Saturday. By accommodating his needs, I now have a more committed and loyal employee.

Also remember to use the impromptu method when applicable. As a reminder, the impromptu method is the PREW method. Answer by giving the following:

P   Point of View

R   Reason

E   Example

W   Wrap-up

This method can be used when you are asked for an opinion on an issue.

When responding to questions, bear in mind the following attributes for which interviewers look:

- Motivation
- Good communication skills
- Company fit
- Good personality
- Positive outlook
- Education
- Dress and appearance
- Grades

- Experience
- Responsibility
- Ability to take initiative
- Ability to be part of a team
- Leadership qualities
- Adaptability
- Sincerity
- Integrity

Answer your questions thoughtfully, reveal the knowledge that you acquired as a result of your research on the company, and market yourself as the ideal candidate.

Before the Interview

- Find out the name of the interviewer, her title, and the pronunciation of her name.
- Gather your résumé, letters of references, visual samples, if necessary, and a copy of your transcripts.
- Dress professionally and show good manners.
- Allow sufficient time to reach the interview site. Plan on arriving 10-15 minutes early.
- Be polite and friendly to the receptionist or secretary. She, in turn, will be able to convey a positive impression of you to her boss before bringing you into the meeting room.
- Practise some deep breathing and relaxation exercises while you are waiting.
- Have a good night's sleep before the interview.

EXERCISES

1. Prepare answers to the 29 questions that interviewers typically ask.
2. Get into pairs. One person will be the interviewer; the other will be the interviewee. Decide on a job position and the name of the organization, company, or

firm you want to work for. Prepare a list of pertinent questions. Conduct a 15-minute interview. Once the interview is over, the interviewer should give feedback to the candidate and suggest improvements that could be made.

3. If you have a video camera at your disposal, redo the interview. Videotape the interview offering your new polished responses. Review the tape. Check to see whether you have conveyed the attributes that interviewers are looking for. Check to see whether your answers are comprehensive, appropriate, and confident.

Tips for Answering Interview Questions

1. When answering the question, "What are your weaknesses?" try and turn a weakness into a strength. You can say: "I am a perfectionist and therefore expect a lot of myself. I sometimes anticipate that others will produce the same high standard of work that I expect of myself. I am learning not to project my expectations onto others." Here you have stated the perceived weakness and demonstrated how you are dealing with it.

2. When answering the question, "What are your strengths?" describe your skills, your knowledge, your strengths, and your values. Remember to relate these to the job position. It will help you to write them down beforehand.

Using a separate piece of paper, fill in answers to the following chart:

FORM 14.1	Interview Preparation Chart
My knowledge: _____	e.g. Legal analysis
_____	Extensive accounting and budgeting experience
_____	Develop and deliver training programs
My skills: _____	e.g. I am a problem-solver
_____	I sell
_____	I operate a computer
My strengths: _____	e.g. Organized
_____	Detail-oriented
_____	Kind, patient
My values: _____	e.g. Integrity
_____	Discipline
_____	Fairness
_____	Respect

FORM 14.2	Practice Chart

Here is a chart that will start you thinking about how you can build a bridge from the employer's needs to your related experience.

Employer Needs
- A competent, confident on-air television broadcaster
- A dependable and reliable employee

Skills & Knowledge
- Four-year degree from Ryerson University
- Trained to operate a video camera
- Completed sports journalism course
- References

Relevant Experience
- Interned at Roger's Sportsnet for one year
- Worked as an on-air reporter for hockey and skiing
- Work began at 9 a.m. daily and I was always punctual and diligent

When the question, "Why should we hire you?" is asked, you could respond in the following way:

"You are looking for a competent on-air broadcaster and I can confidently say that my experience and qualifications will meet your needs. I qualified at Ryerson University after having completed a four-year course in Journalism, with training as a video journalist and on-air reporter. I interned at Roger's Sportsnet for one year and reported on basketball and hockey. I have references from the producer of the show I worked on and would be pleased to share them with you. He speaks about the high quality of my work and my dependability."

EXERCISE

1. Take a sheet of paper and write down, "Ten Reasons To Hire Me."
2. Practise speaking your answers aloud.

Tips for Presenting Yourself Effectively

1. The interview may last from 20 minutes to approximately one hour. Through your nonverbal and verbal communication you want to exhibit confidence, warmth, a positive attitude, and enthusiasm.

2. When you meet the recruiter/interviewer, extend your hand to offer a firm handshake, look him or her directly in the eye, and say, "I'm John Adams. Pleased to meet you, Mr. or Ms. Peters."

3. Wait for the interviewer to offer you a seat. When seated, do not encroach upon the interviewer's space; in other words, don't place your briefcase on the desk or invade his or her personal zone.

4. Don't slouch in your seat or exhibit an attitude that is too relaxed. Sit upright and be alert but not rigid. Establish a friendly atmosphere.

5. The interview will probably begin with comfortable conversation such as a discussion of a current event, last night's baseball game, or the weather. Keep abreast of current events by reading the newspaper.

6. Allow the interviewer to set the tone and take the lead with the questions. When you answer, show thoughtfulness, and reply in a clear, well-projected voice.

7. Listen actively and if you are asked a question which you don't understand, ask the interviewer for clarification. (Refer to Chapter 15 on listening skills in this textbook.)

8. Do not ramble when answering. Be specific, give concrete examples, or share an anecdote that illustrates the point you wish to make.

9. Always tell the truth. Be straightforward yet diplomatic.

10. Do not express negative views about a previous employer.

11. When you sense that the timing is right during a lull in the conversation, this could be the right moment to pose your carefully prepared questions about the company.

12. Don't be afraid to reveal your personality, to laugh, or nod at the appropriate time.

13. Some recent graduates may have had little work experience. In this case the interviewer may ask you a hypothetical question to judge how you would carry out a particular task; he or she may ask, for example, "How would you deal with complaints in your department?" This type of question is designed to gauge how you would perform in the job environment. Take time to plan your answer and organize your thoughts. Then deliver your answer.

14. Before the interview ends, make certain that you have conveyed the points you wish the interviewer to know about you. Tell him or her why you are qualified for this job and project how you can fit into the company's future.

15. Let the interviewer know that you are excited by this position by stating, "I am very interested in this position."

16. Ask when you will be hearing from the employer.

17. Do not overstay your welcome.

18. Thank the interviewer and offer a handshake once more. Exit with erect posture, purposefulness, and confidence.

The Follow-Up

Assess your performance at the interview. Think about how you presented yourself, how you spoke, and how you answered the questions. Did you build rapport with the interviewer? Decide whether you would accept the job offer if it was presented to you.

Send the interviewer a thank-you letter after the interview. Restate your interest in the position.

If you receive no telephone call or written response to your letter, you should follow-up with a telephone call to find out whether a candidate has been selected for the position yet. If a decision has not been made, you may ask when they expect to make their decision. Do not appear too assertive. Always remain polite and respectful.

If you do not land the position, it would be a valuable learning experience for you to ask for feedback from the employer or interviewer. This will help you develop and polish your interviewing skills that will lead to future success.

Reasons for Hiring or Rejecting the Candidate

Top recruiters cite the following reasons for failure during the interviewing process:

- Poor communication skills
- Failure to listen
- Lack of candour and honesty
- Arrogance
- Not a team player
- Trying to take control of the interview
- Offering excuses for job failure
- Giving vague statements
- Speaking in clichés
- Offering prepared, pat answers
- Insincerity

Recruiters were impressed with the following qualities:

- Good communication skills
- Motivation and drive
- A solid track record
- Active listening skills
- Presenting a professional image
- Strong interpersonal skills
- Good manners
- Clear articulation of goals
- Confidence and enthusiasm
- Exhibited knowledge of the corporation, its values, and goals
- Honesty and integrity
- Punctuality
- Demonstration of responsibility
- Ambition
- Capable of handling stress
- Comfortable and relaxed presentation
- A clear career goal
- Knowledge required for the position
- A positive attitude

Being forewarned is being forearmed, so knowing what the recruiter or interviewer is looking for can help shape your demeanour and your responses.

THE RESEARCH INTERVIEW

The research interview is a two-way interaction where the interviewer requires solid oral skills, listening skills, and research skills, as well as the ability to develop rapport with the subject being interviewed.

When we do our research, we can gather information from the library, Internet, organizations, newspapers, journals, magazines, government, and experts. We discussed researching in Chapter 3 so now you have a point of reference in terms of approach. What we are concerned with in this chapter is the personal research interview where we interact with our subject in order to glean information that he or she possesses.

Why do we need a personal interview? We conduct this type of interview when someone is the expert on a topic or possesses specialized knowledge or skills. When your subject is newsworthy or has "inside information," this is the method to employ. If you are doing a project on gene therapy and a leading scientist has just unveiled a new discovery in the *New England Journal of Medicine*, it would add impact to your project if you could include a quotation from the scientist herself by conducting an interview with her. The direct quotation, as opposed to a written summary from the journal, adds more colour and interest to your work.

The following are five stages of the research interview and we will look at each one:

1. Establish the purpose of the interview
2. Plan the interview
3. Prepare your questions
4. Conduct the interview
5. Follow-up

Defining the Purpose

You are about to give a talk on, "How Physicians Can Improve Their Communication Skills with Patients." Now you need to decide on the precise purpose you have in mind when you interview Dr. Field, a psychologist. You have done your research on the courses doctors receive during their training, you have interviewed patients who have encountered problems communicating with their physicians; you now want to learn how Dr. Field, a noted psychologist and communication expert in this field, has learned and enhanced skills and techniques to improve his own interpersonal communication skills.

Write down your purpose in one clearly defined sentence; for example, "My purpose is to elicit information, tips, and techniques to improve the communication skills of physicians."

Planning The Interview

Background Research   Do your background research on your interviewee. Using the example offered above, you would need to know about Dr. Field's academic qualifications, his medical expertise, what his colleagues have to say about him, and what contributions, if any, he has made to medical and psychological journals. Perhaps you might even have access to a patient whom you could interview. Why is he the renowned expert? Does he present at medical conferences? Also, you might want to find out about his family life. Does he have children? Is he a good communicator at home?

Arranging the Interview   You may do so in any one of the following ways: send a letter, send an email, place a telephone call. Introduce yourself by stating your name and the purpose of your interview. Also state the duration of the interview and tell your subject that the interview could be arranged at his or her convenience. It is important to demonstrate that you are flexible because frequently the interviewees are busy people.

If you are making your request by telephone, here is a sample script you may use:

Hello, my name is Brian Thomas and I am a student at the University of Alberta. I am presently conducting research into Effective Communication Skills for Physicians for my psychology class. As you are an expert in this field, I would appreciate it if we could arrange an interview that would last for 20 to 30 minutes. This interview could be arranged at your convenience to fit in with your schedule.

Most people are flattered to be interviewed so do not be reluctant to contact any potential interviewee.

Once you have secured a time to meet or speak on the telephone, be polite and thank the interviewee. If you are doing a person-to-person interview, decide on a location to meet and make sure it is in a venue that is suitable for interviewing. You do not want to choose a setting where there are frequent interruptions or a lot of noise in the background. You may even ask your subject where he or she would prefer to meet. Offer your telephone number so that he or she will be able to reach you in order to pose any questions or reschedule the interview.

Preparing Your Questions   Have an open mind and be ready to improvise once you are in the meeting; prior to the interview, however, prepare your questions thoroughly. Prepare questions that are clear, specific, and intelligent. Avoid posing questions that are hostile or confrontational. Many individuals do not respond well to hypothetical questions. You may need to phrase provocative questions but use language that does not offend. You do not want to discourage the interviewee in any way.

To get more detailed responses, plan open-ended questions. An open-ended question begins with: What, Why, Tell me, How, Describe. When using this type of question, you will get a more complete, descriptive response from your subject: "Tell me how you first developed an interest in communication skills," will be a more effective question than, "Are you interested in communication skills?"

Closed-ended questions usually only invite one-word answers. They begin with the words: Do, Did, Can, Could, Will, Would, Are, and Is. So a question like, "Is your specialty internal medicine?" would likely result in the one-word answer, "Yes."

Do not lead the interviewee into providing the answer you want. You can, however, use probing questions for clarification.

Once you have prepared your list of questions, add an extra three or four in case the interviewee covers the answers to some of the questions you planned but hadn't yet posed. Now practise speaking the questions aloud so that when you actually deliver them they will sound fluent and articulate. Use your tape recorder for practising.

Conducting the Interview Create a professional impression by being punctual and by dressing appropriately. When you introduce yourself, offer a handshake, and thank the person for making the time to meet with you. Establish comfortable conversation and restate the purpose of the interview. You may also restate how long the interview will take. Live up to your promise and shortly before the allotted time comes to an end, warn the interviewee by saying, "We'll have time for one or two more questions." This then gives the interviewee the option of saying, "Well, we can continue for another ten minutes if you wish."

You want to be able to recall as much information as possible once the interview has been completed; my advice would be to use a tape recorder to record the interview. It is necessary to ask permission prior to recording and to ask the subject to sign a release form. The form might look like the one in Form 14-3 below.

FORM 14.3	**Permission Form**

I voluntarily agree to participate in a research interview conducted by Brian Thomas on the topic of "Communication Skills for Physicians." I grant permission for the interview to be tape recorded and transcribed and to be used solely by Brian Thomas for inclusion in his talk on "How Physicians Can Improve Their Communication Skills."

I understand that Brian Thomas may use my name only in regard to the above-mentioned project.

Signed: _____

Date: _____

If the interview is conducted via e-mail or over the telephone, you will still need to obtain written permission. Remember, the verbal agreement to be interviewed does not grant you permission to use, print, or disseminate segments of the interview. You still need to get your subject's written permission.

Now set up the tape recorder. Allow the subject to feel at ease with the microphone and proceed with your questions. Make notes if you feel the need to do so, too. Stay the course with your interview plan. If the conversation veers off course, gently steer it back to the topic at hand. You are the one who needs to keep control of the interview.

To convey accurate information it is crucial that you listen effectively to the answers that are given. You may then think of another question that arises out of an answer and pose it. Don't be too fixed on asking all your questions in the pre-planned order if the interview calls for you to be flexible and go with the flow of information. Do, however, return to your planned questions after the diversion.

Upon completion of the interview you may want to confirm some responses or check for clarification of particular details. If you plan on quoting your subject, check the quote for accuracy. And finally, thank the interviewee for giving up his or her valuable time to meet with you.

The Follow-Up   Display courtesy and appreciation by following up the interview with a thank-you note. You may also make mention of how your subject specifically contributed to the success of your research.

Transcribe your notes and the tape recording as soon as possible after the interview while the comments and answers are still fresh in your mind. Are there any gaps or discrepancies in the information? Will you need a second interview? In addition, make some notes about your general impression of the interviewee for future reference.

You are now ready to evaluate, interpret, select, and utilize all the pertinent and valuable information you have acquired.

EXERCISES

1. An expert on one of your favourite topics/courses is visiting your campus to deliver a talk. You are promoting the lecture and need to interview this expert in order to write promotional literature. Decide on the expert and the topic of the lecture. Plan ten questions you would pose.

2. A Canadian soldier has returned from battle in another country. You are giving a presentation on "The Role of Canadians in Peacekeeping on the World Stage." What questions would you ask him or her? Who else would you interview for your research?

3. You are planning a career in a particular field. Who would provide you with the information you require? Who could be a role model or mentor to you? Plan a list of questions you would pose to this person.

SUMMARY

In this chapter we examined two kinds of interviews, the job interview, which will prepare you for entering the work force, and the research interview, which will assist you when preparing your assignments. During the job interview process, you might encounter the screening interview where candidates are initially interviewed before moving on to the in-depth interview. Prior to the interview you need to do research on the company, firm, association, and executives you want to work for. Find out as much information as possible about the particular position for which you are applying. It is important to pay attention to the visual impression you impart as your appearance and grooming will be judged. Your image is also assessed based on your posture, handshake, manners, sincerity, smile, and interest. You can prepare yourself thoroughly by planning answers to potential interview questions. Also plan a few questions that you would like to pose to the interviewer. When answering questions you can use the SAR formula when responding. Alternatively, you can use the PREW method. Know how to articulate your strengths, values, skills, and pertinent knowledge, and offer the interviewer concrete reasons to hire you for the position. Once you have presented yourself at the interview, thank the interviewer. Follow-up by sending a thank you note to restate your interest in the job.

The purpose of the personal research interview is to gather information. It involves the ability to communicate and listen effectively, to frame pertinent questions, and to have good research skills. There are five stages of the research interview. First, define the purpose of the interview. Second, plan the interview. Third, prepare your questions. Fourth, conduct the interview. Finally, do the follow-up. Once these five stages are complete you can analyze, evaluate, and interpret the material you have gathered. You can now incorporate first-hand research in your assignment.

SUGGESTED READING

Bolles, Richard. *What Colour is Your Parachute*. Berkeley: Ten Speed Press, 1999.

Corcodilos, Nicolas. *New Interview Instruction Book: A Guide to Winning Job Offers using Proven Techniques Developed by Headhunters*. Berkeley: North Bridge Group, 1996.

DeLuca, Matthew. *Best Answers to the 201 Most Frequently Asked Questions*. New York: McGraw-Hill, 1997.

Kennedy, Joyce Lain. *Hook Up, Get Hired*. Toronto: John Wiley & Sons, 1995.

Molloy, John. *New Dress for Success*. New York: Warner Books, 1988.

Swartz, Mark. *Get Wired, You're Hired*. Toronto: Prentice Hall, 1997.

Yate, Martin. *Knock 'Em Dead*. Massachusetts: Adams Media Corporation, 1998.

WEBLINKS

strategis.ic.gc.ca
Canadian company and industry information

www.yahoo.ca
Company Web sites

www.newswire.ca
Newspaper articles on companies

www.cacee.com
Profiles of employers and information on the job search process

www.canada.gc.cawww.gov.on.ca
Government information

www.cybf.ca
Canadian Youth Business Foundation

chronicle.com
Articles and job postings in North America

www.statcan.ca
Statistics Canada

hrdc-drhc.gc.ca/corp/stragpol/arb/jobs/english/index.htm
Job Futures

ADDITIONAL RESOURCES

Directories available at the library:

Scott's Directories—lists details about Canadian companies

Canada Student Employment Guide

Canadian Almanac and Directory

National Directory of Service Companies

Maclean's "Canada's Top 100 Employers"

2000 Canadian Sourcebook

The Canadian Job Directory: The Ultimate Guide to Canada's Hidden Job Market

Canadian Directory of Search Firms

Canada's Top 100 Employers

Canadian Key Business Directory

National Directory of Service Companies

Survey of Industrials

The Career Directory

chapter fifteen

Listening

One of the best ways to persuade others is with your ears—by listening to them.

—Dean Rusk

LEARNING OBJECTIVES

- **To define listening**

- **To improve your listening skills**

- **To identify barriers to effective communication**

- **To understand the listening process**

- **To learn five listening techniques**

As a student you probably spend the greatest portion of your time in school listening. When you enter or re-enter the workforce and embark upon your chosen career, you will probably spend a large portion of your day listening. Doctors listen closely as their patients describe their medical symptoms. Accountants listen to their clients' requirements. Architects listen to understand the concepts that their clients envision. Teachers listen attentively to students in order to assist them in reaching or attaining their educational goals. Career counsellors listen to help students define their career objectives. When conducting research interviews or when you are the interviewer, you need to listen actively.

Whatever your reason for listening—whether listening for entertainment, for evaluation, for information, or for inspiration—practising and focusing on positive active listening skills will enrich your life and enhance your understanding of the world around you.

Why is listening a vital skill? Let's begin with a definition of effective communication. Effective communication is the conveying of thoughts, ideas, information, feelings, and opinions so that they are clearly understood. It is always a two-way process that involves a speaker and a listener. The speaker transmits the message and the listener receives the message.

Hearing and listening are often confused. While hearing is physical, listening is mental. To listen means to pay attention while hearing someone speak or while hearing a sound. We hear with the ears when sounds or stimuli impact or reach them.

Professor John Drakeford (1967) distinguishes between listening and hearing in the following way: "Hearing is a word to describe the physiological sensory processes by which auditory sensations are received by the ears and transmitted to the brain. Listening, on the other hand, refers to a more complex psychological procedure involving interpreting and understanding the significance of the sensory experience." Several decades later, his comments continue to ring true.

Perhaps the old-fashioned word *hearken* encapsulates this process best. It means to listen and to give respectful attention.

How often do we hear, yet we do not listen? And why do we listen? As a student, you are probably spending more than 45 percent of your time listening, and when you enter the workforce you will probably spend more than 70 percent of your working hours communicating.

In order to secure your first job, you will have to listen effectively during the interview process. How well you listen will impact your personal and professional life. It is important to arm yourself with listening skills in order for you to heighten your proficiency in communication.

OBSTACLES TO LISTENING

For the clear, accurate reception of your message, you need to be aware of the obstacles you might encounter. Physical, emotional, and mental obstacles often stand in the way. There are three factors we need to look at, the Where Factor, the Who Factor, and the How Factor.

Where

Where is the act of communication taking place? Is the room comfortable? Is it air-conditioned in the summer and heated during the winter? Is there adequate ventilation? Is there a sufficient amount of seating? Does the listener have an unrestricted view of the speaker? Does the audio or video equipment function efficiently? Is the venue appropriate for conveying your message? Is speaking at the water cooler a sensible place for giving confidential information? Be aware of distractions such as construction noise occurring outside, telephones constantly ringing, and people walking by. Such interruptions can be barriers to effective listening. Try to control your environment as much as you can. Alternatively, switch locations.

Who

Is my message tailored to the age group of the listeners, to their level of understanding, and to their needs? Can they see me? Can they hear me? Have they eaten recently? Are they hungry or thirsty? Is the listener ill? Is he or she comfortable? Lack of physical ease will hinder the reception of your words. Think about how emotions, perception, social obstacles, and assumptions affect how you listen.

Emotions often intrude when we listen. Heightened tension, fear, stress, jealousy, prejudice, preoccupation, inexperience, anger, or embarrassment can inhibit good listening. When you are awaiting the results of your examination, you may experience some degree of stress. As the lecturer reads out the passing grades, you may become momentarily "deaf" prior to hearing your name read out. Clearly your mastery of effective listening skills is hampered by the intrusion of your emotions. When we are angry with a family member, a boss, or co-worker and he or she tries to offer an explanation for his or her behaviour, we are often unwilling to listen while emotions are still raw. Bearing in mind all the emotional factors that can intrude, it is often wiser to reschedule your interaction for a later time when your feelings have been assuaged.

The way in which we **perceive** situations or remarks is affected by such factors as previous experience, age, sex, health, gender, culture, education, and self-concept. Never assume that your listener will attach the same meaning to your message as the one you intended to send. Avoid assuming that others see, think, feel, act, and judge in the same way you do. This is why audience analysis is so important.

The following are two scenarios that demonstrate poor listening:

(i) When a group of refugees arrives in British Columbia, officials listen to their tale and assume they have arrived in Canada searching for prosperity and hoping to benefit from our generous healthcare system. Such assumptions need to be checked. In cases such as this, the officials have assumed a "blame the victim" mentality. These refugees in fact are fleeing grinding poverty and torture meted out by an oppressive regime. They are primarily searching for a safe haven. Contrary to the officials' assumptions, their main intention is not to become a burden to our system.

(ii) A fellow student, Ralph, whom you've known since you began college, approaches you at the coffee shop to tell you about the latest saga in his relationship with his girlfriend, Sonia. You have heard the same sob story numerous times. Your friend repeats the identical pattern of returning to his unsuitable relationship with Sonia. He initiates this discussion again and automatically you assume that he is about to offload with the usual emotional tirade. You stop listening. You tune out mentally before he has finished his tale. However, this time you have put up a barrier to listening effectively to your friend and you miss the key message he is about to deliver. Ralph and Sonia have finally broken up. You made the false assumption that Ralph would repeat the same old information and you were wrong.

Making incorrect assumptions can inhibit your ability to communicate and listen effectively.

We can also encounter obstacles in the **mental** area. Listening is sabotaged when language or jargon is not understood because the speaker has not accurately gauged the educational level of the listener; when highly technical information is presented to a non-technical audience; and when the listener lacks the information or the necessary training to receive the speaker's message.

We must also consider **social** obstacles. In a multicultural society such as Canada we need to be judicious in our choice of words and the channel we use to send our words. Politics, sex, religion, race, gender, and status can be obstacles to effective communication.

In September 2001, the World Conference Against Racism took place in Durban, South Africa. Retired Anglican Archbishop Desmond Tutu wanted states that had participated in slave trading to pay financial reparations. He claimed, "We want to open these wounds; we want to cleanse them, and then we want to pour the balm on them and hope they are going to heal." Vivid language such as Tutu's can transcend social obstacles as he leaves a visual and emotional imprint on the listener that ultimately affects the reception of the message. Tutu aimed to inspire the listener to act through the use of vivid imagery.

Assumptions impede the clear flow of ideas. At a board meeting of top executives, a man with a dishevelled appearance and long, unkempt hair enters and ceremoniously walks to the front of the room. He proceeds to explain a math theory that will affect the production of future computer programs for the company. He is a Ph.D. and a mathematics genius. If listeners had judged him solely by his appearance, they would not have listened further to benefit from his expertise. They would have not been open to new, innovative ideas that could ultimately lead to increased profits for the company.

To make accurate decisions and to respond to the current academic or business environments, we need to listen comprehensively and to be conscious of all the factors that hinder our ability to do so.

Carl Rogers, the noted psychologist, speaks about judgemental listening and its impact on him: "Nothing feels so good as being understood, not evaluated or judged. When I try to share some feeling aspects of myself and my communication is met with evaluation, reassurance, distortion of my meaning, I know what it is to be alone." His comments reiterate the importance of being a good listener so that, as Rogers suggests, the person who is speaking to you will feel acknowledged and will not experience a sense of being alone.

How

How a message is conveyed can either deter your listener or work in your favour. In this high-tech age, a message can be conveyed in person or in print, via radio, television, or e-mail, by messenger or by nature. Select the medium that is appropriate to your message.

(a) A busy accountant will gladly receive her e-mail on her palm pilot.

(b) An elderly woman who rarely leaves her home and has few technical skills might prefer the radio or the newspaper.

(c) Savvy students, professionals, and business people who are not technophobic could use any of the above-mentioned mediums.

(d) For those who prefer face-to-face communication, appearing in person or sending a messenger would be preferable.

(e) Many teenagers receive and gather information from television and the Internet. Getting information from the Internet does not involve listening, but it does involve the reception and the assignment of meaning, two important elements of the listening process. We will discuss these elements shortly.

(f) Nature sends its own brand of messages. Thunder is the precursor to lightning, and lets us know that a storm could be approaching.

(g) The academic may utilize all channels for comprehensive research.

The famous Canadian media philosopher, Marshall McLuhan, has said: "The medium is the message." Be mindful of these words when you begin your planning so that you select the appropriate medium for you, one that will help you achieve your desired objective. Always bear in mind that most people listen selectively and that listening preferences change based on:

- the time of day
- the time the listener has available to listen
- the topic
- the environment in which the message is delivered
- the willingness and energy of the listener

EXERCISES

1. Write down your definition of effective listening.
2. Write down a list of obstacles to good listening.
3. List the names of people you know who listen well.
4. Write down the qualities that make these individuals effective listeners.
5. Objective: For students to be come aware of their own listening ability.

    (a) Divide into groups of three. Person A is designated as the speaker. Person B will be the listener. Person C will be the observer. A and B sit facing each other. C, the observer, sits a little distance away from them ready to make notes of his or her observations.

    (b) The participants can select their own topics of discussion or the instructor can offer suggestions—for example, "Talk about how your life has changed since the September 11, 2001 terrorist attacks and suggest any solutions you may have to deal with terrorists." Speak for about three to five minutes.

    (c) The listener will now repeat back what he or she has heard.

    (d) The observer offers comments on what he or she saw during the interaction, giving comments on body language, eye contact, interruptions, and any encouragement that might have been offered. He or she will also mention any points that the listener omitted when she or he relayed what was heard.

    (e) Repeat this exercise so that each participant has the opportunity to play the listener, the speaker, and the observer.

6. Objective: For students to recognize words that trigger them emotionally and, as a result, hamper effective listening.

    (a) Write a list of words and phrases that trigger a reaction in you.

    (b) List these words on the chalkboard.

    (c) As the instructor calls out the list of words, each student should write down his or her immediate reaction to the words on the list. Instructors should not allow too much time in between calling out each word in order to minimize the tendency to censor or judge responses.

(d) After the students have had a chance to write their responses, the instructor will call out each word and students will share their responses. For example, the word "success" may elicit differing associations such as money, peace, happiness, film star, freedom, or remote. (Note the similarities and differences between the responses of students.)

When swear words, and words with racist, sexual, or political overtones are used, how do you react? Do you tune-out or react emotionally to these words? From the list you have compiled, do many of the same words come up frequently? Once you are aware of words that trigger you, you can then aim to listen more objectively.

Think about individuals you know who are good listeners. Now think about those who do not listen well. Those who listen well do the following:

- exhibit the ability to put aside distractions and focus on the speaker
- remain emotionally neutral
- avoid judgements
- keep an open mind
- do not attach labels to the speaker
- are patient, poised, and involved
- show caring, understanding, and empathy
- respond appropriately

Good listening leads to better problem solving and to better understanding. These skills, in turn, improve personal, professional, and business relationships. If you don't listen, you cannot interview, lead, respond, problem-solve, empathize, learn, or make informed decisions. We can maximize our success by attending to messages in a focused manner.

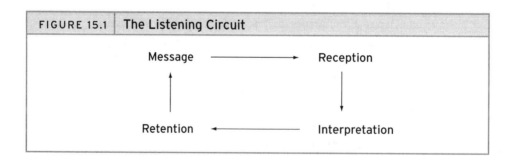

FIGURE 15.1 | **The Listening Circuit**

Message ⟶ Reception

Retention ⟵ Interpretation

Have you ever given much thought to the actual listening process?

1. Message Transfer

    Here the speaker formulates, shapes his or her message, and then articulates his or her thoughts.

2. Reception of the message

    The listener receives the message through the speaker's words voice, tone, accompanying body language, and silences. The reception of the message is affected by our own personal perceptions, education, prior knowledge, sex, gender, prejudices, attitude, self-concept, and willingness to listen.

3. Interpretation

During Stage 3, we attach meaning to the message and interpret it. Here we search our personal frame of reference, our senses, our prior knowledge, our belief system, our emotional and symbolic storehouse, our associations, and our relationship to the words uttered.

It is important to know that listeners respond differently to the same words. If I use the word "house" in my speech, Bob thinks about his bungalow, Cathy thinks about her mansion, and John recalls his cottage. The words "Celine Dion" may elicit the following associations: "Titanic," Quebec, music, or motherhood. The lesson to learn here is to always use precision of language and detail when you feel the audience may misinterpret your meaning. You may say, "Let's define and describe the type of 'house' we are talking about. It is an ancient structure built of stone and marble with tall grey spires reaching skyward."

As we listen and speak, we should be aware of, and sensitive to, certain words, phrases, and topics of discussion: politics, sex, health, race, religion, war, peace, disease, communism, superstitions, abuse, age, abortion, prostitution, obscenity, or drugs.

Invest your words with meaning that bears significance for the listener. If you speak these words, "Mr. James is a pillar of the community," we will likely understand, "Mr. James is an upstanding citizen. He may be a devoted family man. He gives his time to worthy community causes." Now consider this recent Canadian newspaper headline: "Air Transat pilot of Flight 236 is a hero." The article in the newspaper described how the pilot managed to save many lives by averting a disastrous plane crash. However, the pilot's hero status dissolved a day later when the press released his history: he had been convicted of drug trafficking a few years earlier. The pilot descended from hero to criminal within such a short space of time. We need to listen with awareness and suspend judgement until we have all of the facts.

"To a mouse, cheese is cheese; that's why mousetraps work." Wendell Johnson, in *People in Quandaries*, coined this truth. If only it was so simple for humans—we, the listeners, attribute meanings to words.

4. Retaining the Information

This is the stage when we decide whether to remember the information we have heard in order to recall it at a future date. In this age of information overload, we frequently find that the "CD-ROM" of our brain is filled to capacity. We simply have no more room to house information. So we decide what to retain, what to store, and what to delete. In this phase, we will record information that is valuable to us and will have bearing on our lives.

EXERCISES

1. Retention

Objective: To see how much information we can recall.

Instruction: Read the following extract by Jean Chrétien, when he was parliamentary secretary to the Minster of Finance; his comments below are from CBC's *Twenty Million Questions* (1967). Read it only once.

My name is Jean Chrétien, you know, it's Christian in English...my initials are "J.C."like Jesus Christ. I'm six feet high, my mother's name is Mary; I live on the Boulevard Pius XII; at 30 I was at the beginning of my public life; I hope that I will not be crucified—I'm 33.

Now, cover the words you have just read. How many facts can you recall? Notice what you recalled and why you remembered particular points. Did you remember more than seven points? The brain is capable of recalling seven points with relative ease. Do you need to take notes to aid your recall? What have you learned about the amount of information you are capable of retaining?

2. Radio News

Listen to an extended radio news broadcast on CBC Radio. Record this broadcast on a tape recorder while you are listening. Turn off the radio and the recorder. Write down all the news items you have retained from the broadcast. Rewind the tape and listen to the broadcast once more. Make a note of the points you did not recall.

3. Key Messages

Objective: To learn to listen for key messages.

Instruction:

(i) Using the Internet, go to: **www.historychannel.com/speeches/index.html** or **www.historyplace.com/speeches/previous.htm-14k.**

(ii) Select a speech—for example, "I Have A Dream," by Martin Luther King. Listen to it online via Real Audio.

(iii) Listen for the key ideas. You may take notes if this helps you.

(iv) Download the script of the speech. Make copies of the script for your classmates.

(v) Ask members of your class to read the script of the speech.

(vi) After your classmates have read the speech, relay the main ideas of the speech to the class.

(vii) Ask the class to give you feedback and confirm whether your facts are correct. They may include ideas that you have forgotten to mention.

LISTENING TECHNIQUES

Nonverbal Techniques

1. Observe your body language and keep it open. Make sure you adjust your posture to face the speaker.

2. Make eye contact with the speaker. The average duration of comfortable eye contact is five to nine seconds, which is the length of time it takes to articulate the average thought. So look at the speaker and make this nonverbal connection. You can look away periodically and then resume making eye contact again.

3. Nod appropriately, which will make the speaker feel you are listening.

Positive Active Listening Skills

Use the following skills when they are pertinent to the message being conveyed.

Restatement or Paraphrasing   Restate or paraphrase what the speaker has said. You do not have to do so in elaborate detail but repeat the key points the speaker has uttered. Focus on the facts. For example, after your teacher has outlined your assignment, you may use this listening technique and say: "Mrs. Jones, your expectation is that our assignment should be on your desk on Monday, March 18 by 9 a.m. and failure to do so will result in a penalty being imposed." The teacher will feel that you have listened attentively and have grasped the intention of her message. Through the use of restatement, misunderstanding can be avoided.

Clarifying   When using the clarifying technique, we ascertain or confirm that we understand the meaning of the speaker's message. By using this technique, we can clarify whether we have interpreted the message correctly. It also helps us gather further information or facts. The following are some clarifying phrases that you can use:

"So let me understand, what you are saying is..."

"Is this what you mean...?"

"Let me clarify my understanding..."

"As you have conveyed, you see the situation as follows..."

This technique gives the speaker the opportunity to say: "No, that's not what I meant, what I wanted to say was..." or alternatively: "Yes, you've grasped my meaning."

Neutral   This technique encourages the speaker to continue speaking and shows that you are interested in his or her message. Have you ever engaged in a conversation where you emerge saying, "John is an excellent listener. I felt as if he truly heard what I had to say."? Well, all John did was utilize the neutral listening technique. He did the following:

- He nodded appropriately
- He used the following words or phrases:

"Really?"

"And?"

"I see."

"Go on..."

"Uh huh..."

"Of course..."

"I understand."

"That's interesting."

"Tell me more."

"For instance..."

The neutral technique is the oil that lubricates the flow of conversation and ensures that the speaker really feels listened to.

Reflective Technique   Whereas restatement involves the restatement of the facts, when using the reflective technique, the listener labels and states the feelings the speaker has conveyed. In this way you show the speaker that you understand how he or she feels.

This technique involves an element of interpretation. Take note of the speaker's words, which demonstrate feeling, and observe his body language. Try to empathize with him or her and ask yourself, "What would I be feeling if I were in his or her shoes?"

For example, Janet, a student, rushes into the examination room five minutes after the examination has begun. She says: "The route from downtown to the university has been closed off due to a broken water main. Traffic was held up for an extra half hour. I left home with plenty of time to spare and now I will be penalized for a predicament that is beyond my control."

The examiner responds, "I understand that you are frustrated since you have arrived late for the exam and are fearful that you will be penalized." The examiner articulates the feelings of her student by using the words "frustrated" and "fearful." Jane then feels understood.

When using the reflective technique, you can use the following phrases:

"You feel that you were betrayed..."

"You were confused to find..."

"I can appreciate your sadness when..."

"You're angry that you were passed over for the promotion..."

Summarizing   When using this technique, you restate the main themes or ideas that have been expressed by the speaker. You may also include in your summary any emotional components that are pertinent. Summarizing helps to bring the speaker's ideas into clear focus while it presents back to him the relevant information he has communicated.

You can summarize by saying:

"Let's recap the main ideas..."

"So, in summary, what have you expressed...?"

"Here are the key ideas discussed..."

These five techniques will help make you a better listener. Use them judiciously and appropriately.

EXERCISE

Applying the Listening Techniques

Objective: To put into practice the newly learned techniques and test their effectiveness.

a) Get into pairs.

b) A is the speaker. B is the listener.

c) A discusses an event or situation with B. Make certain that there is an emotional component to your topic.

d) B listens and applies all five listening techniques.

e) Reverse the process. B now becomes the speaker. A is the listener who now applies the five listening techniques.

f) In reality we do not always apply all five techniques but, for the purpose of this exercise, it is important to use them all so that you can measure just how well they work in contributing to a more meaningful interaction.

The Benefits of Effective Listening

1. We learn more effectively when we listen effectively.
2. We develop greater understanding of the topic, the problem, and/or the speaker.
3. We improve personal and professional relationships.
4. We lead with more strength when we listen effectively.
5. We become more capable of nurturing good rapport.
6. We shorten meeting time through positive active listening.
7. We reduce stress by applying listening techniques.
8. We increase sales when we listen to the customer.
9. We improve business performance by listening to clients, customers, employers, and employees.
10. Effective listening heightens the enjoyment of the well-turned phrase, the sound of a mellifluous resonant voice, the spell of classical music, and the sounds of nature.

The Chinese characters that make up the words "to listen" are shown below in Figure 15.2.

FIGURE 15.2	To Listen

The symbol to the left represents the ear, the one on the top right represents the eye, and the one on the bottom right represents the heart. This all-encompassing symbol reflects the need to listen not only with our ears but with our eyes and heart as well.

Tips for Effective Listening

First listen, my friend, and then you may shriek and bluster.

—Aristophanes

1. Focus by paying strict attention to the speaker's words and body language.
2. Put all other thoughts out of your mind and stop what you are doing. Keep an open mind.
3. Do not assume you know what the speaker is about to say by completing his sentences. Suspend judgement until the complete message is conveyed.
4. Stop the internal debating, the rehearsal of your response, and the jumping to conclusions.
5. Listen for the central idea or theme and try to understand how other ideas relate to the central idea.
6. Use the listening techniques to give feedback.
7. Listen to understand rather than to contradict or attack the speaker.
8. Pose pertinent questions.
9. Listen without prejudice. Avoid emotional censorship when you receive information you would rather not hear. Be cognizant of words that trigger you emotionally and aim to remain emotionally neutral.
10. Be patient.

SUMMARY

In every walk of life, the ability to listen actively will serve you well. During the communication process the speaker transmits a message, which the listener receives. Hearing is a physical process, whereas listening is a mental process that requires interpreting and understanding the words that have been spoken. Physical, emotional, and mental obstacles often interfere with the reception of the message. A good listener will focus on the speaker, keep an open mind, avoid premature judgements, and remain emotionally neutral. He or she will convey empathy and respond appropriately. There are four steps involved in the listening process. First, a message is sent. Second, it is received by the listener who then attaches meaning to the message. The final stage is the retention of the information. This is when the listener decides whether or not to retain the message in order to recall it in the future. To be a good listener, keep your body language open and make effective eye contact. Five listening skills are presented. Students are encouraged to use restatement, clarifying statements, the neutral technique, the reflective technique, and summarizing. The benefits and rules of effective listening close the chapter.

SUGGESTED READING

Bolton, Robert. *People Skills*. New York: Simon & Schuster Inc., 1986.

Ellis, Richard and Ann McClintock. *If You Take My Meaning: Theory into Practice in Human Communication*. Great Britain: Edward Arnold, 1994.

Johnson, Wendell. *People in Quandaries: The Semantics of Personal Adjustment*. New York: Harper & Row, 1946.

Ross, Raymond S. *Essentials of Speech Communication*. New Jersey: Prentice-Hall, 1984.

Tolela Myers, Gail and Michelle Tolela Myers. People in Quandaries. *The Dynamics of Human Communication: A Laboratory Approach*. New York: McGraw-Hill, 1998.

REFERENCES

Drakeford, John. *The Awesome Power of the Listening Ear*. Texas: Word, 1967. 17.

Sample Speeches

1. STEPHEN LEACOCK

Stephen Leacock's (1869-1944) reputation as oral humorist and a political economist has spread around the world. He taught at McGill University where he was head of the Department of Economics and Political Science. He was best known for his essays, parodies, and short stories.

The Difficulties of Public Speaking by Stephen Leacock

Public speaking is more or less of an ordeal, even for those who have to undertake it constantly. Worse than all is speaking at a dinner, because you have to wait your turn, and you feel it coming for hours. The next time you are at a public dinner, notice the men at the head table who sit and eat celery by the bunch and never stop. Those are the men who are going to speak. Oh, I don't say that trained speakers are nervous. No, no, they wish the chairman would announce that the rest of the meeting is cancelled, because of smallpox, or that the hotel would catch fire or that there would be an earthquake. Oh, but none of them. They are not nervous. But, if speaking is an ordeal to them, what is it to those who have never spoken? Some men go through life and never have to speak. They rise to wealth and standing with a fear of it in the background. Fear with an element of temptation. Such a one was my senior acquaintance of long ago, Mr. Gritterley, no harm to name him, General Manager of one of the Toronto banks. He had just retired without ever speaking in public when a bankers' three-day convention came to town, and they invited Mr. Gritterley to speak at the dinner. He accepted; hung in the wind, blew around in the flame. Finally, on the opening days, he sent a note saying that he had been called out of town for the evening. I saw him around the hotel the next morning. He was telling me how sorry he was to have missed the opportunity to speak. He told me a lot of things he could have said about branch banking. He said that he would have had liked to have a sly joke, very good natured, of course, about the American Treasury System. It's too bad, he said, he'd been called out of town. He even intended, just in an offhand way, to get off one or two quotations from Shakespeare. He had them in his pocket. One read, "I know a bank where time grows." Gritterley thought that would get a laugh, eh! "Too bad," he said, "he couldn't get that off." "But, Mr. Gritterley," I said "you are making a mistake. They didn't have the dinner last night. The trains were so late they only had the inaugural address. The dinner is tonight. You'll probably get an invitation." And, as I spoke, a boy brought it to him on a tray. "So, you see, you will be able to tell them about branch banking." "Yes," said Mr. Gritterley, "yes." "And the jokes about the U.S. Treasury." "Yes," said Mr. Gritterley. "Quite so." All day Gritterley was around the hotel, pulling little bits of Shakespeare out of his pocket; but the thing beat him. In due course, at the dinner, the chairman announced, "I regret very much that Mr. Gritterley will not be able to speak. His speech of which he gave me an outline would have been a great treat. Unfortunately, he had to leave tonight..." his chairman consulted his notes, "for Japan. With your permission, I will take it upon myself to cable our representatives, and I am sure that they will be glad to get up a dinner for Mr. Gritterley at Tokyo." Gritterley got the invitation on board the ship and went right on to Hong Kong. The bankers there received a cable and organized a lunch. Gritterley had gone on to Singapore. But the bankers followed him up, and he left for Calcutta. They lost him somewhere in Tibet. He may have entered a monastery there. For many people that would be preferable to speaking.

[Transcript prepared from original tape recording, Leacock Museum archives, gift of Dr. Carl Spadoni.]

2. WINSTON CHURCHILL

A master of the crisis speech, Winston Churchill gave his "Some chicken! Some neck!" address to the Joint Session of the Canadian Parliament, Ottawa, Canada, December 30, 1941. Churchill's rhetorical style contributed to Britain's resistance during the early dark days of war.

Sir, we did not make this war. We did not seek it. We did all we could to avoid it. We did too much to avoid it. We went so far to try to avoid it as to be almost destroyed by it when it broke upon us, but that dangerous corner has been turned. And with every month and every year that passes we shall confront the evildoers with weapons as plentiful, as sharp and as destructive as those with which they have sought to establish their hateful domination.

We have been concerting the United Pacts and Resolves of more than thirty states and nations to fight on in unity together. And in fidelity, one with another, without any thought except the total and final escalation of the Hitler tyranny, of the Japanese frenzy, and the Mussolini flop.

There will be no halting or half measures. There will be no compromise or parley. These gangs of bandits have sought to darken the light of the world, have sought to stand between the common people of all the lands, and their march forward into their inheritance. They shall, themselves be cast into the pit of death and shame and only when the earth has been cleansed and purged of their crimes and of their villainies will we turn from the task which they have forced upon us—a task which we were reluctant to undertake, but which we shall now most faithfully and punctiliously discharge.

When I warned them that Britain would fight on alone whatever they did, their generals told their Prime Minister and his divided cabinet, "In three weeks, England will have her neck wrung like a chicken." Some chicken! Some neck!

3. CHIEF DAN GEORGE

Chief Dan George [1899-1981] was a man of considerable dignity and a noble spokesperson for his race. He was a chief of the Salish Band in Burrard Inlet, British Columbia. Below is his lament for Confederation Speech, 1967.

How long have I known you, Oh Canada? A hundred years? Yes, a hundred years. And many, many seelanum more. And today, when you celebrate your hundred years, Oh Canada. I am sad for all the Indian people throughout the land.

For I have known you when your forests were mine; when they gave me my meat and my clothing. I have known you in your streams and rivers where your fish flashed and danced in the sun, where the waters said come, come, and eat of my abundance. I have known you in the freedom of your winds. And my spirit, like the winds, once roamed your good lands.

But in the long hundred years since the white man came, I have seen my freedom disappear like the salmon going mysteriously out to sea. The white man's strange customs, which I could not understand, pressed down upon me until I could no longer breathe.

When I fought to protect my land and my home, I was called a savage. When I neither understood nor welcomed this way of life, I was called lazy. When I tried to rule my people, I was stripped of my authority.

My nation was ignored in your history textbooks—they were little more important in the history of Canada than the buffalo that ranged the plains. I was ridiculed in your plays and motion pictures, and when I drank your fire-water, I got drunk—very, very drunk. And I forgot.

Oh Canada, how can I celebrate with you this Centenary, this hundred years? Shall I thank you for the reserves that are left to me of my beautiful forests? For the canned fish of my rivers? For the loss of pride and authority, even among my own people? For the lack of my will to fight back? No! I must forget what's past and gone.

Oh God in Heaven! Give me back the courage of the olden Chiefs. Let me wrestle with my surroundings. Let me again, as in the days of old, dominate my environment. Let me humbly accept this new culture and through it rise up and go on.

Oh God! Like the Thunderbird of old I shall rise again out of the sea; I shall grab the instruments of the white man's success—his education, his skills, and with these new tools I shall build my race into the proudest segment of your society. Before I follow the great Chiefs who have gone before us, Oh Canada, I shall see these things come to pass.

I shall see our young braves and our chiefs sitting in the houses of law and government, ruling and being ruled by the knowledge and freedoms of our great land. So shall we shatter the barriers of our isolation. So shall the next hundred years be the greatest in the proud history of our tribes and nations.

4. ELIE WIESEL

Professor Elie Wiesel of Boston University was imprisoned in Auschwitz and Buchenwald as a teenager. Both his parents and sister died in concentration camps. After the war Wiesel became a journalist and a citizen of the United States. In 1986 he was awarded the Nobel Peace Prize.

A special ceremony attended by thirteen presidents, three kings, and many Nobel laureates took place on the fiftieth anniversary of the liberation of Auschwitz. They assembled to pray for its 1.5 million victims, and it was on this solemn occasion that Wiesel delivered this powerful, finely crafted, haunting speech.

I speak to you as a man who fifty years and nine days ago had no name, no hope, no future, and was known only by his number, A 7713.

I speak as a Jew who has seen what humanity has done to itself by trying to exterminate an entire people and inflict suffering and humiliation and death on so many others.

In this place of darkness and malediction we can but stand in awe and remember its stateless, faceless, and nameless victims. Close your eyes and look: endless nocturnal processions are converging here, and here it is always night. Here heaven and earth are on fire.

Close your eyes and listen. Listen to the silent screams of terrified mothers, the prayers of anguished old men and women. Listen to the tears of children, Jewish children, a beautiful little girl among them, with golden hair, whose vulnerable tenderness has never left me. Look and listen as they quietly walk towards dark flames so gigantic that the planet itself seemed in danger.

All these men and women and children came from everywhere, a gathering of exiles drawn by death.

Yitgadal veyitkadash, Shmay Rabba.

In this kingdom of darkness there were many people. People who came from all the occupied lands of Europe. And then there were the Gypsies and the Poles and the Czechs. It is true that not all the victims were Jews. But all the Jews were victims.

Now, as then, we ask the question of all questions: What was the meaning of what was so routinely going on in this kingdom of eternal night? What kind of demented mind could have invented this system?

And it worked. The killers killed, the victims died, and the world was the world, and everything else was going on, life as usual. In the towns nearby, what happened? In the lands nearby, what happened? Life was going on where God's creation was condemned to blasphemy by the killers and their accomplices.

Yitgadal veyitkadash, Shmay Rabba.

Turning point or watershed, Birkeneau produced a mutation on a cosmic scale, affecting man's dreams and endeavours. After Auschwitz, the human condition is no longer the same. After Auschwitz, nothing will ever be the same.

Yitgadal veyitkadash, Shmay Rabba.

As we remember the solitude and the pain of its victims, let us declare this day marks our commitment to commemorate their death, not to cele-brate our own victory over death.

As we reflect upon the past, we must address ourselves to the present, and the future. In the name of all that is sacred in memory, let us stop the bloodshed in Bosnia, Rwanda, and Chechenia; the vicious and ruthless terror attacks against Jews in the Holy Land. Let us reject and oppose more effec-tively religious fanaticism and racial hate.

Where else can we say to the world, "Remember the mortality of the human condition," if not here?

For the sake of our children, we must remember Birkenau, so that it does not become their future.

Yitgadal veyitkadash, Shmay Rabba.

Weep for thy children whose death was not mourned then; weep for them, our Father in heaven, for they were deprived of their right to be buried, for heaven itself became their cemetery.

5. ALBERT KOHL, ENVIRONMENTAL LAWYER

Albert Kohl is an environmental lawyer with an appreciation of and an interest in the art of public speaking.

The Pause by Albert Kohl

I want to share a secret with you. It is my biggest fear in public speaking—something I flee from like a postman from an angry dog, like a mischievous child from a swarm of bees, like a playboy from a marriage, like a tourist in Pamplona from the charging bulls, like a teenager in his father's car from a stop sign, like a mouse from a cat, like a cat from a dog, like a fly from a frog. [Deep breath.] I think you know what it is...the pause.

I do know that the pause is important, even crucial. It's just that I forget to use it when I'm speaking.

Listen to a speech by a great speaker and notice the pause. John F. Kennedy in his inaugural address did not say, "My fellow Americans ask not what your country can do for you but what you can do for your country." He said, "And so, my fellow Americans: [pause] ask not what your country can do for you—[pause] ask [pause] what you can do for your country."

That's three pauses. It takes me four speeches to accumulate that number of pauses.

The irony of public speaking is that to speak well you have to stop speaking. Not forever, but long enough to catch your breath and let your audience catch its breath. When I started as an articling law student, I was sent to a hearing. All I had to say was, "Your honour, we consent to the adjournment." I practiced this line carefully on the way to court but when my turn came to speak, I couldn't get out a single word. It was all pause. Finally, the judge asked if we consented and I nodded.

In general, you should err on the side of a pause for longer than you might think necessary.

The pause is an essential ingredient of good public speaking. It is the sauce for your pasta. Without it you are just serving noodles.

Pause. Let the words linger in the air like the aroma of a fine dish or like a pleasant ocean breeze billowing through the curtains of a Mediterranean villa on a hot summer day.

The pause gives your audience time not only to hear your words, but also to listen to them, to think about them. The pause is to your speech what digestion is to eating. The pause also tells your audience your speech is worth listening to, that you have something important to say.

And finally, the pause makes your speech sound natural as if you are speaking with your best buddy, even though 300 people in the audience are analyzing whether your tie goes with your shirt. It's like the advertisements for quality makeup—you've got to put it on in order to look natural.

The pause is so important that I create a separate category in public speaking for it. It's the third "P" in prepare, present, pause.

Preparation comes first. No speaker routinely speaks "off the cuff." When Martin Luther King gave his famous "I have a Dream" speech in front of the Lincoln Memorial, he had chosen his words meticulously and practised them before many audiences.

Presentation is how you serve the meal. It is how you look, how you sound, and how you act. It's the only thing some people will remember. But the pause, the gap, is what brings it all together. It is the difference between talking to a crowd and communicating with individuals.

I am not the only one who is stingy with pauses. James C. Humes, in his book on public speaking, says some people rush through speeches as if they are running a gauntlet of swords on a pirate ship.

There are two reasons why I so fear the pause. The first reason has to do with divine retribution. For most of my life, it was during the lull of a pause that I fell asleep. During university lectures, during mass at church, even during conversations. My reputation for dozing was so famous that it became the subject of wagering among my classmates. In one class there was a student who routinely came late for class, and a game was devised where my classmates bet on whether I would fall asleep before the other student arrived.

I no longer fall asleep in class. Probably because after decades of snoozing, I am well rested. But I do fear my listeners will doze off during any pauses, so I rush through my speeches.

The second reason is a bit more complicated. You know that one of the ways people try to feel comfortable as speakers is by imagining that their audience is naked or in their underwear. It's a very Freudian technique. You just want everyone dressed according to the way you feel. You feel terribly vulnerable standing up there all alone. Whatever insecurities you have are amplified. I'm too short, too skinny or too fat, not good-looking, not smart. You are facing the audience, but you are also facing yourself.

You have heard about my work in Guatemala. Some of our trips were physically challenging. Sometimes there was risk involved. But frankly, those dangers were nothing compared to the risks involved in public speaking. You see, the dangers I faced were deniable, and external. It was twenty-five kilometres to the next village. You either made it or you didn't.

In the same way, the dangers the audience poses are fairly easy to calculate. Some won't care about what you have to say, some are preoccupied with family issues, some will like or dislike you. But how you react is harder to quantify, harder to control, and harder to overcome. That's probably why those studies show that people fear death less than public speaking. Death is more easily measured—about six feet under for most of us—than public speaking.

I rush through my speeches and avoid the pause because I fear people will get bored because I have nothing significant to say. That's my insecurity. Others fidget, umm, their heart races; they sweat perhaps because they doubt themselves. Perhaps they think the audience won't like them. There could be a number of other reasons.

When you were three years old you weren't nervous or self-conscious. Indeed you could captivate any audience even by saying the silliest things. So fear must have been learned along the way.

In part, public speaking teaches us how to mask those insecurities, to cover up what happened since we were three years old. We learn techniques, for example, bite your tongue if your mouth gets dry, breathe deeply, fight pirates...

Once when I was playing ice hockey I said to a friend, "I love playing hockey because I can forget all my problems." He replied in a very paternal voice: "Wouldn't it be better to deal with your problems?"

I suspect most of us are here in this class not only because we have the time and desire to learn the techniques of effective public speaking, but also because we are willing to deal with our fears. It is not a well-travelled path.

And so, that's why I say to the brave, we the few who have faced our fear...we will be rewarded. Our reward is the ability to move men and women to change their ways or change their thinking, even to motivate men and women to move mountains. For good or for evil, great speakers have always had the power to change the world. This, my adventurous friends, is the journey we have started and the power that lies ahead.

6. ADRIENNE CLARKSON

The Eulogy for Canada's Unknown Soldier was delivered by Her Excellency the Right Honourable Adrienne Clarkson, Governor General of Canada and Commander-in-Chief of the Canadian Forces, on the occasion of the Funeral for Canada's Unknown Soldier. It was presented at the National War Memorial in Ottawa on May 28, 2000.

Wars are as old as history. Over two thousand years ago, Herodotus wrote, "In peace, sons bury their fathers; in war, fathers bury their sons." Today, we are gathered together as one, to bury someone's son. The only certainty about him is that he was young. If death is a debt we all must pay, he paid before he owed it.

We do not know whose son he was. We do not know his name. We do not know if he was a MacPherson or a Chartrand. He could have been a Kaminski or a Swiftarrow. We do not know if he was a father himself. We do not know if his mother or wife received that telegram with the words "Missing In Action" typed with electrifying clarity on the anonymous piece of paper. We do not know whether he had begun truly to live his life as a truck driver or a scientist, a miner or a teacher, a farmer or a student. We do not know where he came from.

Was it the Prairies whose rolling sinuous curves recall a certain kind of eternity?

Was he someone who loved our lakes and knew them from a canoe?

Was he someone who saw the whales at the mouth of the Saguenay?

Was he someone who hiked in the Rockies or went sailing in the Atlantic or in the Gulf Islands?

Did he have brown eyes?

Did he know what it was to love someone and be loved back?

Was he a father who had not seen his child?

Did he love hockey? Did he play defense?

Did he play football? Could he kick a field goal?

Did he like to fix cars? Did he dream of owning a Buick?

Did he read poetry?

Did he get into fights?

Did he have freckles?

Did he think nobody understood him?

Did he just want to go out and have a good time with the boys?

We will never know the answers to these questions. We will never know him. But we come today to do him honour as someone who could have been all these things and now is no more. We who are left have all kinds of questions that only he could answer. And we, by this act today, are admitting with terrible finality that we will never know those answers.

We cannot know him. And no honour we do him can give him the future that was destroyed when he was killed. Whatever life he could have led, whatever choices he could have made are all shuttered. They are over. We are honouring that unacceptable thing—a life stopped by doing one's duty. The end of a future, the death of dreams.

Yet we give thanks for those who were willing to sacrifice themselves and who gave their youth and their future so that we could live in peace. With their lives they ransomed our future.

We have a wealth of witnesses in Canada to describe to us the unspeakable horror and frightening maelstrom that war brings. What that first World War was like has been described in our poetry, novels, and paintings. Some of our greatest artists came out of that conflict, able to create beauty out of the hell that they had seen. The renowned member of the Group of Seven, F.H. Varley, was one of those artists. Writing in October 1918 he said,

> *You in Canada... cannot realize at all what war is like. You must see it and live it. You must see the barren deserts war has made of once fertile country... see the turned-up graves, see the dead on the field, freakishly mutilated—headless, legless, stomachless, a perfect body and a passive face and a broken empty skull—see your own country-men, unidentified, thrown into a cart, their coats over them, boys dig-ging a grave in a land of yellow slimy mud and green pools of water under a weeping sky. You must have heard the screeching shells and have the shrapnel fall around you, whistling by you—seen the results of it, seen scores of horses, bits of horses lying around in the open— in the street and soldiers marching by these scenes as if they never knew of their presence. Until you've lived this... you cannot know.*

> [With permission of the Varley Estate.]

It is a frightening thing for human beings to think that we could die and that no one would know to mark our grave, to say where we had come from, to say when we had been born and when exactly we died. In honouring this unknown soldier today, through this funeral and this burial, we are embracing the fact of the anonymity and saying that because we do not know him and we do not know what he could have become, he has become more than one body, more than one grave. He is an ideal. He is a symbol of all sacrifice. He is every soldier in all our wars.

Our veterans, who are here with us today, know what it is to have been in battle and to have seen their friends cut down in their youth. That is why remembrance is so necessary and yet so difficult. It is necessary because we must not forget and it is difficult because the pain is never forgotten.

And the sense of loss, what this soldier's family must have felt is cap-tured in a poem by Jacques Brault, the Quebec poet who lost his brother in Sicily in the Second World War, and wrote the poem, *Suite Fraternelle*.

I remember you my brother Gilles lying forgotten in the earth of Sicily...

I know now that you are dead, a cold, hard lump in your throat fear lying heavy in your belly I still hear your twenty years swaying in the blasted July weeds...

There is only one name on my lips, and it is yours Gilles

You did not die in vain Gilles and you carry on through our changing seasons

And we, we carry on as well, like the laughter of waves that sweep across each tearful cove...

Your death gives off light Gilles and illuminates a brother's memories...

The grass grows on your tomb Gilles and the sand creeps up

And the nearby sea feels the pull of your death

You live on in us as you never could in yourself

You are where we will be you open the road for us.

[Jacqes Brault, «suite fraternelle», in *Poèmes*, Editions du Noroît, 2000]

When a word like Sicily is heard, it reverberates with all the far countries where our youth died. When we hear Normandy, Vimy, Hong Kong, we know that what happened so far away, paradoxically, made our country and the future of our society. These young people and soldiers bought our future for us. And for that, we are eternally grateful.

Whatever dreams we have, they were shared in some measure by this man who is only unknown by name but who is known in the hearts of all Canadians by all the virtues that we respect—selflessness, honour, courage and commitment.

We are now able to understand what was written in 1916 by the grandson of Louis Joseph Papineau, Major Talbot Papineau, who was killed two years later: "Is their sacrifice to go for nothing or will it not cement a foundation for a true Canadian nation, a Canadian nation independent in thought, independent in action, independent even in its political organization—but in spirit united for high international and humane purposes...?"

The wars fought by Canadians in the 20th century were not fought for the purpose of uniting Canada, but the country that emerged was forged in the smithy of sacrifice. We will not forget that.

This unknown soldier was not able to live out his allotted span of life to contribute to his country. But in giving himself totally through duty, commitment, love, and honour he has become part of us forever. As we are part of him.

[Published with the kind permission of Her Excellency the Right Honourable Adrienne Clarkson, Governor General of Canada, 2002.]

Index